CH

D0474753

CLICHÉS
AND HOW TO AVOID THEM

by
Michael Munro

CHAMBERS

CHAMBERS

An imprint of Chambers Harrap Publishers Ltd

7 Hopetoun Crescent

Edinburgh, EH7 4AY

First published by Chambers Harrap Publishers Ltd 2005

A CIP catalogue record for this book is available from the British Library.

ISBN 0550 10171 3

Editor: Ian Brookes
Publishing Manager: Patrick White
Prepress Controller: Vienna Leigh
Prepress Manager: Sharon McTeir

Designed and typeset by Chambers Harrap Publishers Ltd, Edinburgh
Printed and bound in Great Britain by Mackays of Chatham Ltd

Introduction

The idea behind this book is simple. Most people use clichés in everyday speech and writing whether they are aware of it or not. For those who would prefer not to use them, this book aims to offer words or phrases that could do the same job in a plainer or less hackneyed way.

What are clichés and what's so bad about using them?

The word 'cliché' was originally French. In the days when all printing was carried out using pages composed from individual letters of metal type, an item called a stereotype was in common use. This was a metal plate that could be inserted into a page, usually consisting of an illustration, but often composed of a phrase which was so often used that it saved time and the compositor's fingers by having it available in permanent form rather than composing it letter by letter every time. The French word for a stereotype was *cliché*. Some attribute an onomatopoeic origin to the word, meaning that it echoed the sound of such a metal plate being slotted into place, but the truth of that need not detain us here.

In English this borrowed word came to mean an expressive and memorable form of words that could be employed ready-made, thus avoiding having to think up something original for every occasion. Through time, however, many of these expressions became overused and overfamiliar. Persistent use of clichés came to suggest laziness and lack of originality in thinking. Many a shining phrase became dull through over-exposure and instead of slotting into place with a crisp click landed with the dull and stultifying thump of inevitability.

Introduction

One man's meat...

If clichés serve only to advertise the fact that one has nothing original or memorable to say, it would probably be as well to avoid them as much as possible. That is the premise behind this book, and that is why it provides you with simple alternatives to clichéd expressions.

Yet the avoidance of clichés is not always so straightforward. We should recognize that many people have no great objection to their use. Some might argue that if the essence of the spoken and written word is communication then a familiar expression will do the job with ease and economy. Furthermore, what strikes one person as a thumping great cliché may be seen by its user as a nicely judged, apposite and succinct turn of phrase. This book is not aimed at turning readers into some kind of Orwellian 'cliché police' attempting to proscribe natural expression. Clichés can often appeal because they are handy (and many people have favourites) and they avoid the necessity of stopping to reflect on something that doesn't matter that much.

However, I do believe we must guard against clichés being used as a substitute for doing any thinking at all. I don't think I'm alone in being irritated by such things as the continual parade of television vox pops in which interviewees can think of nothing better to say than they were 'gobsmacked', 'couldn't believe it', or had experienced 'a nightmare'.

In their *Modern English Usage* (revised edition, 1965), the Fowler brothers stigmatized as a cliché the expression 'own the soft impeachment'. This quotation from Sheridan's *The Rivals* (1775) was then a hackneyed way of saying 'to admit or confess something'; few of us nowadays would own to any impeachment at all, soft or otherwise. It is to be hoped that some of our current bugbears will take the same path to obscurity.

How does this book help?

Essentially the book works like a thesaurus. If an expression pops into the mind at very little prompting, the chances are that it's a cliché. To find an alternative, all the reader has to do is look up the suspect phrase under the alphabetical letter of its first word (ignoring, in most cases, any 'the' or 'a', etc). Once the required entry is located, the reader will be offered a selection of **plain English alternatives** to consider. It would rather defeat the purpose, of course, to simply replace one cliché with another, and to avoid this, readers are also provided with a list of **clichéd alternatives** where tempting but probably undesirable replacements may be identified. In some entries **original alternatives** are shown, expressions that are intended to be striking and novel, or which deserve to be used more widely. If you feel prompted to make use of these, you should act quickly, before they in turn become clichés. Better still, you might try to come up with your own original alternatives to use on occasions when you want your writing to seem especially interesting and fresh.

Some clichés are more deplorable than others, and in recognition of this the entries in this text are graded using a system of one to five stars, in ascending order of objectionableness, and the key to this system is repeated at the foot of the page.

Where interesting information is available on the origins of the expressions this is also shown.

Over to you

In compiling this book I have assumed that readers will actively seek to escape sounding hackneyed, but those who actually enjoy the siren song of old favourites should not feel excluded. Whether you think clichés are the salt of the earth or you would prefer to avoid them like the plague, it is to be hoped that the book has something of interest to all.

A

a bit special ✪✪

PLAIN ENGLISH ALTERNATIVES: talented; skilful; gifted; brilliant; excellent; outstanding

CLICHÉD ALTERNATIVES: out of the top drawer; a bit tasty

■ *Origins* Probably coined by football commentators, who are never content with plain English.

absolutely fabulous ✪

PLAIN ENGLISH ALTERNATIVES: excellent; wonderful; outstanding; superb

CLICHÉD ALTERNATIVES: marvellous; top; unbelievable

■ *Origins* A 1960s catchphrase that was resuscitated in the 1990s when it was used as the title of a popular sitcom.

accidentally on purpose ✪✪

PLAIN ENGLISH ALTERNATIVES: deliberately; intentionally; by design; knowingly

accident waiting to happen ✪✪✪

PLAIN ENGLISH ALTERNATIVES: an inevitable misfortune; a foreseeable setback

CLICHÉD ALTERNATIVES: a deathtrap; a walking disaster area

ace in the hole ✪✪

PLAIN ENGLISH ALTERNATIVES: secret advantage; hidden asset

CLICHÉD ALTERNATIVES: ace up one's sleeve; card up one's sleeve; trick up one's sleeve; trump card

■ *Origins* From the card game poker, in which a card dealt face down (and thus unseen by other players) is described as being 'in the hole'. Obviously, if you have an ace that your opponents do not know about, you may be in a position to surprise them.

Achilles' heel ✪

PLAIN ENGLISH ALTERNATIVES: cause of one's downfall; fatal flaw; fatal weakness; weak spot; vulnerable area

CLICHÉD ALTERNATIVES: chink in one's armour; crack in one's defences; soft underbelly

■ *Origins* From Achilles, a hero in ancient Greek mythology. When he was a baby his mother made him invulnerable by immersing him in the River Styx, all except for the one heel by which she held him. This meant that his heel alone was vulnerable, and it was here that he was later fatally wounded by an arrow.

acid test ✪✪

PLAIN ENGLISH ALTERNATIVES: proof; exacting trial; searching analysis; testing examination

CLICHÉD ALTERNATIVES: baptism of fire

■ *Origins* From the application of a little nitric acid to a piece of metal to determine its gold content.

across the board ✪✪

PLAIN ENGLISH ALTERNATIVES: general; universal; nationwide; company-wide; global

CLICHÉD ALTERNATIVES: blanket; all-inclusive; one size fits all

■ *Origins* From betting on horse races, in which a bet across the board would win money whether the horse came in first, second or third.

actions speak louder than words ✪✪✪

PLAIN ENGLISH ALTERNATIVES: it's what you do that counts, not what you say

CLICHÉD ALTERNATIVES: handsome is as handsome does; talk is cheap; put your money where your mouth is; you can talk the talk, but can you walk the walk?

act of contrition ✪✪✪

PLAIN ENGLISH ALTERNATIVES: apology; amends; penance

CLICHÉD ALTERNATIVES: eating humble pie

- **Origins** A Roman Catholic prayer expressing penitence.

add insult to injury ✪✪

PLAIN ENGLISH ALTERNATIVES: make matters worse; aggravate matters; compound the situation

CLICHÉD ALTERNATIVES: rub it in; rub one's nose in it; make one eat dirt

- **Origins** From the idea of doing someone a bad turn, then making things worse by gloating about it.

address the issue ✪✪✪

PLAIN ENGLISH ALTERNATIVES: take action; do something; apply oneself; set to work

CLICHÉD ALTERNATIVES: take steps; take matters in hand; set the wheels in motion

after a fashion ✪✪

PLAIN ENGLISH ALTERNATIVES: in a way; to a certain extent; to a degree; to some extent

CLICHÉD ALTERNATIVES: in a manner of speaking; in one's own way

after due consideration

PLAIN ENGLISH ALTERNATIVES: eventually; after thinking about it; after deliberation

CLICHÉD ALTERNATIVES: having thought long and hard about it; in due course; in the fullness of time

after one's own heart

PLAIN ENGLISH ALTERNATIVES: of the same opinion; in agreement; just as one would wish

CLICHÉD ALTERNATIVES: like-minded

against one's better judgement

PLAIN ENGLISH ALTERNATIVES: reluctantly; with reluctance; unwillingly; grudgingly; without enthusiasm

aided and abetted

PLAIN ENGLISH ALTERNATIVES: helped; assisted; seconded; supported

■ *Origins* From the legal use relating to someone helping in the commission of a crime.

airs and graces

PLAIN ENGLISH ALTERNATIVES: affectation; affected manners; pretension; pretentious behaviour

alarms/alarums and excursions

PLAIN ENGLISH ALTERNATIVES: fuss; commotion; confusion; agitation; bustle

CLICHÉD ALTERNATIVES: a great to-do; hullabaloo; brouhaha; to-ing and fro-ing; kerfuffle

✪ mild　　　✪✪ highly unoriginal　　　✪✪✪ irritating

■ *Origins* From an Elizabethan stage direction used to indicate a general rushing about waving swords and shouting, essentially intended to suggest a battle going on offstage.

alas and alack ✪✪

PLAIN ENGLISH ALTERNATIVES: unfortunately; regrettably; sad to say

alive and kicking ✪✪✪✪

PLAIN ENGLISH ALTERNATIVES: active; flourishing; healthy; vigorous; still around

CLICHÉD ALTERNATIVES: in the land of the living; in rude health; in fine fettle; fighting fit; still to the fore

alive and well and living in ... ✪✪✪

PLAIN ENGLISH ALTERNATIVES: currently in; to be found in; living in; presently in; located in

all and sundry ✪✪✪

PLAIN ENGLISH ALTERNATIVES: everyone; one and all

CLICHÉD ALTERNATIVES: all comers; every Tom, Dick and Harry; each and every one; the world and his wife

all at sea ✪✪✪

PLAIN ENGLISH ALTERNATIVES: at a loss; disorientated; confused; bewildered; lost

CLICHÉD ALTERNATIVES: at sixes and sevens

■ *Origins* From the idea of mariners being out of sight of land and unsure of where they are.

all done with mirrors ✪✪

PLAIN ENGLISH ALTERNATIVES: deceit; deception; trickery; hocus-pocus; conjuring tricks

CLICHÉD ALTERNATIVES: all smoke and mirrors

- *Origins* From the use of mirrors by stage illusionists.

all ears ✪✪

PLAIN ENGLISH ALTERNATIVES: listening attentively; giving every attention

CLICHÉD ALTERNATIVES: giving one's undivided attention; hanging on someone's every word

all Greek to me ✪✪

PLAIN ENGLISH ALTERNATIVES: unintelligible; incomprehensible

CLICHÉD ALTERNATIVES: a closed book; beyond one's ken; beyond one's understanding; a foreign language; over one's head

- *Origins* In Shakespeare's *Julius Caesar* (Act I, Scene 2), Casca says, 'For mine own part, it was Greek to me.'

all grist to the mill ✪

PLAIN ENGLISH ALTERNATIVES: useful; potentially advantageous; worth having; of use; worthwhile

CLICHÉD ALTERNATIVES: better than a poke in the eye with a sharp stick

- *Origins* Grist is corn for grinding into flour by a mill, and any kind or amount of it is better than nothing.

all hell broke loose ✪✪✪

PLAIN ENGLISH ALTERNATIVES: there was a commotion; there were dreadful consequences; mayhem ensued; dreadful scenes ensued

CLICHÉD ALTERNATIVES: the shit hit the fan

- *Origins* An early, but certainly not the first, use of this is by Milton in *Paradise*

Lost IV.917–8: 'Wherefore thou alone? wherefore with thee / Came not all Hell broke loose?'

all in a day's work ✪✪

PLAIN ENGLISH ALTERNATIVES: normal; customary; to be expected; routine; a matter of course; no trouble

CLICHÉD ALTERNATIVES: no big deal; par for the course

all in the same boat ✪✪

PLAIN ENGLISH ALTERNATIVES: facing the same difficulties; in the same situation; in this together

all-new ✪✪✪✪✪

PLAIN ENGLISH ALTERNATIVES: new; brand-new

■ *Origins* Like many 'snappy' phrases, this came from the USA, and is still more common there than in British English. It's often used in the sales patter for videos, DVDs, animated films, etc. It seems to have arisen as an assurance to the public that they were not being fooled into buying something that was a mixture of new and older material.

all our yesterdays ✪✪

PLAIN ENGLISH ALTERNATIVES: the past; days gone by; history

CLICHÉD ALTERNATIVES: the good (or bad) old days; the long-ago; days of yore

■ *Origins* From Shakespeare's *Macbeth* (Act V, Scene 5): 'And all our yesterdays have lighted fools / The way to dusty death. Out, out, brief candle!' Readers of a certain age will remember it as the title of a popular documentary history TV programme.

all over bar the shouting ✪✪

PLAIN ENGLISH ALTERNATIVES: almost finished; essentially decided; virtually over; the outcome is already clear

✪✪✪✪ toe-curling   ✪✪✪✪✪ diabolical

all over the shop

CLICHÉD ALTERNATIVES: all but over

■ *Origins* Unclear, but one theory is that political elections long ago were decided by a spoken rather than a paper vote (there being far fewer voters in those days), and that, politics being what it is, raised voices were involved before the end. When it had become obvious who would win, the final voice vote was a mere formality.

all over the shop   ✪✪

PLAIN ENGLISH ALTERNATIVES: in disarray; in confusion; untidy; disorganized; chaotic

CLICHÉD ALTERNATIVES: all over the place; higgledy-piggledy

! *Original alternative:* like a crazy woman's knitting

■ *Origins* 'Shop' in this case means a workshop or other place of work, as in *shop steward*.

all-singing, all-dancing   ✪✪✪✪

PLAIN ENGLISH ALTERNATIVES: impressive; advanced; multi-functional; versatile; comprehensive; all-purpose

CLICHÉD ALTERNATIVES: state-of-the-art; top-end

■ *Origins* From publicity material for a musical show, film, etc, keen to impress the public with its multiplicity of talented performers and non-stop action. Loosely and indiscriminately used to describe anything possessed of more than the bog-standard minimum.

all's well that ends well   ✪✪

PLAIN ENGLISH ALTERNATIVES: everything turned out all right in the end; the result was worth the trouble

CLICHÉD ALTERNATIVES: it was all right on the night

    ✪ mild   ✪✪ highly unoriginal   ✪✪✪ irritating

all systems go ✪✪

PLAIN ENGLISH ALTERNATIVES: everything is ready; everything is functioning; we can start now

CLICHÉD ALTERNATIVES: we're ready to go; we're good to go; we're ready to roll

■ *Origins* From the jargon used by NASA from the 1960s onwards, indicating that a space vehicle is ready for launch.

all talk (and no action) ✪✪

PLAIN ENGLISH ALTERNATIVES: insincere; sham; undependable

CLICHÉD ALTERNATIVES: all mouth (and no trousers); a paper tiger; talking a good game

all that glitters is not gold ✪✪✪

PLAIN ENGLISH ALTERNATIVES: don't be fooled by appearances; all is not as it seems

CLICHÉD ALTERNATIVES: appearances can be deceptive

■ *Origins* An old proverb, probably most familiar from Shakespeare (*Merchant of Venice*, Act II, Scene 7), who actually says 'glisters'.

all the best ✪✪

PLAIN ENGLISH ALTERNATIVES: good luck; cheers; best wishes

CLICHÉD ALTERNATIVES: best of luck

all things being equal (which they never are) ✪✪✪

PLAIN ENGLISH ALTERNATIVES: if everything remains the same; if nothing changes; if there are no new developments; *ceteris paribus* (*Latin*)

all things considered ✪✪

PLAIN ENGLISH ALTERNATIVES: taking everything into account

CLICHÉD ALTERNATIVES: all in all; looking at the broad picture; when all is said and done; when you get right down to it

all things to all men

See **be all things to all men**.

all-time ✪✪✪✪

PLAIN ENGLISH ALTERNATIVES: unsurpassed; unbeaten; best-yet; worst-yet; greatest; worst

CLICHÉD ALTERNATIVES: best-ever; worst-ever

■ *Origins* An import from the USA, but increasingly common in British usage. Better avoided as many people object to the sloppiness of suggesting that the thing described cannot be surpassed even in future time, whereas what it really means is 'up to now'.

and all that jazz ✪✪

PLAIN ENGLISH ALTERNATIVES: and all that; and all that sort of thing; and so forth; and so on; and the rest; et cetera

CLICHÉD ALTERNATIVES: and stuff; yada yada yada

■ *Origins* Like jazz itself, originally American.

and lots more ✪

PLAIN ENGLISH ALTERNATIVES: and more; and other stuff; and the rest

■ *Origins* From advertising, especially on TV and radio, where telling you everything the product, programme, etc contains is not enough; you have to suggest that there's even more (too much to detail), even if there isn't any.

angel of mercy ✪✪✪✪

PLAIN ENGLISH ALTERNATIVES: nurse; doctor; member of medical staff

CLICHÉD ALTERNATIVES: modern-day Florence Nightingale

another day, another dollar ✪✪

PLAIN ENGLISH ALTERNATIVES: that's the end of another demanding day

CLICHÉD ALTERNATIVES: all in a day's work

- *Origins* Another US import. Funny how nobody ever says 'another day, another pound'!

another one bites the dust ✪✪✪

PLAIN ENGLISH ALTERNATIVES: yet another failure; that's the end of that

CLICHÉD ALTERNATIVES: another one in a long line of failures; back to the drawing board; there's another one gone

- *Origins* See **bite the dust**.

another think coming

See **you've got another think coming**.

ants in one's pants

See **have ants in one's pants**.

any old how ✪✪

PLAIN ENGLISH ALTERNATIVES: anyhow; any way; carelessly; lackadaisically

CLICHÉD ALTERNATIVES: any way one can

any port in a storm ✪✪✪

PLAIN ENGLISH ALTERNATIVES: help is welcome from any source; one can't spurn any offer of help

CLICHÉD ALTERNATIVES: beggars can't be choosers

- *Origins* From the idea of a ship caught in a storm at sea, abandoning its set course to seek shelter in the nearest harbour.

anything but ✪✪

PLAIN ENGLISH ALTERNATIVES: certainly not; by no means; not at all; not in the least; in no way

CLICHÉD ALTERNATIVES: not the least bit

anything for a quiet life ✪✪

PLAIN ENGLISH ALTERNATIVES: I don't care as long as I get peace; do what you like, but leave me out of it

CLICHÉD ALTERNATIVES: whatever!

anything goes ✪✪

PLAIN ENGLISH ALTERNATIVES: you can do what you like; anything is permissible; there are no rules

CLICHÉD ALTERNATIVES: this is Liberty Hall; the only rule is: there are no rules

apple of one's eye ✪✪

PLAIN ENGLISH ALTERNATIVES: favourite; pet; darling; beloved

CLICHÉD ALTERNATIVES: blue-eyed boy; fair-haired boy (*US*)

■ *Origins* Apparently from the idea of the pupil of the eye being a round ball like an apple.

argue black was white

See **he/she would argue black was white**.

argue the toss ✪✪

PLAIN ENGLISH ALTERNATIVES: dispute a decision; question a ruling; challenge a verdict; refuse to accept what has been decided

CLICHÉD ALTERNATIVES: kick up a fuss; be bolshie; shout the odds

■ *Origins* Presumably from questioning the result of tossing a coin.

armed to the teeth ✪✪✪

PLAIN ENGLISH ALTERNATIVES: heavily-armed; carrying many weapons; armed and ready to fight

CLICHÉD ALTERNATIVES: tooled-up; loaded for bear

■ *Origins* Perhaps from the idea of a fighter carrying so many weapons that he has to hold a knife in his teeth, as pirates are often traditionally depicted.

as a matter of fact ✪✪✪✪✪

PLAIN ENGLISH ALTERNATIVES: in fact; actually; in actuality

CLICHÉD ALTERNATIVES: in point of fact; it so happens

as an added bonus/extra ✪✪✪

PLAIN ENGLISH ALTERNATIVES: as well; included

CLICHÉD ALTERNATIVES: into the bargain; thrown in

Note: This expression is rendered doubly undesirable by being not only clichéd but tautological (a bonus or extra is necessarily 'added').

as and when ✪✪

PLAIN ENGLISH ALTERNATIVES: when suitable; whenever appropriate

CLICHÉD ALTERNATIVES: when and only when; if and only if

as cool as a cucumber ✪✪

PLAIN ENGLISH ALTERNATIVES: calm; perfectly self-possessed; unfazed; not in the least bothered; nonchalant

CLICHÉD ALTERNATIVES: as cool as you please; cool, calm and collected; ice cool

> ❗ *Original alternative:* like a duck on a pond

as easy as falling off a log ✪✪

PLAIN ENGLISH ALTERNATIVES: simple; straightforward; effortless; no bother; no trouble

CLICHÉD ALTERNATIVES: child's play; simplicity itself; a doddle; like taking candy from a baby; a walk in the park

as fit as a fiddle ✪✪

PLAIN ENGLISH ALTERNATIVES: in the best of condition; in top form; very healthy; in excellent shape

CLICHÉD ALTERNATIVES: as fit as a butcher's dog; as sound as a bell; fighting fit; in the pink; in good nick; in tip-top condition

■ *Origins* Perhaps from the exertions of a fiddler rather than the instrument itself.

as it happens ✪✪✪✪

PLAIN ENGLISH ALTERNATIVES: actually; in fact

CLICHÉD ALTERNATIVES: as a matter of fact

Note: In most cases this is a mere verbal filler and can be dropped altogether with no loss of meaning.

as it turns out ✪✪✪

PLAIN ENGLISH ALTERNATIVES: apparently; eventually; in the end; after all

CLICHÉD ALTERNATIVES: it transpires that; as it happens

as it were ✪✪

PLAIN ENGLISH ALTERNATIVES: in other words; in a way; as one might put it; in a sense

CLICHÉD ALTERNATIVES: so to speak; in a manner of speaking; to coin a phrase

ask for it ✪✪

PLAIN ENGLISH ALTERNATIVES: be provocative; court danger; invite trouble

CLICHÉD ALTERNATIVES: look for trouble; tempt fate; trail one's coat

as luck would have it ✪✪✪

PLAIN ENGLISH ALTERNATIVES: fortunately; fortuitously; by chance; luckily

CLICHÉD ALTERNATIVES: as it chanced; as it turned out

as old as the hills ✪✪

PLAIN ENGLISH ALTERNATIVES: aged; ancient; superannuated; archaic; antiquated; antediluvian

CLICHÉD ALTERNATIVES: out of the ark; past its sell-by date; as old as Methuselah

> **!** *Original alternative:* so old that their parents used to give them their pocket money in groats

as sure as fate/death ✪✪

PLAIN ENGLISH ALTERNATIVES: surely; without a doubt; doubtless(ly); indubitably; inevitably; inexorably

CLICHÉD ALTERNATIVES: as surely as night follows day; without a shadow of a doubt

as the saying goes ✪✪✪

PLAIN ENGLISH ALTERNATIVES: in other words; as some people say

CLICHÉD ALTERNATIVES: as they say; to coin a phrase; as some would have it

as thick as two short planks ✪✪

PLAIN ENGLISH ALTERNATIVES: not very clever/bright/smart; dim; dim-witted; dense; slow

CLICHÉD ALTERNATIVES: not the sharpest tool in the box; no genius; no rocket scientist; no Einstein; no mastermind

at all costs ✪✪

PLAIN ENGLISH ALTERNATIVES: no matter what it takes; regardless of the sacrifice involved; regardless of the price to be paid; whatever else happens

CLICHÉD ALTERNATIVES: at any cost; at any price

at a loose end ✪✪

PLAIN ENGLISH ALTERNATIVES: with nothing to do; idle; unemployed; unoccupied

CLICHÉD ALTERNATIVES: kicking one's heels; twiddling one's thumbs

■ *Origins* Referring to a length of thread or rope that is not tied up neatly and therefore appears useless or extraneous, as in a piece of weaving or one of a ship's ropes.

at any rate ✪✪

PLAIN ENGLISH ALTERNATIVES: whatever happens; whatever may happen; no matter what happens; in any case

CLICHÉD ALTERNATIVES: at all events

at daggers drawn ✪✪

PLAIN ENGLISH ALTERNATIVES: mutually hostile; on bad terms; enemies

CLICHÉD ALTERNATIVES: spoiling for a fight; pistols at dawn; not on the best of terms

■ *Origins* An image of two people squaring up to each other, relations having deteriorated to the point at which they are threatening to use weapons.

at death's door ✪✪

PLAIN ENGLISH ALTERNATIVES: at the point of death; dying; near death;

moribund; dangerously ill; critically ill; likely to die; *in extremis* (*Latin*)

CLICHÉD ALTERNATIVES: on one's deathbed; with one foot in the grave; not long for this world; knocking on heaven's door; on the way out; about to meet one's maker; heading for the last roundup

at long last ✪✪

PLAIN ENGLISH ALTERNATIVES: eventually; finally; after a long delay

CLICHÉD ALTERNATIVES: at length

at one fell swoop ✪

PLAIN ENGLISH ALTERNATIVES: simultaneously; all at once; all together

CLICHÉD ALTERNATIVES: in one go

■ **Origins** From Shakespeare's *Macbeth* (Act IV, Scene 3), in which Macduff is told of Macbeth's slaughter of his wife and children and compares this to the swoop of a bird of prey on its victims: 'What, all my pretty chickens, and their dam, / At one fell swoop?'

at one's earliest convenience ✪✪

PLAIN ENGLISH ALTERNATIVES: soon; now; immediately; right away; as soon as possible; without delay

CLICHÉD ALTERNATIVES: asap; instanter; by return of post

at one's wits' end ✪✪

PLAIN ENGLISH ALTERNATIVES: at a loss; overwhelmed; in despair; not knowing what to do

CLICHÉD ALTERNATIVES: at the end of one's tether/rope; driven to distraction

at sixes and sevens ✪✪

PLAIN ENGLISH ALTERNATIVES: in confusion; in disarray; in a mess; disorganized; chaotic

CLICHÉD ALTERNATIVES: all at sea; higgledy-piggledy

■ *Origins* Probably from games with dice.

at the crack of dawn ✪✪

PLAIN ENGLISH ALTERNATIVES: in the early morning; at daybreak; at dawn; at sunrise; at sunup; at first light

CLICHÉD ALTERNATIVES: at break of day; at cockcrow; at sparrow-fart

■ *Origins* It is unclear why dawn should crack, unless it's the sound of day breaking.

at the drop of a hat ✪✪

PLAIN ENGLISH ALTERNATIVES: immediately; right away; without delay; at once; instantly

CLICHÉD ALTERNATIVES: just like that; without more ado

■ *Origins* Presumably from the old practice of using the dropping of someone's hat as a signal to start a race or fight.

at the end of the day ✪✪✪✪✪

PLAIN ENGLISH ALTERNATIVES: finally; in the end; ultimately; when everything has been taken into consideration

CLICHÉD ALTERNATIVES: in the final analysis; in the final reckoning; when all is said and done; when one gets right down to it

at the end of one's rope/tether ✪✪

PLAIN ENGLISH ALTERNATIVES: at the limit of one's patience/endurance; pushed to the limits; exasperated; desperate

CLICHÉD ALTERNATIVES: up to here with it; at one's wits' end; on the brink; driven to distraction

■ *Origins* Presumably from the idea of a tethered domestic animal reaching the end of its rope and being unable to go any further.

at the last minute ✪✪

PLAIN ENGLISH ALTERNATIVES: at the latest possible time; as time runs out

CLICHÉD ALTERNATIVES: at the eleventh hour; in the nick of time

at this moment in time ✪✪✪✪✪

PLAIN ENGLISH ALTERNATIVES: now; just now; right now; at the moment; at this point; currently

CLICHÉD ALTERNATIVES: as of now; at this point in time; at this juncture; as we speak; in the current situation

Auld Reekie ✪

PLAIN ENGLISH ALTERNATIVES: Edinburgh; Scotland's capital

CLICHÉD ALTERNATIVES: the Athens of the north; Edina

■ *Origins* Literally 'Old Smoky', this came from the persistent cloud of smoke from the city's multitude of household coal fires.

avid reader ✪✪

PLAIN ENGLISH ALTERNATIVES: someone who enjoys reading; enthusiastic reader

CLICHÉD ALTERNATIVES: voracious reader; bookworm; a great one for books

avoid (something) like the plague ✪✪✪✪

PLAIN ENGLISH ALTERNATIVES: shun; keep well away from; have nothing whatsoever to do with; remain aloof from

CLICHÉD ALTERNATIVES: give a wide berth to; steer well clear of; not touch with a bargepole

axe to grind ✪✪

PLAIN ENGLISH ALTERNATIVES: grievance; personal motive; ulterior motive

CLICHÉD ALTERNATIVES: reasons of one's own; a bone to pick

B

backhanded compliment ✪✪

PLAIN ENGLISH ALTERNATIVES: double-edged remark; equivocal praise;
ambiguous comment; sarcastic remark

CLICHÉD ALTERNATIVES: faint praise

back in the day ✪✪✪✪✪

PLAIN ENGLISH ALTERNATIVES: earlier; in the past; in those days; at one time

CLICHÉD ALTERNATIVES: in the (good) old days; way back when; in days of
yore

back of beyond ✪✪

PLAIN ENGLISH ALTERNATIVES: a remote spot; the wilds; an out-of-the-way
place; the backwoods

CLICHÉD ALTERNATIVES: the middle of nowhere; somewhere off the beaten
track; the sticks; beyond the black stump (*Australian*)

> **!** *Original alternative:* out where the buses don't
> run

back to square one ✪✪

PLAIN ENGLISH ALTERNATIVES: back where you started; right back at the
beginning; no further forward

CLICHÉD ALTERNATIVES: back to the drawing board

■ *Origins* Probably from the type of board game in which landing on an unlucky
square means you have to go back to the start.

back to the drawing board ✪✪

PLAIN ENGLISH ALTERNATIVES: let's try another approach; a complete re-think is necessary

CLICHÉD ALTERNATIVES: back to square one; that's torn it; another one bites the dust

back (someone) to the hilt ✪✪

PLAIN ENGLISH ALTERNATIVES: support unreservedly; fully endorse; give full support

CLICHÉD ALTERNATIVES: be right behind; be with all the way

■ *Origins* From a rather gruesome display of solidarity involving sticking one's knife or sword into a mutual enemy as far as it can penetrate.

bag and baggage ✪✪

PLAIN ENGLISH ALTERNATIVES: with all one's belongings; with all one possesses; completely

CLICHÉD ALTERNATIVES: with all one's goods and chattels; with all one's worldly goods; lock, stock and barrel

bald as a coot ✪✪

PLAIN ENGLISH ALTERNATIVES: bald; completely bald; hairless; balding; bald-headed; thinning; receding

CLICHÉD ALTERNATIVES: follically challenged; a slaphead; thin on top

■ *Origins* The coot is a water-bird that has a noticeable white area on the front of its head.

ball is in your court, the ✪✪

PLAIN ENGLISH ALTERNATIVES: the initiative lies with you; you must make the next move; the decision is up to you

CLICHÉD ALTERNATIVES: it's your move; it's up to you; the ball is at your feet; piss or get off the pot; put up or shut up

ballpark figure ✪✪✪✪

PLAIN ENGLISH ALTERNATIVES: approximate figure; rough estimate; rough guess

CLICHÉD ALTERNATIVES: guesstimate

■ *Origins* Its American origin is given away by the fact that 'ballpark' is an exclusively American word, meaning 'a baseball ground'. Being in the same ballpark as someone or something else is far from a guarantee of close proximity.

bang one's head against a brick wall ✪✪

PLAIN ENGLISH ALTERNATIVES: waste one's time; waste one's efforts; try in vain

CLICHÉD ALTERNATIVES: talk till one is blue in the face; spit into the wind; get nowhere; perform the labours of Sisyphus

bang to rights ✪✪✪

PLAIN ENGLISH ALTERNATIVES: in the act; fairly; conclusively; with no hope of getting away

CLICHÉD ALTERNATIVES: fair and square; red-handed; in flagrante delicto; stitched up like a kipper

barking up the wrong tree ✪✪

PLAIN ENGLISH ALTERNATIVES: misled; mistaken; on the wrong track; astray; off target

CLICHÉD ALTERNATIVES: labouring under a wrong (or false) impression; way off; backing the wrong horse

■ *Origins* Quite simply, this is what a hunting dog is literally doing when it is confidently signalling that it has 'treed' its quarry, while in fact the hunted creature has sneakily transferred to the branches of another tree.

bat an eye(lid) ✪✪

PLAIN ENGLISH ALTERNATIVES: be surprised; show surprise; react; flinch

CLICHÉD ALTERNATIVES: betray the least concern; be up and down

bat out of hell

See **like a bat out of hell**.

batten down the hatches ✪✪

PLAIN ENGLISH ALTERNATIVES: prepare for trouble/a crisis; be ready for an emergency

- *Origins* On board sailing ships, battens were strips of wood used to secure things. In particular, they would be nailed down to hold in place a tarpaulin covering a hatchway, to keep water from finding its way below decks during rough weather.

battle royal ✪✪

PLAIN ENGLISH ALTERNATIVES: brawl; confrontation; hostilities; free-for-all; general melée; bitter struggle; fierce fight; tussle; scrimmage; set-to

CLICHÉD ALTERNATIVES: donnybrook; the mother of all battles; one hell of a row

- *Origins* From cockfighting, meaning 'a fight between several birds at one time'.

be-all and end-all ✪✪

PLAIN ENGLISH ALTERNATIVES: only thing that matters; main issue; decisive point; most important thing

CLICHÉD ALTERNATIVES: whole shooting-match; name of the game; only game in town

be all things to all men ✪✪

PLAIN ENGLISH ALTERNATIVES: please everyone; accommodate everyone

CLICHÉD ALTERNATIVES: please all of the people all of the time; chop and change

■ *Origins* Based on the words of St Paul in the Bible: 'I am made all things to all men, that I might by all means save some.' (*1 Corinthians*).

bear with one ✪✪

PLAIN ENGLISH ALTERNATIVES: be patient; make allowances for one; give one a chance; let one finish

CLICHÉD ALTERNATIVES: hold one's horses

beat about the bush ✪✪

PLAIN ENGLISH ALTERNATIVES: not come to the point; procrastinate; hesitate; prevaricate; hedge

CLICHÉD ALTERNATIVES: hum and haw; shilly-shally

■ *Origins* From hunters beating bushes with sticks in order to flush out any birds hiding within.

beat a hasty retreat ✪✪

PLAIN ENGLISH ALTERNATIVES: flee; decamp; withdraw; make off; run off; run away; clear out; scarper

CLICHÉD ALTERNATIVES: clear off sharpish; make oneself scarce; head for the hills; run for it; take to one's heels

be a thing of the past ✪✪

PLAIN ENGLISH ALTERNATIVES: be outmoded; be outdated; be passé; be a relic; be antiquated; be archaic; belong to another era; be past one's prime

CLICHÉD ALTERNATIVES: be ancient history; be over the hill; be yesterday's man; be consigned to the dustbin of history; belong in a museum

beauty sleep

See **get one's beauty sleep**.

beaver away ✪

PLAIN ENGLISH ALTERNATIVES: work hard; toil away; work tirelessly; sweat; put in long hours

CLICHÉD ALTERNATIVES: keep one's nose to the grindstone; peg away; work all the hours (God sends); keep hard at it

■ *Origins* From the idea of the dam-building beaver as a particularly industrious creature.

be cruel to be kind ✪✪

PLAIN ENGLISH ALTERNATIVES: be utterly frank; deal frankly with someone; be firm; speak the truth although it hurts

CLICHÉD ALTERNATIVES: show tough love; tell it like it is

bed of roses ✪✪

PLAIN ENGLISH ALTERNATIVES: ease; comfort; a comfortable situation

CLICHÉD ALTERNATIVES: comfort zone; life of Riley; easy street; lap of luxury; roses all the way

bee in one's bonnet ✪✪

PLAIN ENGLISH ALTERNATIVES: obsession; *idée fixe*; fixation; preoccupation; hobby-horse

CLICHÉD ALTERNATIVES: complex; a thing about something

been there, done that, got the T-shirt ✪✪✪✪

PLAIN ENGLISH ALTERNATIVES: I am not impressed; that's nothing

CLICHÉD ALTERNATIVES: so what; that's so last year; join the club

bee's knees, the ✪✪

PLAIN ENGLISH ALTERNATIVES: the greatest; wonderful; the best

before you can say Jack Robinson

CLICHÉD ALTERNATIVES: the cat's pyjamas; the cat's whiskers; the dog's bollocks; something else; the best thing since sliced bread; God's gift; all that

> **!** *Original alternative:* the kipper's knickers

■ *Origins* This seems to have been invented as a piece of slang in the USA in the 1920s, but no-one quite knows why.

before you can say Jack Robinson   ✪✪

PLAIN ENGLISH ALTERNATIVES: right away; immediately; instantly; before you know it; before you know what's happening

CLICHÉD ALTERNATIVES: like a flash; like a shot; before you can say knife; before you can turn round; before you have time to blink; in the twinkling of an eye

■ *Origins* Wouldn't it be fun to pinpoint an individual Mr Robinson? However, it seems the name was probably chosen at random.

beggar description   ✪✪

PLAIN ENGLISH ALTERNATIVES: outdo one's powers of description; be impossible to describe; be utterly indescribable; be too extraordinary to describe

CLICHÉD ALTERNATIVES: defy description

be gobsmacked   ✪✪✪✪✪

PLAIN ENGLISH ALTERNATIVES: be surprised; be shocked; be astounded; be taken aback; be incredulous; be nonplussed; be speechless

CLICHÉD ALTERNATIVES: be unable to believe it; be unable to believe one's eyes

■ *Origins* Presumably from looking as if one has just been slapped in the face.

behind the eight ball ✪✪✪✪

PLAIN ENGLISH ALTERNATIVES: in trouble; in an awkward situation; in an uncomfortable position

CLICHÉD ALTERNATIVES: in shtook; up the creek without a paddle; up a gum tree

■ *Origins* From the game of pool, in which the ball bearing the number eight is the last to be potted. Players are penalized if they hit the wrong ball, and if your target ball is obscured by the eight ball it really makes things difficult.

behind the scenes ✪✪

PLAIN ENGLISH ALTERNATIVES: in secret; clandestinely; privately; out of the public eye; in camera

CLICHÉD ALTERNATIVES: sub rosa; on the quiet

■ *Origins* From the world of theatre, referring to what takes place offstage, whether being part of the plot reported by an actor as having happened, or merely a Shakespearean player smoking an anachronistic cigarette.

be history ✪✪✪✪

PLAIN ENGLISH ALTERNATIVES: be finished; be forgotten

CLICHÉD ALTERNATIVES: be all washed up; be a thing of the past; be yesterday's man; have no future

be left holding the baby ✪✪

PLAIN ENGLISH ALTERNATIVES: be abandoned; be deserted; be left to take responsibility

CLICHÉD ALTERNATIVES: be left to carry the can; be left in the lurch; be left high and dry

bells and whistles ✪

PLAIN ENGLISH ALTERNATIVES: accessories; additional features; gimmicks

CLICHÉD ALTERNATIVES: added extras

- *Origins* From the actual bells and whistles attached to fairground organs in order to generate even more noise.

below par

PLAIN ENGLISH ALTERNATIVES: in poor health; slightly unwell; ailing; indisposed; in low spirits; poorly

CLICHÉD ALTERNATIVES: under the weather; not up to snuff; off-colour; out of sorts

- *Origins* Not, as might be assumed, from golf but from the stock market, where a share that is selling below par is going for less than its nominal value.

below the belt

PLAIN ENGLISH ALTERNATIVES: unfair; against the rules; cowardly; unscrupulous

CLICHÉD ALTERNATIVES: not in the spirit of the thing

- *Origins* From the boxing rule outlawing punching an opponent any lower on the body than the waist.

be my guest

PLAIN ENGLISH ALTERNATIVES: help yourself; do as you please; go ahead

CLICHÉD ALTERNATIVES: feel free; make yourself at home; *mi casa, su casa* (*Spanish*); go for it; go for your life; get stuck in; whatever you say

bend or lean over backwards

PLAIN ENGLISH ALTERNATIVES: make every effort; do one's utmost; try one's hardest; spare no effort; do all one can

CLICHÉD ALTERNATIVES: pull out all the stops

beneath contempt

PLAIN ENGLISH ALTERNATIVES: despicable; contemptible; disgraceful; shameful; mean

CLICHÉD ALTERNATIVES: the lowest of the low

best bet ✪✪

PLAIN ENGLISH ALTERNATIVES: best chance; wisest course of action; most likely way of proceeding

CLICHÉD ALTERNATIVES: way to go

best bib and tucker ✪✪

PLAIN ENGLISH ALTERNATIVES: dress clothes; best clothes; your best; smartest clothes

CLICHÉD ALTERNATIVES: glad rags; full fig; best gear

■ *Origins* *Bib* refers to an old-fashioned shirt-front for a man, and tucker was a piece of material tucked over a woman's low-cut bodice.

best-ever ✪✪✪✪✪

PLAIN ENGLISH ALTERNATIVES: finest; greatest; unsurpassed; unparalleled; unequalled; leading; supreme; outstanding

CLICHÉD ALTERNATIVES: all-time best

Note: Many people object to this expression, which was originally American, because the 'ever' strictly suggests not only the past but the limitless future. A purist would insist on saying 'best until now', 'currently unsurpassed', 'current best' or a similar formula, but the point is lost on increasing numbers of users.

best of British (luck) ✪✪

PLAIN ENGLISH ALTERNATIVES: good luck; good fortune

CLICHÉD ALTERNATIVES: all the best; lots of luck; all the luck in the world

best thing since sliced bread ✪✪✪

PLAIN ENGLISH ALTERNATIVES: a wonder; a marvel; a wonderful thing

CLICHÉD ALTERNATIVES: a boon to all mankind; brilliant; the best thing yet

best thing that ever happened to me (him, her, you, etc) ✪✪✪

PLAIN ENGLISH ALTERNATIVES: a great boon; wonderful; marvellous

CLICHÉD ALTERNATIVES: stroke of luck; piece of luck

be thankful for small mercies ✪✪

PLAIN ENGLISH ALTERNATIVES: consider oneself fortunate; appreciate what one has; be grateful that things aren't worse

CLICHÉD ALTERNATIVES: know when one is well off; count one's blessings

be that as it may ✪✪

PLAIN ENGLISH ALTERNATIVES: despite that; in spite of that; however; while that is the case; notwithstanding

CLICHÉD ALTERNATIVES: that said

be there for someone ✪✪✪✪✪

PLAIN ENGLISH ALTERNATIVES: give someone one's support/help/sympathy; help someone out; do all one can to help; give emotional support

CLICHÉD ALTERNATIVES: stand by someone; provide someone with a shoulder to cry on

bet one's bottom dollar ✪✪

PLAIN ENGLISH ALTERNATIVES: risk all; gamble everything; stake everything; be absolutely sure; be absolutely certain; feel confident; depend upon it

CLICHÉD ALTERNATIVES: bet one's boots; bet one's ass (US); put one's shirt on it; count on it

■ *Origins* As the currency unit indicates, this was originally American and refers to a gambler working his way down through a stack of coins until only one is left to wager.

better half ✪✪✪✪✪

PLAIN ENGLISH ALTERNATIVES: wife; husband; partner

CLICHÉD ALTERNATIVES: her indoors; the little woman; significant other

better judgement

See **against one's better judgement**.

between a rock and a hard place ✪✪✪

PLAIN ENGLISH ALTERNATIVES: in a dilemma; faced with two undesirable alternatives

CLICHÉD ALTERNATIVES: between Scylla and Charybdis; between the devil and the deep blue sea; in a cleft stick; on the horns of a dilemma

between Scylla and Charybdis ✪✪

PLAIN ENGLISH ALTERNATIVES: in a dilemma; faced with two undesirable alternatives

CLICHÉD ALTERNATIVES: between a rock and a hard place; between the devil and the deep blue sea; in a cleft stick; on the horns of a dilemma

■ *Origins* In Greek mythology Scylla and Charybdis were a couple of monsters who each haunted a side of the Straits of Messina, snapping up sailors whose vessels strayed too near. Thus, to be forced to choose between one or the other would mean disaster either way.

between the devil and the deep blue sea ✪✪

PLAIN ENGLISH ALTERNATIVES: in a dilemma; faced with two undesirable alternatives

CLICHÉD ALTERNATIVES: between a rock and a hard place; between Scylla and Charybdis; in a cleft stick; on the horns of a dilemma

■ *Origins* Choosing between going to hell or drowning is not much of a choice, but there is a theory that the devil referred to here is not Old Nick at all. On sailing ships the devil was a name for a seam where the deck joined the side of the ship. A sailor positioned between this and the water (for example, hanging by ropes to paint the vessel's side or trying to clamber aboard) would be in a potentially highly dangerous situation. See also **devil to pay**.

between you and me (and the bedpost, gatepost, etc) ✪✪

PLAIN ENGLISH ALTERNATIVES: in confidence; confidentially; in secrecy

CLICHÉD ALTERNATIVES: just between us

betwixt and between ✪✪

PLAIN ENGLISH ALTERNATIVES: neither one thing nor the other; intermediate

CLICHÉD ALTERNATIVES: neither fish, flesh, nor fowl; in a grey area

beyond a joke ✪✪

PLAIN ENGLISH ALTERNATIVES: not funny; no longer funny; no joke; a serious matter

CLICHÉD ALTERNATIVES: no laughing matter; not in the least bit funny; past a joke

beyond a shadow of doubt ✪✪

PLAIN ENGLISH ALTERNATIVES: certain; certainly; quite certainly; sure; surely; doubtless; doubtlessly; unquestionable; unquestionably; irrefutable; irrefutably

CLICHÉD ALTERNATIVES: without a doubt

beyond one's wildest dreams ✪✪

PLAIN ENGLISH ALTERNATIVES: more than one ever imagined possible; fantastic(ally)

CLICHÉD ALTERNATIVES: past imagining; undreamt-of

beyond the pale   ✪✪

PLAIN ENGLISH ALTERNATIVES: unacceptable; intolerable; objectionable; insupportable; uncivilized

CLICHÉD ALTERNATIVES: not quite the thing; not people like us

■ *Origins* In Irish history, the English Pale was a name for the area of the country on which the invading English had succeeded in imposing total dominance. Anyone living outside this hallowed realm was clearly not the kind of person one would invite to tea.

big cheese   ✪✪

PLAIN ENGLISH ALTERNATIVES: important person; boss; chief; VIP

CLICHÉD ALTERNATIVES: big enchilada; big noise; bigwig; head cook and bottle-washer; honcho; head honcho; top banana

biggest fan   ✪✪

PLAIN ENGLISH ALTERNATIVES: admirer; supporter; devotee; enthusiast; lover

CLICHÉD ALTERNATIVES: fervent admirer; number one fan

big time, the   ✪✪

PLAIN ENGLISH ALTERNATIVES: the highest level; the top level

CLICHÉD ALTERNATIVES: the heights; the big league

big-time   ✪✪

PLAIN ENGLISH ALTERNATIVES: greatly; considerably; enthusiastically; to a great extent

CLICHÉD ALTERNATIVES: in a big way; to the max

bite the bullet   ✪✪

PLAIN ENGLISH ALTERNATIVES: steel oneself; endure

bite the dust

CLICHÉD ALTERNATIVES: take it like a man; put a brave face on it; keep a stiff upper lip; grit one's teeth

■ *Origins* From the practice in the days before anaesthetics of giving a wounded soldier a bullet to grip in his teeth to stop him from crying out in pain when he was operated on.

bite the dust   ✪✪

PLAIN ENGLISH ALTERNATIVES: die; come to an end; fail finally; perish; fall

CLICHÉD ALTERNATIVES: come to a sticky end; pop one's clogs; shuffle off this mortal coil; buy it; kick the bucket; go belly up; peg out; join the choir invisible; join the majority

■ *Origins* Most people assume this comes from Westerns (where it certainly is common), but in fact there are examples of its use dating back to the mid-18th century, *not* referring to expiring Native Americans!

bite the hand that feeds one   ✪✪

PLAIN ENGLISH ALTERNATIVES: be ungrateful; show ingratitude

bits and pieces   ✪✪

PLAIN ENGLISH ALTERNATIVES: odds and ends; things; possessions; accoutrements; stuff

CLICHÉD ALTERNATIVES: bits and bobs; goods and chattels; odds and sods; worldly goods

black sheep   ✪✪

PLAIN ENGLISH ALTERNATIVES: disgrace; ne'er-do-well; scapegrace

CLICHÉD ALTERNATIVES: skeleton in the cupboard; blot on one's escutcheon; the one we don't talk about

blast from the past ✪✪✪

PLAIN ENGLISH ALTERNATIVES: former hit; old standard; old favourite

CLICHÉD ALTERNATIVES: golden oldie; oldie but goodie; trip down memory lane; one from the back catalogue

blazing inferno ✪✪✪✪

PLAIN ENGLISH ALTERNATIVES: fire; flames; conflagration; blaze

CLICHÉD ALTERNATIVES: towering inferno; flaming hell

bleed like a stuck pig ✪✪

PLAIN ENGLISH ALTERNATIVES: bleed heavily; lose a lot of blood

CLICHÉD ALTERNATIVES: welter in one's gore; bleed to death; feel one's life-blood ebbing away

blessing in disguise ✪✪

PLAIN ENGLISH ALTERNATIVES: unexpected benefit; actually a good thing

■ *Origins* From an 18th-century hymn, 'Ev'n Crosses from his sov'reign Hand / Are Blessings in Disguise.'

bloodcurdling scream ✪✪

PLAIN ENGLISH ALTERNATIVES: loud scream; terrifying scream

CLICHÉD ALTERNATIVES: cry to waken the dead; spine-tingling scream; eldritch wail

bloody but unbowed ✪✪

PLAIN ENGLISH ALTERNATIVES: wounded but not defeated; proud in defeat

CLICHÉD ALTERNATIVES: down but not out; with one's head held high

■ *Origins* From a poem by W E Henley (1849–1903), English editor, critic and poet, 'Under the bludgeonings of chance / My head is bloody, but unbowed.'

blot one's copybook ✪✪

PLAIN ENGLISH ALTERNATIVES: err; make a mistake; blunder; spoil one's record

CLICHÉD ALTERNATIVES: let oneself slip; take one's eye off the ball; go astray; let the side down

▪ *Origins* From the idea of a scholar copying something down and carelessly making a blot with the pen.

blot on the landscape ✪✪

PLAIN ENGLISH ALTERNATIVES: eyesore

CLICHÉD ALTERNATIVES: carbuncle; monstrous carbuncle

blow hot and cold ✪✪

PLAIN ENGLISH ALTERNATIVES: change one's mind; be irresolute; be undependable; vacillate

CLICHÉD ALTERNATIVES: chop and change; come and go

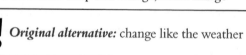

! *Original alternative:* change like the weather

blow one away ✪✪✪

PLAIN ENGLISH ALTERNATIVES: impress; astonish; amaze

CLICHÉD ALTERNATIVES: knock out; rock one's world; turn one's head around; take one's breath away

blow one's mind ✪✪

PLAIN ENGLISH ALTERNATIVES: impress; astonish; amaze

CLICHÉD ALTERNATIVES: knock one out; turn one's head around; rock one's world; blow one away; take one's breath away

blow one's own trumpet ✪✪

PLAIN ENGLISH ALTERNATIVES: boast; brag; congratulate oneself; swagger

CLICHÉD ALTERNATIVES: sing one's own praises; talk oneself up; talk big; show off

> **!** *Original alternative:* act as one's own
> personal PR company

■ *Origins* From the medieval practice of announcing the arrival of a knight at a tourney by having a herald blow a trumpet.

blow the cobwebs away ✪✪

PLAIN ENGLISH ALTERNATIVES: clear one's head; wake one up

CLICHÉD ALTERNATIVES: straighten one out

blow the whistle ✪✪

PLAIN ENGLISH ALTERNATIVES: inform; expose; reveal what is going on; tell the authorities

CLICHÉD ALTERNATIVES: blow the gaff; go public; let the cat out of the bag; spill the beans; blow wide open

■ *Origins* Perhaps from the idea of a sports referee blowing a whistle to signal an infringement and stop play, or of a police officer blowing to summon help in apprehending a criminal.

blue-eyed boy ✪✪

PLAIN ENGLISH ALTERNATIVES: favourite; pet; darling

CLICHÉD ALTERNATIVES: apple of one's eye; fair-haired boy (*US*)

blue murder

See **scream blue murder**.

bob's your uncle

PLAIN ENGLISH ALTERNATIVES: the thing is done; everything is sorted out; it's as easy as that

CLICHÉD ALTERNATIVES: no sooner said than done; that's it; that's that; there you are

> ! *Original alternative:* you're home and hosed

body blow

PLAIN ENGLISH ALTERNATIVES: blow; severe blow; knock; reverse; setback; factor contributing to one's downfall

CLICHÉD ALTERNATIVES: nail in one's coffin; one in the eye

■ *Origins* From boxing, meaning 'a blow that may well knock the wind out of the victim'.

boffin

PLAIN ENGLISH ALTERNATIVES: scientist; expert; specialist; technical advisor

CLICHÉD ALTERNATIVES: backroom boy; rocket scientist; techie

bog-standard

PLAIN ENGLISH ALTERNATIVES: ordinary; standard; plain; basic; common; unexceptional

CLICHÉD ALTERNATIVES: run-of-the-mill; common-or-garden; vanilla

bold as brass

PLAIN ENGLISH ALTERNATIVES: impudent; cheeky; immodest; impertinent

CLICHÉD ALTERNATIVES: brass-necked; in-your-face

bolt from the blue ✪✪

PLAIN ENGLISH ALTERNATIVES: surprise; unlooked-for event; shock

CLICHÉD ALTERNATIVES: bombshell; eye-opener; a turn-up for the books; shock-horror revelation

■ *Origins* The 'bolt' in this case refers to a lightning bolt, proverbial for being sudden and shocking.

bone of contention ✪✪

PLAIN ENGLISH ALTERNATIVES: argument; issue; point of dispute; disputed point

CLICHÉD ALTERNATIVES: bone to pick; moot point; sore point; vexed question

■ *Origins* The idea is of dogs scrapping over an animal bone.

boot is on the other foot, the ✪✪

PLAIN ENGLISH ALTERNATIVES: the positions are reversed; things have changed

CLICHÉD ALTERNATIVES: it's a different kettle of fish; the worm has turned; the lunatics have taken over the asylum

bore one to tears ✪✪

PLAIN ENGLISH ALTERNATIVES: tire; stultify; be tedious; weary

CLICHÉD ALTERNATIVES: make one yawn; send one to sleep; bore the pants off one; bore one rigid

> **!** *Original alternative:* make one prefer to stick pins in one's eyes

born with a silver spoon in one's mouth ✪✪

PLAIN ENGLISH ALTERNATIVES: born into wealth; privileged

---

bosom buddy

Clichéd alternatives: blue-blooded; born into the purple

■ *Origins* From the traditional gift of a silver spoon to a newborn child from a godparent.

bosom buddy/chum/friend/pal   ✪✪

Plain English alternatives: close friend; dear friend; intimate

Clichéd alternatives: alter ego; boon companion; crony; china; homeboy (US); fidus Achates; friend of one's bosom

■ *Origins* Close enough to merit being hugged to one's bosom.

bottom line   ✪✪✪✪

Plain English alternatives: basic truth; plain truth; essence; ultimate criterion; essential fact; what really matters

Clichéd alternatives: nub of the matter; nitty-gritty; crux of the matter

■ *Origins* From the final total shown on an accounts document, determining whether a profit or loss has been made.

bow and scrape   ✪✪

Plain English alternatives: be subservient; ingratiate oneself; abase oneself

Clichéd alternatives: kowtow; suck up; kiss ass; brown-nose

box of tricks   ✪

Plain English alternatives: repertoire; resources; equipment; toolbag

Clichéd alternatives: bag of tricks

■ *Origins* From the literal box of tricks and props used by a stage magician.

break the ice   ✪✪

Plain English alternatives: allow people to relax; lighten things up; dispel people's inhibitions

CLICHÉD ALTERNATIVES: break down the barriers; start the ball rolling

■ *Origins* Breaking the ice allows a frozen river to flow, or a ship to make progress in frozen seas.

break the mould ✪✪

PLAIN ENGLISH ALTERNATIVES: change everything; make radical changes; make wholesale changes; start anew; make a new beginning

CLICHÉD ALTERNATIVES: start from scratch; out with the old, in with the new

■ *Origins* The allusion is to a mould that has been used to cast many copies of something being deliberately broken because something new is now to be made instead. In phrases such as 'when they made her they broke the mould' the idea is that there will be no more like the person in question, whether this is accounted a good thing or not.

breathe new life into something/someone ✪✪

PLAIN ENGLISH ALTERNATIVES: inspire; reanimate; lend fresh impetus to; reawaken one's interest

CLICHÉD ALTERNATIVES: be a breath of fresh air

breath of fresh air ✪✪

PLAIN ENGLISH ALTERNATIVES: new and refreshing influence; new life; new inspiration; new impetus

CLICHÉD ALTERNATIVES: breath of spring

bribery and corruption ✪✪✪✪

PLAIN ENGLISH ALTERNATIVES: dishonesty; graft; fraudulency; jobbery; backhanders

CLICHÉD ALTERNATIVES: shady dealings; funny business; jiggery-pokery

Note: This qualifies as a cliché because it is one of those pairs that are always used together, as if either bribery or corruption on its own were not sufficiently deplorable.

bright and breezy ✪✪

PLAIN ENGLISH ALTERNATIVES: alert; animated; cheery; nonchalant; vivacious; chirpy; light-hearted

CLICHÉD ALTERNATIVES: bright as a button; bright-eyed and bushy-tailed

bright-eyed and bushy-tailed ✪✪✪✪✪

PLAIN ENGLISH ALTERNATIVES: alert; animated; cheery; nonchalant; vivacious; chirpy; light-hearted; keen; ready

CLICHÉD ALTERNATIVES: bright as a button; bright and breezy; fresh as a daisy

■ *Origins* The bushy tail is that of a squirrel, sitting alert to danger or opportunities.

bring home the bacon ✪✪

PLAIN ENGLISH ALTERNATIVES: succeed; triumph

CLICHÉD ALTERNATIVES: do the business; do the necessary; take care of business; carry off the prize

bring someone up to speed ✪✪✪

PLAIN ENGLISH ALTERNATIVES: fully inform someone; bring someone up to date

CLICHÉD ALTERNATIVES: make someone aware of the full facts; put someone in the picture; give someone the full SP

bring the house down ✪✪

PLAIN ENGLISH ALTERNATIVES: be a great success; be acclaimed; earn great applause

CLICHÉD ALTERNATIVES: be applauded to the echo; make the rafters ring; have them rolling in the aisles; get a standing ovation

bring to book ✪✪

PLAIN ENGLISH ALTERNATIVES: arrest; bring to trial; reprimand

CLICHÉD ALTERNATIVES: call to account; bring to justice; carpet; haul over the coals; tear a strip off; make one account for oneself

briny, the ✪

PLAIN ENGLISH ALTERNATIVES: the sea; the ocean

CLICHÉD ALTERNATIVES: the waves; the seven seas; the ocean wave; the deep; the drink

brownie points ✪✪✪

PLAIN ENGLISH ALTERNATIVES: praise; credit; recognition; commendation

CLICHÉD ALTERNATIVES: kudos; pat on the back

■ *Origins* Some say this comes from the Brownie Guides and refers to members gaining merits or badges, while others believe it is more to do with 'brown-nosing'.

buck stops here, the ✪✪✪

PLAIN ENGLISH ALTERNATIVES: the responsibility is mine; I will take responsibility; leave it to me

CLICHÉD ALTERNATIVES: it's my pigeon; it's down to me

■ *Origins* See **pass the buck**.

bumper to bumper ✪✪

PLAIN ENGLISH ALTERNATIVES: busy; heavy; congested

CLICHÉD ALTERNATIVES: chock-a-block

burn the candle at both ends ✪✪

PLAIN ENGLISH ALTERNATIVES: overdo it; overtax oneself; exhaust oneself

burn the midnight oil   ✪✪

PLAIN ENGLISH ALTERNATIVES: work late; study late; stay up late working

CLICHÉD ALTERNATIVES: swot; cram

bury the hatchet   ✪✪

PLAIN ENGLISH ALTERNATIVES: make peace; be reconciled; cease hostilities

CLICHÉD ALTERNATIVES: let bygones be bygones

■ *Origins* Apparently from a Native American custom of physically burying weapons as a demonstration that fighting was over.

buy into   ✪✪✪✪

PLAIN ENGLISH ALTERNATIVES: endorse; support; subscribe to; accept

CLICHÉD ALTERNATIVES: get behind; take on board

by all accounts   ✪✪

PLAIN ENGLISH ALTERNATIVES: apparently; it seems; as general opinion would have it

CLICHÉD ALTERNATIVES: they say; it is said; as the story goes

by a long chalk

See **not by a long chalk**.

by and large   ✪✪

PLAIN ENGLISH ALTERNATIVES: on the whole; generally speaking; in general terms

CLICHÉD ALTERNATIVES: more or less; pretty much

■ *Origins* In nautical terms, sailing *by* means sailing with the sails trimmed very closely so as to allow the vessel to move as closely as possible into the wind; sailing *large* means sailing with a following wind. Thus, sailing *by and large* would cover most types of voyaging.

by hook or by crook ✪✪

PLAIN ENGLISH ALTERNATIVES: by any means necessary; one way or another

CLICHÉD ALTERNATIVES: whatever it takes; any which way; by fair means or foul

■ *Origins* Perhaps from a feudal custom of allowing tenants to take firewood from a tree using a shepherd's crook and a billhook.

by leaps and bounds ✪✪

PLAIN ENGLISH ALTERNATIVES: splendidly; swimmingly; rapidly

CLICHÉD ALTERNATIVES: like nobody's business; at a rate of knots; at a fair old pace

by the same token ✪✪

PLAIN ENGLISH ALTERNATIVES: similarly; at the same time; in the same way

by the skin of one's teeth ✪✪

PLAIN ENGLISH ALTERNATIVES: narrowly; only just; by a narrow margin; by the narrowest of margins

CLICHÉD ALTERNATIVES: by a whisker; at the last minute; just and no more; by a hair's-breadth; by a hair

■ *Origins* From the Bible (*Job* 19.20): 'I am escaped with the skin of my teeth.'

C

call a spade a spade ✪✪

PLAIN ENGLISH ALTERNATIVES: be frank; speak plainly; be direct

CLICHÉD ALTERNATIVES: not mince one's words; talk turkey; give it to one straight from the shoulder

■ *Origins* Apparently the result of a mistranslation of a Greek expression meaning 'to call a basin a basin' (rather than trying to pass it off as a vase).

call it a day ✪✪

PLAIN ENGLISH ALTERNATIVES: stop; stop working; give up; quit; discontinue

CLICHÉD ALTERNATIVES: call a halt; pack it in; knock off; down tools; say enough is enough; throw in the towel

■ *Origins* From the idea of deciding that one can stop working because a day's work has been accomplished no matter whether or not a full working day has elapsed.

callow youth ✪✪

PLAIN ENGLISH ALTERNATIVES: youth; young person; tyro; ingénu(e)

CLICHÉD ALTERNATIVES: greenhorn; someone who is still wet behind the ears; young whippersnapper; fledgling

Note: The word 'callow' originally meant 'too young to have started shaving', so think twice before using this expression to describe a girl!

calm before the storm ✪✪✪

PLAIN ENGLISH ALTERNATIVES: peaceful interlude; deceptive calm

can of worms ✪✪✪

PLAIN ENGLISH ALTERNATIVES: complex problem; difficult situation; unpredictable situation

CLICHÉD ALTERNATIVES: Pandora's box

■ *Origins* Some say that this comes from the idea of an angler opening up a can full of wriggling live worms to be used as bait, while another opinion is that the can is one thought to contain fresh food which turns out to be full of maggots.

captain of industry ✪✪

PLAIN ENGLISH ALTERNATIVES: industrialist; business magnate

CLICHÉD ALTERNATIVES: fat cat; baron; big wheel

card up one's sleeve ✪✪

PLAIN ENGLISH ALTERNATIVES: secret advantage; hidden asset

CLICHÉD ALTERNATIVES: ace in the hole; ace up one's sleeve; card up one's sleeve; trick up one's sleeve; trump card

■ *Origins* From the idea that concealing an additional card besides those one is known to hold can supply an unexpected advantage in card games.

carry a torch for someone ✪✪

PLAIN ENGLISH ALTERNATIVES: suffer unrequited love for someone; love someone in vain

CLICHÉD ALTERNATIVES: suffer the pangs of unrequited love for someone; worship someone from afar; have a thing for someone

■ *Origins* The torch symbolizes love or passion, and this idea is also found in such expressions as *torch-singer* and *torch-song*.

carry the can ✪✪

PLAIN ENGLISH ALTERNATIVES: be blamed; take the blame; accept responsibility

CLICHÉD ALTERNATIVES: take the rap; put one's hands up

catch one's death of cold

■ *Origins* This seems to come from military slang, referring to a scapegoat being left holding an empty container after being only one of several unentitled persons involved in disposing of its contents.

catch one's death of cold ✪✪

PLAIN ENGLISH ALTERNATIVES: catch a bad cold; contract a heavy cold

CLICHÉD ALTERNATIVES: catch the mother and father of all colds; be laid low by the cold

catch one's drift ✪✪

PLAIN ENGLISH ALTERNATIVES: understand; follow; catch on; twig; see; get it

CLICHÉD ALTERNATIVES: get the picture; hear what one is saying

■ *Origins* 'Drift' here means the direction in which something is driven or carried by a current at sea.

catch someone red-handed ✪✪✪

PLAIN ENGLISH ALTERNATIVES: catch someone in the act

CLICHÉD ALTERNATIVES: catch someone in flagrante delicto; catch someone with their hand in the till; catch someone with a smoking gun

■ *Origins* Originally applied to a killer, apprehended so quickly after the crime that their hands are still stained with blood.

catch someone's eye ✪✪

PLAIN ENGLISH ALTERNATIVES: attract someone's attention; be seen

CLICHÉD ALTERNATIVES: be spotted by someone

catch someone with their pants or trousers down ✪✪

PLAIN ENGLISH ALTERNATIVES: take someone unawares; catch someone unprepared; take someone by surprise; catch someone off-guard

CLICHÉD ALTERNATIVES: catch someone napping; catch someone on the hop; blindside someone; sneak up on someone

Catch-22 situation ✪✪✪✪✪

PLAIN ENGLISH ALTERNATIVES: dilemma; quandary; impossible position

CLICHÉD ALTERNATIVES: no-win situation; lose-lose situation

▪ *Origins* From the novel *Catch-22* by Joseph Heller (1961), which refers to a rule applying to US bomber pilots in World War II. Essentially, it boils down to the idea that a pilot could only be grounded if he was insane, but if he sought to be grounded he was demonstrating sanity, and so he would have to keep flying missions. The phrase is often used rather loosely to refer to any difficult situation.

cat's pyjamas or **whiskers, the** ✪✪

PLAIN ENGLISH ALTERNATIVES: the greatest; wonderful; the best

CLICHÉD ALTERNATIVES: the bee's knees; the dog's bollocks; something else; the best thing since sliced bread; God's gift; all that

▪ *Origins* Like *the bee's knees*, this comes from 1920s US slang. While a feline's whiskers are clearly of great use, the attribution of excellence to its pyjamas seems to be entirely arbitrary.

chain reaction ✪✪

PLAIN ENGLISH ALTERNATIVES: a situation in which one event causes another

CLICHÉD ALTERNATIVES: domino effect; knock-on effect; vicious circle

▪ *Origins* From science, especially nuclear science, where it was originally used to refer to the triggering of one chemical reaction, which led to another, and so on.

chalk and cheese ✪✪

PLAIN ENGLISH ALTERNATIVES: completely different (things); dissimilar; unlike; not comparable; utterly different; incompatible

CLICHÉD ALTERNATIVES: poles apart; worlds apart; (from) two different worlds

champing at the bit ✪✪

PLAIN ENGLISH ALTERNATIVES: impatient; agog; chafing; eager

CLICHÉD ALTERNATIVES: hot to trot; like a cat on hot bricks; straining at the leash; mad for it

■ *Origins* From an impatient or nervous horse relieving its feelings by gnawing the bit in its mouth.

chance one's arm or luck ✪✪

PLAIN ENGLISH ALTERNATIVES: take a chance; take a risk; run a risk; try one's luck

CLICHÉD ALTERNATIVES: push one's luck; try it on; have a go; take the plunge

■ *Origins* Probably from throwing a speculative punch in boxing.

chance would be a fine thing ✪✪

PLAIN ENGLISH ALTERNATIVES: there is not much hope of that; it's unlikely I'll ever be given the opportunity; I only wish I had the opportunity

CLICHÉD ALTERNATIVES: I should be so lucky

change one's tune ✪✪

PLAIN ENGLISH ALTERNATIVES: change one's attitude; change one's opinions; adopt a different stance; have a change of mind; say something different

CLICHÉD ALTERNATIVES: sing a different song

chapter and verse ✪✪✪

PLAIN ENGLISH ALTERNATIVES: the full details; the complete facts

CLICHÉD ALTERNATIVES: the whole thing down in black and white; the whole rigmarole; the lowdown

■ *Origins* References to a specific line of the Bible are given by stating the number of the chapter in which it appears and then the number of the verse within the chapter.

chapter of accidents ✪✪

PLAIN ENGLISH ALTERNATIVES: series of unfortunate events; series of accidents

CLICHÉD ALTERNATIVES: catalogue of misery; one damn thing after another

■ *Origins* An early use is as a chapter heading in *Tom Brown's Schooldays* (1857).

chattering classes ✪✪

PLAIN ENGLISH ALTERNATIVES: literati; intelligentsia; intellectuals; cognoscenti; media commentators

CLICHÉD ALTERNATIVES: media types

cheap and cheerful ✪✪

PLAIN ENGLISH ALTERNATIVES: economic but practical; inexpensive but attractive; bargain

CLICHÉD ALTERNATIVES: mid-range

cheap and nasty ✪✪

PLAIN ENGLISH ALTERNATIVES: second-rate; shoddy; poor-quality; tatty; tawdry

CLICHÉD ALTERNATIVES: cheapo; poxy; scuzzy; bargain-basement

cheap at half the price ✪✪

PLAIN ENGLISH ALTERNATIVES: overpriced; high-priced; not very cheap at all

CLICHÉD ALTERNATIVES: over the odds; steep

cheek by jowl

Note: Some people unthinkingly use this expression in direct contradiction of its meaning to refer to something that is a bargain. This is a good reason for avoiding it altogether.

cheek by jowl ✪✪

Plain English alternatives: side by side; close together; in close proximity

Clichéd alternatives: on top of one another

chequered career ✪✪

Plain English alternatives: a life of mixed fortune; an eventful life

Clichéd alternatives: a life of ups and downs; a dubious past; a history; a past

■ *Origins* The meaning of 'chequered' here is having alternations of black and white, like a chessboard, symbolizing bad and good luck, or dishonourable and honourable actions.

cheque's in the post, the ✪✪✪✪✪

Plain English alternatives: payment is imminent; payment is in hand; you will receive payment soon

Clichéd alternatives: the money's on its way

■ *Origins* Often referred to as 'the oldest cliché in the book', it clearly cannot predate the invention of the cheque, but has been in use ever since as a favourite way of stalling creditors.

chew the fat ✪✪

Plain English alternatives: argue; gossip; chat; chatter; converse

Clichéd alternatives: argue the toss; rabbit on; shoot the breeze

■ *Origins* From a comparison between the movements of a person's mouth and face while speaking to the similar movement made while eating.

chink in one's armour ✪✪

Plain English alternatives: weakness; weak point; vulnerable point; flaw; defect; shortcoming

Clichéd alternatives: Achilles' heel; soft underbelly; crack in one's defences

■ *Origins* From a literal gap in a warrior's otherwise reliable armour, through which a fatal arrow or blade might find a way.

chip on one's shoulder ✪✪

Plain English alternatives: grievance; bitterness; resentment; readiness to take offence; quarrelsome nature

Clichéd alternatives: chip on both shoulders

■ *Origins* This originated in America in the 19th century, and refers to the practice of challenging someone to fight by placing a woodchip on your shoulder and daring the other person to knock it off. It was introduced into Britain by US servicemen in World War II.

chop, the ✪✪

Plain English alternatives: death; dismissal; discharge; the sack; redundancy

Clichéd alternatives: one's P45; one's marching orders; one's books; one's cards; the boot; the elbow; the high jump; the old heave-ho; the push; the bum's rush; the order of the boot

■ *Origins* Presumably from execution by having one's head chopped off.

chop and change ✪✪

Plain English alternatives: keep making changes; vacillate; fluctuate; be indecisive

Clichéd alternatives: blow hot and cold; be unable to make one's mind up; keep coming and going

■ *Origins* The original meaning is 'to buy and sell, to barter or exchange', and lacks the pejorative element of indecisiveness.

chorus of disapproval

PLAIN ENGLISH ALTERNATIVES: widespread disapproval; general censure; public opprobrium

chosen few, the

PLAIN ENGLISH ALTERNATIVES: the elite; the elect; the best; the pick; the favoured; the privileged

CLICHÉD ALTERNATIVES: those and such as those (*Scottish*)

claim to fame

PLAIN ENGLISH ALTERNATIVES: accomplishment; achievement; attainment; gift; talent; feat

CLICHÉD ALTERNATIVES: unique selling point

clean sweep

See **make a clean sweep**.

clear as mud

PLAIN ENGLISH ALTERNATIVES: not at all clear; unclear; obscure; impenetrable; confusing; unintelligible

clear the air

PLAIN ENGLISH ALTERNATIVES: simplify the situation; reduce tension; dispel misunderstandings

CLICHÉD ALTERNATIVES: get it all out in the open; put things right; sort it all out

clear the decks

PLAIN ENGLISH ALTERNATIVES: clear up; tidy up; prepare for action

CLICHÉD ALTERNATIVES: get everything shipshape and Bristol-fashion; get things squared away

■ *Origins* As you might expect, this was originally a naval expression, referring to the practice aboard a ship preparing for battle of removing any clutter on the decks that might impede the use of the guns.

climate of opinion ✪✪✪✪

PLAIN ENGLISH ALTERNATIVES: general opinion; public opinion; complex of opinions; critical atmosphere; general mood; prevailing mood; temper; ambience; attitudes

CLICHÉD ALTERNATIVES: way the wind blows

cloak-and-dagger ✪✪

PLAIN ENGLISH ALTERNATIVES: undercover; secret; secretive; clandestine

CLICHÉD ALTERNATIVES: James Bond-style

■ *Origins* From 16th-century Spanish swashbuckling dramas known as *comedias de capa y espada* (literally, cape and sword comedies), the term somehow being transposed to matters of espionage and intrigue.

close, but no cigar ✪✪

PLAIN ENGLISH ALTERNATIVES: you were almost correct; you were close but not close enough

CLICHÉD ALTERNATIVES: tough luck; you were almost there; you nearly had it then

■ *Origins* Originally American, this refers to a cigar being given as a prize, for example at a fairground.

close call/shave/thing ✪✪

PLAIN ENGLISH ALTERNATIVES: narrow escape; near thing

CLICHÉD ALTERNATIVES: a close-run thing; a near-run thing; a touch-and-go situation

clutching at straws

- *Origins* The fact that a shave or incident may be uncomfortably close is obvious enough, but why a call? One explanation is that this comes from baseball, where a decision made by the umpire is referred to as a call, and a difficult decision may be described as 'too close to call'.

clutching at straws ✪✪

PLAIN ENGLISH ALTERNATIVES: acting out of desperation; applying a remedy known to be inadequate; trying everything; clinging to forlorn hopes; indulging in wishful thinking

CLICHÉD ALTERNATIVES: trying everything in the book; hoping against hope

- *Origins* From the proverb 'a drowning man will clutch at a straw'.

coast is clear, the ✪✪

PLAIN ENGLISH ALTERNATIVES: there is no danger; there is no obstacle; there is nothing to prevent our action

CLICHÉD ALTERNATIVES: nobody's looking; we can make a clean getaway

- *Origins* Probably from the idea of smugglers operating while the revenue cutter is out of sight.

cock-and-bull story ✪✪✪

PLAIN ENGLISH ALTERNATIVES: fabrication; lie; rigmarole; fiction; canard

CLICHÉD ALTERNATIVES: tall story; tall tale; porky pie

- *Origins* From traditional fables involving talking cocks and bulls.

cocktail of drugs ✪✪✪✪

PLAIN ENGLISH ALTERNATIVES: mixture of drugs; number of different drugs; several drugs at once

cold feet

See **get cold feet**.

cold shoulder, the ✪✪

PLAIN ENGLISH ALTERNATIVES: a rebuff; a cut; discouragement; rejection; a snub; ostracism

CLICHÉD ALTERNATIVES: a chilly reception

■ *Origins* It has been suggested that this derives from a medieval snub of offering cold shoulder of mutton (normally servants' fare) to guests as a sign that they were not welcome. However, a much less strained explanation is that it refers to turning away from someone one does not wish to speak to.

come a cropper ✪✪

PLAIN ENGLISH ALTERNATIVES: fall; fall headlong; fall heavily; fail badly; flop

CLICHÉD ALTERNATIVES: come a purler; come unstuck; come to grief; fall flat on one's face; go belly-up; go head over heels; crash and burn; come to a sticky end

■ *Origins* Perhaps from the phrase 'neck and crop', meaning 'completely'.

come apart at the seams ✪✪

PLAIN ENGLISH ALTERNATIVES: fall to pieces; suffer a breakdown; collapse

CLICHÉD ALTERNATIVES: crack up; fall apart; flip one's lid; go to pieces; lose it

come clean ✪✪

PLAIN ENGLISH ALTERNATIVES: confess; tell the truth; make a frank admission

CLICHÉD ALTERNATIVES: make a full and frank confession; fess up; make a clean breast of it; get it off one's chest

come down on someone like a ton of bricks ✪✪

PLAIN ENGLISH ALTERNATIVES: reprimand someone severely; punish someone severely

CLICHÉD ALTERNATIVES: throw the book at someone; haul someone over the coals; kill someone; murder someone; nail someone's hide to the wall; put the fear of God into someone; come down heavily on someone

come hell or high water

PLAIN ENGLISH ALTERNATIVES: no matter what (happens or transpires); come what may

CLICHÉD ALTERNATIVES: let the cards fall as they may; in the teeth of all opposition; come rain or shine

come home to roost

PLAIN ENGLISH ALTERNATIVES: recoil upon oneself; rebound on one

CLICHÉD ALTERNATIVES: come back to haunt one

- *Origins* From the habit of chickens going back to their roosts for the night.

come onstream

PLAIN ENGLISH ALTERNATIVES: come into operation; come into use; be implemented; be introduced; be brought in; start being used

CLICHÉD ALTERNATIVES: be rolled out; be ushered in; come into play

come rain or shine

PLAIN ENGLISH ALTERNATIVES: no matter what (happens or transpires); come what may

CLICHÉD ALTERNATIVES: let the cards fall as they may; come hell or high water; one way or another

come to a sticky end

PLAIN ENGLISH ALTERNATIVES: meet with disaster; end badly; end disastrously

CLICHÉD ALTERNATIVES: come a cropper; come unstuck; go belly-up; go the way of all flesh; come to grief; crash and burn; tank (*US*)

come to grief   ✪✪

PLAIN ENGLISH ALTERNATIVES: fail; meet with disaster; flop; be ruined; come to nothing

CLICHÉD ALTERNATIVES: come a cropper; come unstuck; go belly-up; go to the wall; come to a sticky end; crash and burn; tank (*US*)

common or garden   ✪✪

PLAIN ENGLISH ALTERNATIVES: ordinary; everyday; common; commonplace; plain; stock

CLICHÉD ALTERNATIVES: bog-standard; vanilla; run-of-the-mill

■ *Origins* A reference to ordinary, non-exotic, species of plants that may grow in any garden.

consign to oblivion   ✪✪

PLAIN ENGLISH ALTERNATIVES: reject; get rid of; forget about; dismiss from one's mind

CLICHÉD ALTERNATIVES: forget something ever existed

conspicuous by one's absence   ✪✪✪✪

PLAIN ENGLISH ALTERNATIVES: absent; missing; not in attendance; not around; elsewhere; not there

CLICHÉD ALTERNATIVES: nowhere to be seen (or found); not in evidence

cook someone's goose   ✪✪

PLAIN ENGLISH ALTERNATIVES: spoil one's plans; ruin one's chances; defeat someone; ruin someone; put paid to someone

CLICHÉD ALTERNATIVES: do for someone; rain on someone's parade; hang someone out to dry; put the mockers on someone

cook the books   ✪✪

PLAIN ENGLISH ALTERNATIVES: falsify accounts; swindle

CLICHÉD ALTERNATIVES: fiddle the accounts

cool as a cucumber

See **as cool as a cucumber**.

cool, calm and collected   ✪✪

PLAIN ENGLISH ALTERNATIVES: calm; perfectly self-possessed; unfazed; not in the least bothered; nonchalant

CLICHÉD ALTERNATIVES: as cool as a cucumber, as cool as you please; ice cool

cost an arm and a leg   ✪✪

PLAIN ENGLISH ALTERNATIVES: be very expensive; be high-priced; be extortionate

CLICHÉD ALTERNATIVES: cost a bomb; cost a fortune; cost a packet; cost the earth

couldn't care less

See **I couldn't care less**.

cover all the bases   ✪✪

PLAIN ENGLISH ALTERNATIVES: cover everything; be comprehensive; take in everything

CLICHÉD ALTERNATIVES: run the whole gamut

- *Origins* From baseball, in which this means to have a man at each base ready to receive a throw.

crack of dawn

See **at the crack of dawn**.

crack troops   ✪✪✪✪

PLAIN ENGLISH ALTERNATIVES: elite troops; elite forces

cream of the crop   ✪✪

PLAIN ENGLISH ALTERNATIVES: the best; the elite; the pick; the flower

CLICHÉD ALTERNATIVES: the *crème de la crème*

cross swords   ✪✪

PLAIN ENGLISH ALTERNATIVES: come into conflict; enter into a dispute; come up against one another; have dealings

CLICHÉD ALTERNATIVES: fall out; have a run-in

cross the Rubicon   ✪✪

PLAIN ENGLISH ALTERNATIVES: commit oneself; take an irrevocable step; take an action from which there is no turning back

CLICHÉD ALTERNATIVES: burn one's boats (or bridges)

■ *Origins* In Roman times the Rubicon was a river marking the border between Cisalpine Gaul and Rome proper. When Julius Caesar led an army towards Rome across this river in defiance of the Senate he was effectively initiating civil war.

cross to bear   ✪✪

PLAIN ENGLISH ALTERNATIVES: burden; affliction; trial; sorrow

■ *Origins* A Biblical reference to Jesus carrying the cross on which he was to be crucified, but also highly symbolic.

crying out for attention ✪✪

PLAIN ENGLISH ALTERNATIVES: urgent; importunate; pressing; blatant; obtrusive

CLICHÉD ALTERNATIVES: sticking out like a sore thumb

cry one's eyes out ✪✪

PLAIN ENGLISH ALTERNATIVES: weep copiously; howl; blubber; blub; sob; boo-hoo

CLICHÉD ALTERNATIVES: be in floods of tears; cry like a baby

cup that cheers, the ✪✪✪✪✪

PLAIN ENGLISH ALTERNATIVES: tea; a cup of tea

CLICHÉD ALTERNATIVES: a cuppa; a brew

■ *Origins* Altered from a line in a poem by William Cowper (*The Task*, 1785): 'The cups that cheer but not inebriate'.

cut a long story short

See **to cut a long story short**.

cut and dried ✪✪

PLAIN ENGLISH ALTERNATIVES: decided; settled; fixed; ready; prearranged

■ *Origins* Refers to lengths of cut wood being left to dry out before being ready for use.

cut no ice ✪✪

PLAIN ENGLISH ALTERNATIVES: fail to impress; count for nothing; be of no account; have no effect; have no influence; make no difference; make no impression

CLICHÉD ALTERNATIVES: make not a hap'orth of difference; be neither here nor there; butter no parsnips

cut one some slack   ✪✪

PLAIN ENGLISH ALTERNATIVES: be less critical; be less insistent; give one some leeway; give one a chance

CLICHÉD ALTERNATIVES: give one a break; give one room to manoeuvre

■ *Origins* The 'slack' refers to an amount of slack rope that someone can work with.

cut the mustard   ✪✪

PLAIN ENGLISH ALTERNATIVES: do what is required; perform well; be efficient; succeed

CLICHÉD ALTERNATIVES: do the necessary; get the job done; make the grade; make the cut

■ *Origins* Apparently a reference to harvesting mustard plants.

cutting-edge   ✪✪✪✪✪

PLAIN ENGLISH ALTERNATIVES: avant-garde; groundbreaking; ultramodern; pioneering

CLICHÉD ALTERNATIVES: up-to-the-minute; pushing the envelope

cut to the chase   ✪✪✪

PLAIN ENGLISH ALTERNATIVES: get to the point; be succinct

CLICHÉD ALTERNATIVES: cut a long story short; don't beat about the bush

■ *Origins* From the movies, in which a dull film can always be livened up by abandoning tedious exposition or clunky dialogue in favour of an action sequence such as a car chase.

D

dab hand

PLAIN ENGLISH ALTERNATIVES: expert; master/mistress; wizard; ace; virtuoso; whiz

CLICHÉD ALTERNATIVES: past master

daddy of them all, the

PLAIN ENGLISH ALTERNATIVES: the best; the biggest; the greatest

CLICHÉD ALTERNATIVES: the dog's bollocks; the mother of all …

daggers drawn

See **at daggers drawn**.

damp squib

PLAIN ENGLISH ALTERNATIVES: fiasco; failure; flop; debacle; let-down; disappointment

CLICHÉD ALTERNATIVES: cock-up

dance attendance on someone

PLAIN ENGLISH ALTERNATIVES: serve someone assiduously; carry out someone's every wish

CLICHÉD ALTERNATIVES: cater to someone's every whim; be at someone's beck and call; be unable to do enough for someone; wait on someone hand and foot

■ *Origins* Perhaps from the tradition of a bride being expected to dance with every guest at her wedding.

darken someone's door ✪✪

PLAIN ENGLISH ALTERNATIVES: appear; visit; turn up; come to call; show up

CLICHÉD ALTERNATIVES: make an appearance; put in an appearance; show one's face

> **❗** *Original alternative:* darken someone's towels (*One of the Marx Brothers' movies contains the immortal line, 'Go! And never darken my towels again!'*)

Davy Jones's locker ✪✪

PLAIN ENGLISH ALTERNATIVES: the sea; the bottom of the sea; an ocean grave

CLICHÉD ALTERNATIVES: a watery grave

■ *Origins* Davy Jones is a traditional sailors' name for the evil spirit of the sea, a nautical Old Nick. References in print to his locker (which means a chest) date back to the 1720s.

day in, day out ✪✪

PLAIN ENGLISH ALTERNATIVES: daily; every day; indefinitely; constantly; continually; unceasingly

CLICHÉD ALTERNATIVES: one day after another

daylight robbery ✪✪

PLAIN ENGLISH ALTERNATIVES: blatant over-charging; extortion; over-pricing

CLICHÉD ALTERNATIVES: charging an arm and a leg

■ *Origins* A robbery committed in broad daylight rather than under cover of darkness is all the more shocking in its effrontery.

days are numbered, one's ✪✪

PLAIN ENGLISH ALTERNATIVES: one will not survive much longer; one does not have long to live; one is obsolescent

CLICHÉD ALTERNATIVES: one is on the way out; the writing is on the wall

> **!** *Original alternative:* one's jacket is on a shaky nail

■ *Origins* Perhaps from a biblical allusion (*Daniel* 5). At Belshazzar's feast a disembodied hand wrote the following Aramaic words on the wall: *mene, mene, tekel, upharsin*, which have been interpreted as 'numbered, numbered, weighed, divisions'. The prophet Daniel took this to forecast the imminent downfall of Belshazzar. See also **writing is on the wall, the**.

dead as a dodo ✪✪✪

PLAIN ENGLISH ALTERNATIVES: dead; deceased; defunct; extinct; forgotten

CLICHÉD ALTERNATIVES: pushing up daisies; no longer with us; dead and gone; dead as a doornail; no more; history

■ *Origins* The dodo was a large flightless bird, native to the island of Mauritius, which was not sufficiently streetwise to avoid being rendered extinct by scavenging sailors in the 17th century.

dead as a doornail ✪✪✪

PLAIN ENGLISH ALTERNATIVES: dead; deceased; defunct; extinct; forgotten

CLICHÉD ALTERNATIVES: pushing up daisies; no longer with us; dead and gone; dead as a dodo; no more; history

dead from the neck up ✪✪

PLAIN ENGLISH ALTERNATIVES: deeply stupid; impenetrably stupid; invincibly stupid; cretinous; brain-dead; halfwitted; moronic; dumb

CLICHÉD ALTERNATIVES: thick as two short planks; slow on the uptake; not the sharpest tool in the box

dead in the water ✪✪

PLAIN ENGLISH ALTERNATIVES: helpless; powerless; finished; done-for; unable to move; impotent; disabled; prostrate

CLICHÉD ALTERNATIVES: gone for a Burton

■ *Origins* From the idea of a ship being unable to make any progress, whether a sailing ship becalmed or a powered vessel that has broken down.

dead ringer ✪✪✪

PLAIN ENGLISH ALTERNATIVES: double; image; exact copy; duplicate; twin; clone; doppelgänger

CLICHÉD ALTERNATIVES: spitting image; spit and image; dead spit

■ *Origins* A 'ringer' is a horse or athlete substituted for another in order to mislead the poor punters betting on the race.

dead to the world ✪✪

PLAIN ENGLISH ALTERNATIVES: sound asleep; fast asleep; deeply asleep; unconscious

CLICHÉD ALTERNATIVES: out for the count; out of it

deliver best practice ✪✪✪✪✪

PLAIN ENGLISH ALTERNATIVES: do a good job; do an exemplary job; work well; perform efficiently

CLICHÉD ALTERNATIVES: meet one's targets

demon drink, the ✪✪

PLAIN ENGLISH ALTERNATIVES: alcohol; strong drink; spirituous liquors

CLICHÉD ALTERNATIVES: the hard stuff; the bottle; strong waters; the sauce

devil to pay, the ✪✪

PLAIN ENGLISH ALTERNATIVES: dreadful consequences; evil consequences;

serious trouble; ructions

CLICHÉD ALTERNATIVES: hell to pay; all kinds of trouble; trouble in store

■ *Origins* 'Devil' here means a seam on a ship's deck, and to pay it means to waterproof it by painting it with tar. In fact, the full form of the phrase is 'the devil to pay and no pitch hot'. See also **between the devil and the deep blue sea**.

diamond geezer ✪✪✪

PLAIN ENGLISH ALTERNATIVES: admirable fellow; splendid chap; first-rate fellow; brick

CLICHÉD ALTERNATIVES: gem; stand-up guy; wonderful human being; one of nature's gentlemen; a gentleman, a scholar and a fine judge of whisky

dicing with death ✪✪

PLAIN ENGLISH ALTERNATIVES: taking great (or unnecessary) risks; risking one's life; exposing oneself to danger

CLICHÉD ALTERNATIVES: gambling with one's life; living dangerously; flirting with danger; playing with fire; going in harm's way; skating on thin ice; putting one's life on the line; risking life and limb

■ *Origins* 'Dicing' here means gambling on throws of dice against a personified figure of Death.

didn't see that one coming

See **I didn't see that one coming**.

die is cast, the ✪✪

PLAIN ENGLISH ALTERNATIVES: there is no turning back; an irrevocable step has been taken

■ *Origins* 'Die' is the little-used singular form of 'dice'. The expression is a translation of the Latin *alea iacta est*, said to have been uttered by Julius Caesar on taking the decisive step of crossing the Rubicon to initiate a civil war. See also **cross the Rubicon**.

die the death ✪✪

PLAIN ENGLISH ALTERNATIVES: fail utterly; fail to impress; bomb; flop

CLICHÉD ALTERNATIVES: go down like a lead balloon

■ *Origins* Originally used in the theatre of performers failing to get a reaction from an audience.

different ballgame, a ✪✪✪

PLAIN ENGLISH ALTERNATIVES: a different matter; not the same thing at all; something else again; another situation entirely

CLICHÉD ALTERNATIVES: a whole new ballgame; something completely different; another story altogether

■ *Origins* An import from the USA, as shown by the fact that the ballgame is a game of baseball.

different strokes for different folks ✪✪

PLAIN ENGLISH ALTERNATIVES: each to his/her own taste; we're not all the same

CLICHÉD ALTERNATIVES: to each his own; one man's meat is another man's poison; it wouldn't do if we all thought the same way

dirty work at the crossroads ✪

PLAIN ENGLISH ALTERNATIVES: foul play; dishonourable practices; skulduggery; criminal activity; illegal activity; underhandedness; suspicious goings-on; trickery; double-dealing; jiggery-pokery

CLICHÉD ALTERNATIVES: funny business

■ *Origins* Perhaps because people denied a Christian burial were formerly buried at a crossroads, or perhaps simply because a crossroads is a good place to ambush someone.

do a U-turn ✪✪

PLAIN ENGLISH ALTERNATIVES: go back on what one has previously said;

reverse one's policy; have a complete change of mind; flip-flop; back-pedal

CLICHÉD ALTERNATIVES: undergo a Damascene conversion; take the opposite tack

■ *Origins* From motoring, referring to a U-shaped turn made to reverse one's direction of travel.

does a bear shit in the woods?   ✪✪✪✪

PLAIN ENGLISH ALTERNATIVES: of course!; naturally!; obviously!; what do you think?

CLICHÉD ALTERNATIVES: you bet; do ducks fly south for the winter?; is the Pope a Catholic?

■ *Origins* This phrase began life as an American smart response to a needless question.

dog eat dog   ✪✪

PLAIN ENGLISH ALTERNATIVES: ruthless competition; unbridled individualism

CLICHÉD ALTERNATIVES: devil take the hindmost; every man for himself; a free-for-all; nature red in tooth and claw

dog's bollocks, the   ✪✪✪✪

PLAIN ENGLISH ALTERNATIVES: the best; the greatest; the finest; something excellent; something superlative

CLICHÉD ALTERNATIVES: the cat's pyjamas; the cat's whiskers; something else; the best thing since sliced bread

■ *Origins* This one is relatively recent, having become popular in the 1990s, but the reasoning behind elevating canine testicles to the epitome of quality is not immediately apparent.

dog's breakfast or dinner   ✪✪

PLAIN ENGLISH ALTERNATIVES: mess; shambles; jumble; state of disarray

dolce vita ✪✪

PLAIN ENGLISH ALTERNATIVES: a life of luxury; a life of ease; a life of wealth and indulgence

CLICHÉD ALTERNATIVES: the life of Riley

■ *Origins* From Italian, meaning 'sweet life', popularized by the film *La Dolce Vita* made in 1960 by Federico Fellini (which, incidentally, is also responsible for giving the world the term 'paparazzi').

done to death ✪✪

PLAIN ENGLISH ALTERNATIVES: repeated too often; overused; overdone

CLICHÉD ALTERNATIVES: milked for all it's worth

■ *Origins* From the theatre, referring to an act, joke, etc that has been used so often that it has become hackneyed.

donkey's years ✪✪✪

PLAIN ENGLISH ALTERNATIVES: a long time; years; years and years; ages; an age; forever

CLICHÉD ALTERNATIVES: till the cows come home; yonks

■ *Origins* A pun on a donkey's ears, which are always long.

don't call us, we'll call you ✪✪✪✪

PLAIN ENGLISH ALTERNATIVES: you don't get the job; your application has been unsuccessful

CLICHÉD ALTERNATIVES: we'll get back to you; forget it

Note: While this literally means 'we will let you know', it inevitably signifies rejection and was popularized as the archetypal verdict at the end of an indifferent audition.

don't get me wrong ✪✪

PLAIN ENGLISH ALTERNATIVES: don't misunderstand me; don't be misled; let me make myself clear

don't get your knickers in a twist

CLICHÉD ALTERNATIVES: don't get the wrong idea; don't run away with the idea that …; let me spell it out for you; read my lips

don't get your knickers in a twist ✪✪

PLAIN ENGLISH ALTERNATIVES: stay calm; keep cool; keep your head; don't get upset; maintain your composure (or sangfroid)

CLICHÉD ALTERNATIVES: keep your cool; don't get into a tizzy; don't lose the plot

> **!** *Original alternative:* don't get your Calvins in a clinch

don't go there ✪✪✪✪

PLAIN ENGLISH ALTERNATIVES: don't mention that; don't talk about that; that topic is taboo

CLICHÉD ALTERNATIVES: don't even think about it; don't go any further; that subject is off limits; that's not on the agenda

don't hold your breath ✪✪

PLAIN ENGLISH ALTERNATIVES: don't expect a quick result; there's no point in waiting; nothing is likely to happen; it's a waste of time to expect anything

CLICHÉD ALTERNATIVES: you'll be lucky; dream on; don't count on it

don't judge a book by its cover ✪✪

PLAIN ENGLISH ALTERNATIVES: don't trust first appearances; what is inside is most important

CLICHÉD ALTERNATIVES: all is not what it seems; appearances can be deceptive; it's what's on the inside that counts; there may be more to this than meets the eye; what you see isn't always what you get

don't rock the boat ✪✪

PLAIN ENGLISH ALTERNATIVES: don't upset the status quo; don't make a fuss; don't cause trouble; don't stir things up; don't create difficulties

CLICHÉD ALTERNATIVES: let sleeping dogs lie

doom (and gloom) merchants ✪✪

PLAIN ENGLISH ALTERNATIVES: pessimists; defeatists

CLICHÉD ALTERNATIVES: merchants of doom; Cassandras; wet blankets

do-or-die ✪✪

PLAIN ENGLISH ALTERNATIVES: desperate; despairing

CLICHÉD ALTERNATIVES: death-or-glory; win-or-bust; kill-or-cure; last-ditch

■ *Origins* Military, referring to an attack or other action that must succeed if the side making it is to gain victory or even survive.

do someone proud ✪✪

PLAIN ENGLISH ALTERNATIVES: treat someone lavishly; be generously hospitable to someone; do everything one can for someone

CLICHÉD ALTERNATIVES: pull out the stops for someone; push the boat out for someone; spare no expense for someone

do the dirty on someone ✪✪

PLAIN ENGLISH ALTERNATIVES: cheat someone; deceive someone; swindle someone; take advantage of someone

CLICHÉD ALTERNATIVES: play a dirty trick on someone; pull a fast one on someone

dot the i's and cross the t's ✪✪✪

PLAIN ENGLISH ALTERNATIVES: pay attention to detail; get the details right; be meticulous; finalize the details

CLICHÉD ALTERNATIVES: put the finishing touches to something; get everything just so

double Dutch ✪✪

PLAIN ENGLISH ALTERNATIVES: gibberish; gobbledegook; jargon; unintelligible language

CLICHÉD ALTERNATIVES: all Greek; mumbo-jumbo

doubting Thomas ✪✪

PLAIN ENGLISH ALTERNATIVES: sceptic; doubter; unbeliever; pessimist

CLICHÉD ALTERNATIVES: person of little faith

■ *Origins* From St Thomas, the apostle described in the New Testament (*John* 20.25) as being unwilling to believe that Christ had risen from the dead until he had physical proof.

down and out ✪✪

PLAIN ENGLISH ALTERNATIVES: destitute; poverty-stricken; homeless; indigent

CLICHÉD ALTERNATIVES: on one's uppers; on the street; in queer street; on the breadline

■ *Origins* From boxing, referring to a fighter who has not only been knocked down but has been counted out and has lost the fight.

down at heel ✪✪

PLAIN ENGLISH ALTERNATIVES: slovenly; slatternly; unkempt; untidy; in reduced circumstances

CLICHÉD ALTERNATIVES: the worse for wear

■ *Origins* Having to wear worn-out shoes with the heels trodden down is an obvious sign of poverty.

down but not out ✪✪

PLAIN ENGLISH ALTERNATIVES: wounded but not defeated; proud in defeat

CLICHÉD ALTERNATIVES: bloody but unbowed; with one's head held high

down in the mouth ✪✪

PLAIN ENGLISH ALTERNATIVES: in low spirits; out of spirits; depressed; sad; unhappy; disheartened; crestfallen; dispirited; blue; down; low; glum

CLICHÉD ALTERNATIVES: down in the dumps

▪ *Origins* From the idea that the corners of a person's mouth turn downwards when they are sad.

down on one's luck ✪✪

PLAIN ENGLISH ALTERNATIVES: needy; in reduced circumstances; unfortunate

CLICHÉD ALTERNATIVES: strapped for cash; short of the readies

down the drain ✪✪

PLAIN ENGLISH ALTERNATIVES: wasted; gone; lost; thrown away; frittered away

CLICHÉD ALTERNATIVES: down the Swanee

down the hatch ✪✪

PLAIN ENGLISH ALTERNATIVES: cheers; good health; prosit

CLICHÉD ALTERNATIVES: here's mud in your eye; here's looking at you; bottoms up

> **!** *Original alternative:* through the teeth and past the gums, look out belly, here it comes!

down-to-earth ✪✪

PLAIN ENGLISH ALTERNATIVES: hard-headed; sensible; realistic; practical; forthright; plain-speaking; grounded

CLICHÉD ALTERNATIVES: no-nonsense; matter-of-fact; with one's head screwed on right; with both feet on the ground

- *Origins* A down-to-earth person is the opposite of airy-fairy, is unlikely to build castles in the air, and never has their head in the clouds.

draw a blank ✪✪

PLAIN ENGLISH ALTERNATIVES: find nothing; get no result; be unlucky

CLICHÉD ALTERNATIVES: come back empty-handed; get no joy

- *Origins* Probably from a losing lottery ticket.

dream on ✪✪

PLAIN ENGLISH ALTERNATIVES: it's not going to happen; it'll never happen

CLICHÉD ALTERNATIVES: you'll be lucky; in your dreams; you're kidding yourself; never in a million years; don't count on it

dream team ✪✪✪✪

PLAIN ENGLISH ALTERNATIVES: ideal combination; optimum partnership; perfect pairing

CLICHÉD ALTERNATIVES: dream ticket

dressed up to the nines ✪✪

PLAIN ENGLISH ALTERNATIVES: wearing one's best; in one's best clothes; well-dressed

CLICHÉD ALTERNATIVES: dressed to kill; dressed up like a dog's dinner; in full fig; in one's best bib and tucker; in one's glad rags; well turned-out

- *Origins* Unclear. Some think it's a reference to nine being a mystic number and thus symbolizing perfection.

drinking in the last chance saloon ✪✪

PLAIN ENGLISH ALTERNATIVES: on one's last chance; having only one more chance; facing the end; all but finished

CLICHÉD ALTERNATIVES: on death row; on its last legs; on the way out; behind the eight ball

■ *Origins* Probably from the American West, in which a saloon might advertise itself as the last chance for a drink before the desert, etc.

drink like a fish ✪✪✪

PLAIN ENGLISH ALTERNATIVES: drink heavily; drink to excess; drink too much; be intemperate; be an alcoholic; be a drunkard

CLICHÉD ALTERNATIVES: be a lush; be an alky; drink like one has hollow legs

■ *Origins* An odd simile, since fish could be said not to drink at all, but as they are continually surrounded by liquid and often swim with their mouths open it's easy to see the connection.

drive a coach and horses through ✪✪

PLAIN ENGLISH ALTERNATIVES: demolish; nullify; dismiss; brush aside

CLICHÉD ALTERNATIVES: make a nonsense of; set at nought

drive a hard bargain ✪✪

PLAIN ENGLISH ALTERNATIVES: bargain uncompromisingly; be a tough negotiator

drive one to drink ✪✪

PLAIN ENGLISH ALTERNATIVES: be highly exasperating; be maddening; be infuriating; be unendurable; be a great nuisance

CLICHÉD ALTERNATIVES: drive one up the wall; drive one crazy; be more than flesh and blood can stand; try the patience of a saint

■ *Origins* From the idea of someone resorting to alcohol to calm themselves down.

drive one up the wall ✪✪

PLAIN ENGLISH ALTERNATIVES: be highly exasperating; be maddening; be infuriating; try one's patience

CLICHÉD ALTERNATIVES: get in one's hair; get on one's nerves; get on one's wick; get one's goat; drive one to distraction; drive one to drink

drop a brick ✪✪

PLAIN ENGLISH ALTERNATIVES: blunder; be indiscreet; be tactless; say the wrong thing

CLICHÉD ALTERNATIVES: drop a clanger; put one's foot in it; make a bloomer; make a gaffe; commit a faux pas

▪ *Origins* Apparently the expression arose at Cambridge University when the Sergeant-Major of a group of student military volunteers shouted an order so loudly that building workers dropped their bricks in alarm.

drop a clanger ✪✪

PLAIN ENGLISH ALTERNATIVES: blunder; be indiscreet; be tactless; say the wrong thing

CLICHÉD ALTERNATIVES: drop a brick; put one's foot in it; make a bloomer; make a gaffe; commit a faux pas

▪ *Origins* Probably from the idea of dropping something that makes a loud noise when it hits the floor, thus exposing one's clumsiness to all and sundry.

drop in the ocean ✪✪

PLAIN ENGLISH ALTERNATIVES: a tiny amount; a negligible amount; nowhere near enough

CLICHÉD ALTERNATIVES: a drop in the bucket

drop of a hat

See **at the drop of a hat**.

dry as a bone ✪✪

PLAIN ENGLISH ALTERNATIVES: arid; parched; moistureless; dehydrated; desiccated; dried up

CLICHÉD ALTERNATIVES: bone-dry

dry as dust ✪✪

PLAIN ENGLISH ALTERNATIVES: dull; tedious; uninteresting; boring; dreary; ho-hum; tiresome

CLICHÉD ALTERNATIVES: as dull as ditchwater

dull as ditchwater ✪✪

PLAIN ENGLISH ALTERNATIVES: dull; tedious; uninteresting; boring; dreary; ho-hum; insipid; stale; tiresome; sleep-inducing; yawn-inducing; mind-numbing

CLICHÉD ALTERNATIVES: dry as dust; crashingly boring

dyed-in-the-wool ✪✪

PLAIN ENGLISH ALTERNATIVES: confirmed; thorough; thoroughgoing; out-and-out; genuine; through-and-through; inveterate; entrenched; fixed

CLICHÉD ALTERNATIVES: deep-dyed; complete and utter

■ *Origins* Wool that was dyed before it was spun was said to retain its colour better.

E

each and every   ✪✪

PLAIN ENGLISH ALTERNATIVES: each; each one; all; every

CLICHÉD ALTERNATIVES: every single

eager beaver   ✪✪✪

PLAIN ENGLISH ALTERNATIVES: enthusiast; zealot; volunteer

CLICHÉD ALTERNATIVES: glutton for punishment

■ *Origins* Originally American. It seems that 'beaver' was chosen merely as the creature whose name rhymed most closely with 'eager', as the beaver is usually thought of as being industrious rather than keen. See also **beaver away**.

eagle eye   ✪✪

PLAIN ENGLISH ALTERNATIVES: fine eyesight; eye for detail; sharp eye; vigilance; circumspection

CLICHÉD ALTERNATIVES: watchful eye; all-seeing eye; gimlet eye; hawklike gaze

earn a crust   ✪✪

PLAIN ENGLISH ALTERNATIVES: make a living; pursue one's livelihood

CLICHÉD ALTERNATIVES: earn an honest buck; keep the wolf from the door; put food on the table; make a few bob

easy street

See **on easy street**.

eat humble pie ✪✪✪✪

PLAIN ENGLISH ALTERNATIVES: accept humiliation; be humiliated; be humbled; humble oneself; abase oneself; admit one was wrong

CLICHÉD ALTERNATIVES: eat one's words; eat crow; eat dirt

■ *Origins* Altered from 'umble pie', that is, a pie made from the umbles (entrails) of a deer. This would only be eaten by humble people such as servants.

eat one's heart out ✪✪✪

PLAIN ENGLISH ALTERNATIVES: pine away; brood; worry; grieve; be jealous

eat one's words ✪✪

PLAIN ENGLISH ALTERNATIVES: admit one was wrong; withdraw what one has said; take back what one has said

CLICHÉD ALTERNATIVES: eat humble pie

economical with the truth ✪✪✪✪

PLAIN ENGLISH ALTERNATIVES: mendacious; dishonest; false; untruthful; deceptive

CLICHÉD ALTERNATIVES: less than honest; not entirely truthful

■ *Origins* The phrase came to attention during a prominent trial in 1986, when Sir Robert Armstrong, a high-ranking civil servant, denied that a letter he had written contained a lie. He said, 'It contains a misleading impression, not a lie. It was being economical with the truth.'

elbow grease ✪✪

PLAIN ENGLISH ALTERNATIVES: application; effort; hard work; vigour

elementary, my dear Watson ✪✪

PLAIN ENGLISH ALTERNATIVES: it's obvious; it's simple; it's straightforward

CLICHÉD ALTERNATIVES: it's not rocket science; there's nothing to it

■ *Origins* Sherlock Holmes, of course. But the formula never occurs in the writings of his creator, Sir Arthur Conan Doyle. The nearest he came to it seems to have been in the story *The Crooked Man*: '"Excellent!" I cried [I, being Watson, the narrator]. "Elementary," said he.' The well-known form of the phrase was put in the great detective's mouth later by a movie scriptwriter.

eleventh hour   ✪✪

PLAIN ENGLISH ALTERNATIVES: the last minute; the very last moment

CLICHÉD ALTERNATIVES: the nick of time

■ *Origins* Probably from the Biblical parable (*Matthew* 20.1–16) in which workers are described as labouring in a vineyard. A dispute arises over why those who had worked a full day were paid the same as those who only started at the eleventh hour of the day (approximately 5pm).

end it all   ✪✪

PLAIN ENGLISH ALTERNATIVES: commit suicide; kill oneself; take one's own life

CLICHÉD ALTERNATIVES: do oneself in; top oneself

end of story   ✪✪✪

PLAIN ENGLISH ALTERNATIVES: there is no more to be said; and that's all there is to it

CLICHÉD ALTERNATIVES: and that's that; and that's it; enough said; full stop; period

end of the line or **road**   ✪✪

PLAIN ENGLISH ALTERNATIVES: the end; the limit; the finish

CLICHÉD ALTERNATIVES: the last hurrah

enough said   ✪✪✪

PLAIN ENGLISH ALTERNATIVES: there is no more to be said; need one go on?

CLICHÉD ALTERNATIVES: you can guess the rest; 'nuff said; I rest my case

every man Jack ✪✪

PLAIN ENGLISH ALTERNATIVES: one and all; everybody; everyone; every single one; each one

CLICHÉD ALTERNATIVES: all and sundry; each and every one

everything but the kitchen sink ✪✪✪

PLAIN ENGLISH ALTERNATIVES: absolutely everything; every conceivable thing

CLICHÉD ALTERNATIVES: the lot; the whole kit and caboodle; the whole shooting match

everything in the garden's lovely ✪✪✪✪

PLAIN ENGLISH ALTERNATIVES: all is well; things couldn't be better

CLICHÉD ALTERNATIVES: all is for the best in the best of all possible worlds; everything is peachy; God's in His heaven, all's right with the world

- *Origins* From the title of a music-hall song written in 1898.

every Tom, Dick and Harry ✪✪✪

PLAIN ENGLISH ALTERNATIVES: anyone at all; anybody; one and all; everybody; everyone; every single one; each one

CLICHÉD ALTERNATIVES: all and sundry; every man Jack; the world and his brother

every which way ✪✪✪✪✪

PLAIN ENGLISH ALTERNATIVES: in all directions; in every direction; in disorder; in disarray

CLICHÉD ALTERNATIVES: all over the shop (or place)

F

face the music   ✪✪

PLAIN ENGLISH ALTERNATIVES: accept the consequences; accept one's punishment without complaint

CLICHÉD ALTERNATIVES: take what's coming to you; put on a bold front; take it on the chin; take it like a man

■ *Origins* Opinions differ, some saying the reference is to a stage performer facing the orchestra (and the audience), others postulating that the original meaning referred to a soldier facing those trying him at a court martial (including a drummer).

fact of the matter, the   ✪✪

PLAIN ENGLISH ALTERNATIVES: the fact; the truth; the reality; the essence

CLICHÉD ALTERNATIVES: the actual fact

faint heart never won fair maid   ✪✪

PLAIN ENGLISH ALTERNATIVES: take courage; be bold; be brave

CLICHÉD ALTERNATIVES: go for it; get stuck in; have a go; nothing ventured, nothing gained

> **!** *Original alternative:* you've got to be in it to win it

fair and square   ✪

PLAIN ENGLISH ALTERNATIVES: fairly; honestly; justly; in a straightforward way

CLICHÉD ALTERNATIVES: the hard way

fair crack of the whip, a   ✪✪

PLAIN ENGLISH ALTERNATIVES: a fair chance (or opportunity); an even chance; fair play

CLICHÉD ALTERNATIVES: a level playing field; a sporting chance

fair sex, the   ✪✪✪✪

PLAIN ENGLISH ALTERNATIVES: the female sex; women; womankind

CLICHÉD ALTERNATIVES: the distaff side

fair to middling   ✪✪

PLAIN ENGLISH ALTERNATIVES: well enough; fairly well; reasonably well

CLICHÉD ALTERNATIVES: not bad

fall about (laughing)   ✪

PLAIN ENGLISH ALTERNATIVES: laugh hysterically; laugh uncontrollably; collapse with laughter

CLICHÉD ALTERNATIVES: be in stitches; roll about laughing; be rolling in the aisles; split one's sides; wet oneself

fall by the wayside   ✪✪

PLAIN ENGLISH ALTERNATIVES: drop out; fail to finish; give up

CLICHÉD ALTERNATIVES: be found wanting

■ *Origins* An allusion to a parable in the New Testament (*Luke* 8.5) in which some of a sower's seeds fall onto the path beside the field and so fail to grow.

fall foul of   ✪✪

PLAIN ENGLISH ALTERNATIVES: clash with; quarrel with; come into conflict with; fall out with

CLICHÉD ALTERNATIVES: cross swords with

■ *Origins* A nautical reference. When one vessel comes into accidental contact with another they are said to fall foul of one another.

fall on deaf ears ✪✪

PLAIN ENGLISH ALTERNATIVES: be ignored; be disregarded; go unheard; go unheeded

famous last words! ✪✪

PLAIN ENGLISH ALTERNATIVES: don't be so sure; don't prejudge the matter

CLICHÉD ALTERNATIVES: don't count your chickens until they are hatched; don't bet on it; I wouldn't count on it

■ *Origins* The suggestion is that people may express hopes or expectations that come to nothing because their death intervenes.

far and wide ✪✪

PLAIN ENGLISH ALTERNATIVES: all about; all around; all over; everywhere

CLICHÉD ALTERNATIVES: far and near; to the four corners of the globe; all over the place

far be it from me ✪✪✪✪

PLAIN ENGLISH ALTERNATIVES: I am reluctant; I am far too humble; it is not my place; I wouldn't presume

CLICHÉD ALTERNATIVES: God forbid

far cry, a ✪✪

PLAIN ENGLISH ALTERNATIVES: a long way; quite a way; a substantial distance

CLICHÉD ALTERNATIVES: a long haul; a good way

far from it ✪✪

PLAIN ENGLISH ALTERNATIVES: on the contrary; not at all; not in the least; not in the slightest

CLICHÉD ALTERNATIVES: not a bit of it

far from the madding crowd ✪✪✪✪

PLAIN ENGLISH ALTERNATIVES: in seclusion; in a peaceful place; away from the hurly-burly

CLICHÉD ALTERNATIVES: away from it all

■ *Origins* Made popular by being used as the title of a novel by Thomas Hardy, this comes from a line in *An Elegy in a Country Churchyard* (1750) by Thomas Gray: 'Far from the madding crowd's ignoble strife'. The word 'madding' can mean either 'behaving as if mad' or 'tending to drive one mad'.

fast and furious ✪✪

PLAIN ENGLISH ALTERNATIVES: hectic(ally); rapid(ly); vigorous(ly); frenetic(ally); eager(ly); uproarious(ly)

CLICHÉD ALTERNATIVES: thick and fast; like nobody's business

fat chance ✪✪

PLAIN ENGLISH ALTERNATIVES: little likelihood; no chance; little prospect

CLICHÉD ALTERNATIVES: no way

fate worse than death, a

PLAIN ENGLISH ALTERNATIVES: a dreadful fate; a degrading ordeal

CLICHÉD ALTERNATIVES: a fate too shocking to contemplate; a fate to be avoided at all costs

■ *Origins* In Victorian literature or melodrama this was a staple euphemism for a woman's loss of virtue, as by rape or seduction.

feather in one's cap ✪✪

PLAIN ENGLISH ALTERNATIVES: achievement to be proud of; accomplishment; honour; coup; triumph

■ *Origins* The reference is to the feathered headdress of a Native American warrior, to which he was entitled to add another feather for each enemy he killed.

feel-good factor ✪✪✪✪

PLAIN ENGLISH ALTERNATIVES: sense of optimism; sense of wellbeing

CLICHÉD ALTERNATIVES: good feeling

feeling no pain ✪✪

PLAIN ENGLISH ALTERNATIVES: drunk; tipsy; merry; tight

CLICHÉD ALTERNATIVES: tired and emotional; half seas over; rather the worse for drink; under the influence; three sheets in the wind

feel in one's bones ✪✪

PLAIN ENGLISH ALTERNATIVES: sense; know instinctively; intuit; have an intuition; divine

CLICHÉD ALTERNATIVES: feel in one's water; have a funny feeling; have a hunch

few and far between ✪✪✪✪

PLAIN ENGLISH ALTERNATIVES: scarce; rare; seldom met with

CLICHÉD ALTERNATIVES: thin on the ground; scarce as hen's teeth; in short supply

field day

See **have a field day**.

fighting fit ✪✪

PLAIN ENGLISH ALTERNATIVES: in fine condition; in good shape; physically fit

CLICHÉD ALTERNATIVES: in the pink; fit as a fiddle; in tip-top condition

fight like cat and dog ✪✪

PLAIN ENGLISH ALTERNATIVES: fight continually; quarrel constantly

CLICHÉD ALTERNATIVES: fight like Kilkenny cats

fight tooth and nail ✪✪

PLAIN ENGLISH ALTERNATIVES: fight bitterly; fight desperately; fight to the finish; struggle with all one's might

CLICHÉD ALTERNATIVES: fight to the bitter end; fight to the death; fight as if one's life depended on it

▪ *Origins* From the idea of people fighting so desperately that they will bite or scratch their opponent.

fill or fit the bill ✪✪

PLAIN ENGLISH ALTERNATIVES: be adequate; be suitable; be what's required; be what's needed; fulfil the purpose; meet the demand

CLICHÉD ALTERNATIVES: do the business; do the trick; pass muster; tick all the boxes

▪ *Origins* Probably from the theatre, where a bill or poster would be used to list the entertainments on offer, and one that was filled with names would of course be more attractive than one full of spaces.

filthy lucre ✪✪✪✪

PLAIN ENGLISH ALTERNATIVES: money; wealth; sordid gain; riches

CLICHÉD ALTERNATIVES: the readies

▪ *Origins* A biblical reference (*1 Timothy* 3.3): 'Not given to wine, not greedy of filthy lucre'.

find it in one's heart ✪✪

PLAIN ENGLISH ALTERNATIVES: be willing; bring oneself; be able to bring oneself; convince oneself

find oneself ✪✪✪✪✪

PLAIN ENGLISH ALTERNATIVES: come to terms with oneself; discover one's true character; find one's vocation

CLICHÉD ALTERNATIVES: discover what one is all about; get in touch with one's true self

fine-tooth comb

See **go through something with a fine-tooth comb**.

firing on all cylinders ✪✪

PLAIN ENGLISH ALTERNATIVES: working well; working perfectly; working at full strength; performing to capacity; fully functioning; in good working order

■ *Origins* From the cylinders containing the pistons of an internal-combustion engine, as in a car.

first and foremost ✪✪

PLAIN ENGLISH ALTERNATIVES: firstly; in first place; most importantly; to begin with

CLICHÉD ALTERNATIVES: first cab off the rank

first water

See **of the first water**.

fish out of water

See **like a fish out of water**.

fit as a fiddle

See **as fit as a fiddle**.

fit the bill

See **fill the bill**.

flash in the pan ✪✪

PLAIN ENGLISH ALTERNATIVES: brief but unsustained success

CLICHÉD ALTERNATIVES: nine days' wonder

■ *Origins* In an old musket or pistol, the *pan* was a cavity in which a small amount of priming powder was placed. When the trigger was pulled, the flintlock would strike a spark to ignite the powder in the pan, which would in turn ignite the main charge of powder inside the barrel, thus firing the bullet. Sometimes, however, the powder in the pan would ignite (providing an initial promising *flash*) but fail to set off the main charge.

flavour of the month ✪✪✪

PLAIN ENGLISH ALTERNATIVES: current favourite

CLICHÉD ALTERNATIVES: person of the moment

■ *Origins* Originally from the US, where ice-cream sellers promoted a particular flavour each month in the attempt to induce customers to try different ones.

flea in one's ear ✪✪

PLAIN ENGLISH ALTERNATIVES: stinging rebuff; rebuke; reproof; reprimand; earful

CLICHÉD ALTERNATIVES: dusty answer

■ *Origins* From a dog being highly upset by the presence of a flea in its ear.

fleeting glimpse ✪✪

PLAIN ENGLISH ALTERNATIVES: glance; peek; gander; peep; sight; shufti; brief look; brief sight; quick look

flotsam and jetsam ✪✪

PLAIN ENGLISH ALTERNATIVES: detritus; scraps; oddments; miscellaneous items

CLICHÉD ALTERNATIVES: odds and ends; bits and pieces

■ *Origins* Strictly, flotsam means items found floating on the sea after a shipwreck, while jetsam refers to items jettisoned from a ship and washed up on a shore.

fly-by-night ✪✪

PLAIN ENGLISH ALTERNATIVES: irresponsible; untrustworthy; unreliable; shady

CLICHÉD ALTERNATIVES: here today, gone tomorrow; cowboy

fly in the ointment ✪✪

PLAIN ENGLISH ALTERNATIVES: flaw; drawback; catch; nuisance; irritation

CLICHÉD ALTERNATIVES: thorn in one's flesh

■ *Origins* From a biblical allusion (*Ecclesiastes* 10.1): 'Dead flies cause the ointment of the apothecary to send forth a stinking savour: so doth a little folly him that is in reputation for wisdom and honour.'

fly off the handle ✪✪

PLAIN ENGLISH ALTERNATIVES: lose one's temper; become exasperated; get angry; get mad; blow up; fire up

CLICHÉD ALTERNATIVES: lose one's rag; lose the plot; go ballistic; lose it big time; go off at the deep end; see red

■ *Origins* Probably from the idea of the head of an axe or hammer parting company with the handle when swung, thus zooming off and possibly causing indiscriminate damage.

follow suit ✪✪

PLAIN ENGLISH ALTERNATIVES: copy someone; do the same; do what someone else has done

CLICHÉD ALTERNATIVES: follow in someone's footsteps; take the same path

■ *Origins* From certain card games in which the other players are obliged to play a card of the same suit as that played by the first player in each round.

food for thought ✪✪

PLAIN ENGLISH ALTERNATIVES: something to think about; something worth considering; something to ponder; something to mull over

footloose and fancy-free ✪✪

PLAIN ENGLISH ALTERNATIVES: single; unattached; with no commitments; having no ties

CLICHÉD ALTERNATIVES: young, free and single

■ *Origins* Footloose does not literally mean 'having one's feet unencumbered' but comes from a nautical usage referring to the foot of a sail being unsecured and able to flap about.

for a song ✪✪

PLAIN ENGLISH ALTERNATIVES: cheaply; inexpensively; cut-price; for a bargain price; for very little

CLICHÉD ALTERNATIVES: for next to nothing

■ *Origins* Perhaps from the low price of a ballad sold as sheet-music in the streets.

for a start ✪✪

PLAIN ENGLISH ALTERNATIVES: as a preliminary consideration; in the first place; to begin with; firstly; first off

CLICHÉD ALTERNATIVES: for starters; for a kick-off; first cab off the rank

for dear life ✪✪

PLAIN ENGLISH ALTERNATIVES: as if to save one's life; desperately; urgently

CLICHÉD ALTERNATIVES: as if one's life depended on it; like grim death

for the hell of it ✪✪

PLAIN ENGLISH ALTERNATIVES: for fun; for laughs; for no particular reason; because one can

CLICHÉD ALTERNATIVES: for kicks

for the high jump ✪✪

PLAIN ENGLISH ALTERNATIVES: condemned; about to be punished; facing a reprimand

CLICHÉD ALTERNATIVES: done for; for it; in for it

for the life of one ✪✪

PLAIN ENGLISH ALTERNATIVES: try as one might; no matter how hard one tries; even though one's life depended on it

CLICHÉD ALTERNATIVES: to save one's life

forty winks ✪✪

PLAIN ENGLISH ALTERNATIVES: a short nap; a brief sleep; a catnap; a doze

fraught with danger ✪✪

PLAIN ENGLISH ALTERNATIVES: dangerous; perilous; risky; chancy

free, gratis and for nothing ✪✪✪✪✪

PLAIN ENGLISH ALTERNATIVES: free; free of charge; at no cost; for nothing; without charge

CLICHÉD ALTERNATIVES: on the house

fresh as a daisy ✪✪

PLAIN ENGLISH ALTERNATIVES: bright; vigorous; refreshed; vivacious

CLICHÉD ALTERNATIVES: bright-eyed and bushy-tailed; bright and breezy; bright as a button

- *Origins* The daisy closes up on itself in the evening but opens up again each morning.

from hell ✪✪✪

PLAIN ENGLISH ALTERNATIVES: of the worst possible kind; abominable; atrocious; dreadful; awful; hellish; damnable

from pillar to post ✪✪

PLAIN ENGLISH ALTERNATIVES: from one difficulty to another

CLICHÉD ALTERNATIVES: hither and thither; all over the place

- *Origins* This is an image from real tennis, in which the ball often rebounds from the pillars and posts of the covered court.

from start to finish ✪✪

PLAIN ENGLISH ALTERNATIVES: from beginning to end; throughout

CLICHÉD ALTERNATIVES: all along the line; all the way; from first to last

from the cradle to the grave ✪✪

PLAIN ENGLISH ALTERNATIVES: all one's life; throughout one's life; from birth to death

CLICHÉD ALTERNATIVES: all the days of one's life

from the word go ✪✪

PLAIN ENGLISH ALTERNATIVES: from the (very) beginning; from the start

CLICHÉD ALTERNATIVES: from the kick-off; from the get-go

- *Origins* From the action of starting a race by shouting 'Go!'

from time immemorial ✪✪

PLAIN ENGLISH ALTERNATIVES: from a time beyond memory; from the very earliest times; from the distant past

full monty, the

CLICHÉD ALTERNATIVES: time out of mind

full monty, the ✪✪✪✪

PLAIN ENGLISH ALTERNATIVES: everything; the whole thing; the entirety

CLICHÉD ALTERNATIVES: the lot; the whole kit and caboodle; the whole shooting match; the works

■ *Origins* There is no general consensus on this. Among the more plausible theories are (a) that it refers to a full English breakfast, as insisted upon by Field Marshal Montgomery (known as 'Monty') during World War II; and (b) that it means a full three-piece suit provided by the well-known tailor Montague Burton. Certainly, the phrase became more widely known when it was used as a title of a British film about male strippers (1997), in which it refers to a state of complete nakedness.

full of beans ✪✪

PLAIN ENGLISH ALTERNATIVES: in high spirits; full of energy; fired-up; animated; vigorous; feisty

CLICHÉD ALTERNATIVES: full of pep; full of get-up-and-go

■ *Origins* Beans are traditionally believed to provide energy, and even to have aphrodisiac qualities.

full stop ✪✪

PLAIN ENGLISH ALTERNATIVES: there is no more to be said; and that's all there is to it

CLICHÉD ALTERNATIVES: end of story; and that's that; and that's it; enough said; period

fun and games ✪✪

PLAIN ENGLISH ALTERNATIVES: diversion; entertainment; amusing goings-on; amusement; excitement; laughs; sport; frolics

CLICHÉD ALTERNATIVES: a carry-on; funny business; high jinks

  ✪ mild   ✪✪ highly unoriginal   ✪✪✪ irritating

G

gainful employment ✪

PLAIN ENGLISH ALTERNATIVES: paid work; a job; remunerative work

game is not worth the candle, the ✪✪

PLAIN ENGLISH ALTERNATIVES: it's not worth it; it's not worth the expense (or trouble)

■ *Origins* From the days when candles were the sole source of light and one had to reckon whether or not the stakes involved in a game of cards were worth the expense of the candle needed to light it.

game plan ✪✪✪✪

PLAIN ENGLISH ALTERNATIVES: tactics; strategy; scheme
CLICHÉD ALTERNATIVES: plan of campaign

generous to a fault ✪✪

PLAIN ENGLISH ALTERNATIVES: very generous; over-generous; open-handed; liberal; bountiful
CLICHÉD ALTERNATIVES: free with one's money

gentleman and a scholar, a ✪✪

PLAIN ENGLISH ALTERNATIVES: an admirable person; a man of culture
CLICHÉD ALTERNATIVES: a gentleman, a scholar and a fine judge of whisky; one of nature's gentlemen; a man of honour

get a life ✪✪

PLAIN ENGLISH ALTERNATIVES: start living life to the full; find something worthwhile to do

get a result ✪✪✪

PLAIN ENGLISH ALTERNATIVES: win; succeed; score

CLICHÉD ALTERNATIVES: pull it off; make it; get somewhere; score a victory

■ *Origins* From the jargon of professional football, where 'a result' means an outcome to a match in which points are gained, that is, a victory or draw but not a defeat.

get away from it all ✪✪✪

PLAIN ENGLISH ALTERNATIVES: go on holiday; take a holiday; have a break; take a vacation; take time off

CLICHÉD ALTERNATIVES: take off somewhere; go somewhere far from the madding crowd; head for the hills; recharge one's batteries; have some downtime; have some 'me' time

get cold feet ✪✪✪

PLAIN ENGLISH ALTERNATIVES: be too scared to go through with it; lose one's nerve

CLICHÉD ALTERNATIVES: bottle it; bottle out; chicken out; crap out; lose one's bottle; show one's yellow streak

get down to brass tacks ✪✪

PLAIN ENGLISH ALTERNATIVES: come to the point; consider the practical details; face up to reality; deal with the essential issues

CLICHÉD ALTERNATIVES: get down to the nitty-gritty

■ *Origins* Opinions differ, but the most likely explanation is that 'brass tacks' is Cockney rhyming slang for 'facts'.

get hold of the wrong end of the stick   ✪✪

PLAIN ENGLISH ALTERNATIVES: be mistaken; be under a misapprehension; have the wrong idea; misunderstand; form the wrong impression

CLICHÉD ALTERNATIVES: get it all wrong

get in on the act   ✪✪

PLAIN ENGLISH ALTERNATIVES: join in; take part; participate; get involved

CLICHÉD ALTERNATIVES: have a hand in something; play a part

■ *Origins* From American vaudeville theatre, where performers would want to be associated with an act that was popular.

get in on the ground floor   ✪✪✪

PLAIN ENGLISH ALTERNATIVES: be in from the beginning; be involved from the start

CLICHÉD ALTERNATIVES: be in on it from day one

get one's act together   ✪✪✪

PLAIN ENGLISH ALTERNATIVES: get (oneself) organized; sort oneself out

CLICHÉD ALTERNATIVES: get it together; get a grip on oneself; pull oneself together; clean up one's act; pull one's socks up; pull one's finger out; get oneself sorted; shape up or ship out

get one's beauty sleep   ✪✪

PLAIN ENGLISH ALTERNATIVES: go to bed; get some sleep; retire for the night

CLICHÉD ALTERNATIVES: get one's head down; get some shuteye; hit the sack; stack up some Z's

■ *Origins* From the belief that sleep, especially before midnight, helps keep you young and beautiful.

get one's comeuppance   ✪✪

PLAIN ENGLISH ALTERNATIVES: receive one's deserved punishment; be punished; be chastised

CLICHÉD ALTERNATIVES: get one's just deserts; get what's coming to one; get it in the neck

get one's ducks in a row   ✪✪✪✪✪

PLAIN ENGLISH ALTERNATIVES: make preparations; be fully prepared; get (oneself) organized; sort oneself out; put things in order; get everything ready

CLICHÉD ALTERNATIVES: get it together; get sorted

■ *Origins* Originally American, perhaps alluding to the way in which ducklings follow their mother in a line.

get one's goat   ✪✪

PLAIN ENGLISH ALTERNATIVES: annoy; exasperate; irk; vex; rile; irritate

CLICHÉD ALTERNATIVES: do one's head in; drive one up the wall; get on one's nerves; get on one's wick; get one's back up; get one's dander up; rub one up the wrong way; set one's teeth on edge

■ *Origins* There appears to be no convincing explanation of why removing a person's goat should be particularly vexing.

get one's kit off   ✪✪✪

PLAIN ENGLISH ALTERNATIVES: undress; strip; disrobe; take off one's clothes

CLICHÉD ALTERNATIVES: peel off

■ *Origins* Kit here probably refers to the sportswear that someone would take off before the post-exertion shower.

get one's marching orders   ✪✪

PLAIN ENGLISH ALTERNATIVES: be dismissed; be discharged; be asked to leave

CLICHÉD ALTERNATIVES: get the elbow; get the old heave-ho; be shown the door

- *Origins* From a military unit receiving orders to march to a certain place.

get real ✪✪✪

PLAIN ENGLISH ALTERNATIVES: be realistic; be sensible; make sense; don't be silly

CLICHÉD ALTERNATIVES: come back down to earth; wise up; wake up and smell the coffee

get something off one's chest ✪

PLAIN ENGLISH ALTERNATIVES: admit to something; confess something; come out with something; declare something openly; own up to something

CLICHÉD ALTERNATIVES: make a clean breast of it; come clean

get the message ✪✪

PLAIN ENGLISH ALTERNATIVES: twig; catch on; get it; understand; see; grasp

CLICHÉD ALTERNATIVES: see the light

get to the bottom of something ✪✪

PLAIN ENGLISH ALTERNATIVES: explain something; find out the facts about something; discover the truth about something; find an explanation for something; solve something

CLICHÉD ALTERNATIVES: unravel the mystery

gird up one's loins ✪✪

PLAIN ENGLISH ALTERNATIVES: get ready; gird oneself; prepare for action; ready oneself

CLICHÉD ALTERNATIVES: roll one's sleeves up

- *Origins* From the Bible, in which people often prepare for action by tucking up the ends of their garments so as not to have their legs impeded.

give a wide berth to ✪✪

PLAIN ENGLISH ALTERNATIVES: avoid; keep away from; shun; keep one's distance from

CLICHÉD ALTERNATIVES: avoid like the plague; steer well clear of

▪ *Origins* From the nautical practice of allowing plenty of room for a ship to swing round while at anchor.

give it one's best shot ✪✪✪

PLAIN ENGLISH ALTERNATIVES: try one's hardest; make every effort; do one's best

CLICHÉD ALTERNATIVES: do one's damnedest; give one hundred and ten per cent; go for it; go for broke; make an all-out effort; give it one's all; pull out all the stops

give one's eye teeth ✪✪

PLAIN ENGLISH ALTERNATIVES: give anything; do anything; do anything in one's power; sacrifice anything; go to any lengths

CLICHÉD ALTERNATIVES: give one's right arm; move heaven and earth

▪ *Origins* The eye teeth are the canine teeth, positioned below the eyes. While surrendering them would indeed be a sacrifice, it is difficult to imagine why anyone else would want them.

give one the creeps ✪✪

PLAIN ENGLISH ALTERNATIVES: disgust; horrify; repulse; revolt; creep one out

CLICHÉD ALTERNATIVES: give one the shivers; make one's flesh creep

give someone a bum steer ✪✪

PLAIN ENGLISH ALTERNATIVES: misinform someone; mislead someone; misguide someone; give someone the wrong information

CLICHÉD ALTERNATIVES: give someone duff gen; send someone off on a wild-goose chase

■ *Origins* Originally an American expression, 'bum' here means 'wrong' or 'no good' (as in 'a bum note'), while 'steer' means 'an act of steering'.

give someone a piece of one's mind ✪

PLAIN ENGLISH ALTERNATIVES: tell someone what one thinks of them; reprimand someone; rebuke someone; tell someone off

CLICHÉD ALTERNATIVES: give someone a dressing down; give someone a telling-off; let someone know what one thinks in no uncertain terms

give someone short shrift ✪✪

PLAIN ENGLISH ALTERNATIVES: give someone summary treatment; treat someone unsympathetically; be unsympathetic; be hard on someone; treat someone peremptorily

CLICHÉD ALTERNATIVES: give someone a hard time; send someone away with a flea in their ear

■ *Origins* 'Shrift' here means 'confession or absolution from sins', and 'short shrift' refers to the brief time for this granted to someone who was about to be executed.

give someone the third degree ✪✪✪

PLAIN ENGLISH ALTERNATIVES: interrogate someone ruthlessly; question someone brutally; cross-examine someone; grill someone; bully someone

CLICHÉD ALTERNATIVES: put the screws on someone

■ *Origins* Originally American, the idea behind this phrase is that, like a third-degree burn, this level of questioning is most painful for the victim.

give up the ghost ✪✪

PLAIN ENGLISH ALTERNATIVES: die; expire; pass away; pass on

CLICHÉD ALTERNATIVES: breathe one's last; kick the bucket; peg out; snuff it; pop one's clogs; join the majority

give up the ghost

■ *Origins* From the Bible (*Job* 14.10): 'Man dieth, and wasteth away: yea, man giveth up the ghost.'

gloves are off, the ✪✪

PLAIN ENGLISH ALTERNATIVES: now the fight begins in earnest; there will be no more holding back; no mercy will be shown

CLICHÉD ALTERNATIVES: no punches will be pulled; no prisoners will be taken; no more Mr Nice Guy

■ *Origins* Refers to pugilists fighting without gloves, thus allowing punches to do serious damage.

go belly up ✪✪

PLAIN ENGLISH ALTERNATIVES: die; expire; fail; flop; go bankrupt; go out of business

CLICHÉD ALTERNATIVES: cash in one's chips; peg out; crash and burn; go bust; go to the wall; go under

■ *Origins* The image here is of a dead fish floating upside down.

go by the board ✪✪

PLAIN ENGLISH ALTERNATIVES: be discarded; be abandoned; be lost; be thrown out; be forgotten

CLICHÉD ALTERNATIVES: go out (of) the window

■ *Origins* From nautical usage, meaning the same as 'go overboard'.

go down a treat ✪✪

PLAIN ENGLISH ALTERNATIVES: be well received; be popular; be successful; be a hit

CLICHÉD ALTERNATIVES: go down well; hit the spot

✪ mild ✪✪ highly unoriginal ✪✪✪ irritating

go down like a lead balloon ✪✪✪

PLAIN ENGLISH ALTERNATIVES: be poorly received; fail; flop; misfire; meet with a cool reception; bomb; make a poor impression

CLICHÉD ALTERNATIVES: get nowhere

go down that road ✪✪✪✪

PLAIN ENGLISH ALTERNATIVES: pursue that line; take that approach; follow that course

CLICHÉD ALTERNATIVES: take that path

go figure ✪✪✪

PLAIN ENGLISH ALTERNATIVES: try to understand it; give it some thought; see if you can work it out; go away and think about it; try to puzzle it out

CLICHÉD ALTERNATIVES: mull it over

■ *Origins* Originally American, based on the US usage 'figure it out'.

go for broke ✪✪

PLAIN ENGLISH ALTERNATIVES: make an all-out effort; make every effort; try one's hardest; go all-out; gamble everything

CLICHÉD ALTERNATIVES: give it one's all; give it one's best shot; pull out all the stops

go for it ✪✪✪✪✪

PLAIN ENGLISH ALTERNATIVES: go ahead; give it a try; make every effort; try one's hardest

CLICHÉD ALTERNATIVES: have a go; give it one's best shot

go for the jugular ✪✪

PLAIN ENGLISH ALTERNATIVES: attack without mercy; set out to inflict the utmost damage; be merciless; be ruthless

go from strength to strength

CLICHÉD ALTERNATIVES: go in for the kill

go from strength to strength   ✪✪

PLAIN ENGLISH ALTERNATIVES: get better and better; progress successfully; have uninterrupted success; improve progressively

CLICHÉD ALTERNATIVES: have a chain of successes

go haywire   ✪✪

PLAIN ENGLISH ALTERNATIVES: become erratic; become chaotic; behave crazily; go wrong; malfunction

CLICHÉD ALTERNATIVES: go crazy; go wild; be all over the place; go mental

- *Origins* An American expression referring to the unpredictable behaviour of the springy wire used to secure bundles of hay.

going great guns   ✪✪

PLAIN ENGLISH ALTERNATIVES: doing well; doing brilliantly; succeeding; making great progress; performing well

CLICHÉD ALTERNATIVES: going like a bomb

- *Origins* Presumably from the noise and activity of firing heavy cannon.

go in one ear and out the other   ✪✪

PLAIN ENGLISH ALTERNATIVES: make no impression; fail to make any impression; be ignored

CLICHÉD ALTERNATIVES: be lost on someone; fall on deaf ears

go into overdrive   ✪✪

PLAIN ENGLISH ALTERNATIVES: begin working at the optimum; hit one's or its peak; perform at one's best

CLICHÉD ALTERNATIVES: pull out all the stops; hit top form

- *Origins* From motor cars, referring to a gearing device that increases speed.

golden opportunity ✪✪

PLAIN ENGLISH ALTERNATIVES: great chance; ideal opportunity; perfect opportunity

CLICHÉD ALTERNATIVES: chance in a million

gone for a Burton ✪✪

PLAIN ENGLISH ALTERNATIVES: dead; destroyed; lost; missing; ruined; done for

CLICHÉD ALTERNATIVES: gone the way of all flesh; gone to meet his or her maker; have bought it; have had it

■ *Origins* From RAF slang in World War II, meaning 'missing or shot down', especially in the sea. There are various explanations, but the likeliest is that it means 'gone for a drink', that is, a pint of Burton ale.

good as gold ✪✪

PLAIN ENGLISH ALTERNATIVES: very well behaved; very good; perfectly behaved

good old days ✪✪

PLAIN ENGLISH ALTERNATIVES: the past; one's heyday

CLICHÉD ALTERNATIVES: days of yore; days of old

good time was had by all, a ✪✪

PLAIN ENGLISH ALTERNATIVES: it was a great success; everyone had fun; everyone enjoyed themselves

CLICHÉD ALTERNATIVES: it was a roaring success

goose that lays the golden eggs

See **kill the goose that lays the golden eggs**.

go overboard   ✪✪

PLAIN ENGLISH ALTERNATIVES: be highly enthusiastic; show great enthusiasm

CLICHÉD ALTERNATIVES: rave; be wild; lose one's head

▪ *Origins* From the idea of being so excited that one is liable to jump, or fall, from a ship.

go pear-shaped   ✪✪✪

PLAIN ENGLISH ALTERNATIVES: go awry; go wrong; break down; fall apart

CLICHÉD ALTERNATIVES: go out of kilter; go to pieces; come to grief; go phut

▪ *Origins* It's not entirely clear why the shape of a pear means failure, but one suggestion is that the image is of a ball or balloon that is leaking air and losing its roundness.

gory details   ✪✪

PLAIN ENGLISH ALTERNATIVES: unpleasant details; distasteful details; gruesome facts; whole unpleasant story

CLICHÉD ALTERNATIVES: chapter and verse

go scot-free   ✪✪

PLAIN ENGLISH ALTERNATIVES: escape punishment; pay no penalty; go unpunished; be unscathed; be uninjured

CLICHÉD ALTERNATIVES: get away with it; get off with it; come out without a scratch

▪ *Origins* Scot here is nothing to do with Caledonia, but is an old word meaning 'a payment', especially a tax.

go the extra mile   ✪✪✪✪

PLAIN ENGLISH ALTERNATIVES: do more than is expected; do more than is necessary; put in even more effort

CLICHÉD ALTERNATIVES: give one hundred and ten per cent

- *Origins* From the Bible (*Matthew* 5.41): 'And whosoever compel thee to go a mile go with him two.'

go the whole hog ✪✪

PLAIN ENGLISH ALTERNATIVES: commit oneself fully; be thorough; do a thorough job; hold nothing back

CLICHÉD ALTERNATIVES: give it one's all; go for broke; pull out all the stops; see it through to the end; go all the way; go to town

- *Origins* Various explanations have been offered, but perhaps the most likely is that in Virginia butchers would sell a whole hog more cheaply than the total amount they would charge for all the individual cuts.

go through something with a fine-tooth comb ✪✪✪✪

PLAIN ENGLISH ALTERNATIVES: investigate something thoroughly; sift something; search through something carefully; examine something in detail

CLICHÉD ALTERNATIVES: put something under the microscope

- *Origins* From the use of a comb with narrow teeth set closely together to comb through hair searching for lice. It is important to remember that the image refers to a comb with fine teeth, and not a fine one used to comb the teeth.

go to rack and ruin ✪✪

PLAIN ENGLISH ALTERNATIVES: be neglected; fall to pieces; collapse; decay; be allowed to deteriorate

CLICHÉD ALTERNATIVES: fall into disrepair; go to the dogs

- *Origins* 'Rack' here is a variant of 'wrack', meaning 'destruction'.

go to the dogs ✪✪

PLAIN ENGLISH ALTERNATIVES: be ruined; deteriorate; fall to pieces

CLICHÉD ALTERNATIVES: go to rack and ruin

- *Origins* Referring to unwanted or spoiled food being fed to dogs.

go to town   ✪✪

PLAIN ENGLISH ALTERNATIVES: be enthusiastic; be thorough; do a thorough job; make a good job of something

CLICHÉD ALTERNATIVES: go the whole hog; go all the way; pull out all the stops; set to with a will

■ *Origins* The saying arose in America and refers to country dwellers going into a town for a treat.

go with a bang   ✪✪

PLAIN ENGLISH ALTERNATIVES: go well; be a great success; be a huge success

CLICHÉD ALTERNATIVES: go down a bomb

■ *Origins* From the idea of a firework exploding in a spectacularly pleasing way.

go without saying   ✪✪✪

PLAIN ENGLISH ALTERNATIVES: be self-evident; be obvious; be clear; be plain

CLICHÉD ALTERNATIVES: be manifestly true

■ *Origins* From the French expression *cela va sans dire*.

greased lightning

See **like grease lightning**.

great unwashed, the   ✪✪

PLAIN ENGLISH ALTERNATIVES: common people; crowd; mob; general public; masses; rabble

CLICHÉD ALTERNATIVES: hoi polloi; the plebs

green about the gills ✪✪

PLAIN ENGLISH ALTERNATIVES: ill; sickly; pale; pallid; wan; white

CLICHÉD ALTERNATIVES: white as a sheet

green light ✪✪

PLAIN ENGLISH ALTERNATIVES: permission to proceed; consent; encouragement; assent; authorization

CLICHÉD ALTERNATIVES: go-ahead; thumbs-up

- *Origins* From the green traffic light that means 'go'.

grin and bear it ✪✪

PLAIN ENGLISH ALTERNATIVES: endure it stoically; put up with it

CLICHÉD ALTERNATIVES: stick it out; get on with it; put a brave face on it; make the best of it; hang tough

grind to a halt ✪✪

PLAIN ENGLISH ALTERNATIVES: stop; come to a stop; come to a standstill; run down; stall

CLICHÉD ALTERNATIVES: run out of steam

- *Origins* From the idea of a machine slowing down and stopping because something is making it jam.

grit one's teeth ✪✪

PLAIN ENGLISH ALTERNATIVES: show determination; be dogged

CLICHÉD ALTERNATIVES: roll up one's sleeves

guiding light ✪✪

PLAIN ENGLISH ALTERNATIVES: guide; model; lodestar; inspiration; mentor; paradigm; exemplar

CLICHÉD ALTERNATIVES: guiding star

H

halcyon days ✪✪

PLAIN ENGLISH ALTERNATIVES: happy times; good times; heyday

CLICHÉD ALTERNATIVES: good old days; time of one's life

■ *Origins* Halcyon is an old name for the kingfisher, which in legend laid its eggs in a nest floating on the sea, which remained calm while they hatched.

halfway house ✪✪

PLAIN ENGLISH ALTERNATIVES: midway point; central position; compromise; accommodation

CLICHÉD ALTERNATIVES: middle ground

■ *Origins* Literally, an inn or a house between two points on a journey.

hand in glove ✪✪

PLAIN ENGLISH ALTERNATIVES: in collusion; intimate; co-operating; in close association

CLICHÉD ALTERNATIVES: in cahoots

■ *Origins* As close together as a glove is to the hand inside it.

handle with kid gloves ✪✪

PLAIN ENGLISH ALTERNATIVES: treat carefully; treat gently; treat sensitively; be careful with

CLICHÉD ALTERNATIVES: handle with care

■ *Origins* Gloves made from kidskin are proverbially soft and therefore ideal for handling fragile objects.

hand over fist ✪✪

PLAIN ENGLISH ALTERNATIVES: steadily and rapidly; quickly

CLICHÉD ALTERNATIVES: like nobody's business; by the barrowload

■ *Origins* The image is of a sailor climbing or descending a rope by hand, with one hand grasping firmly while the other reaches out to grab another hold.

hang in there ✪✪✪

PLAIN ENGLISH ALTERNATIVES: persist; persevere; hold firm; hold on; stand firm; keep going; don't give up

CLICHÉD ALTERNATIVES: stay the course; keep one's chin up; hang tough

■ *Origins* Probably from the idea of a boxer hanging on to an opponent or the ropes in an effort to stay in the fight.

happy as a sandboy ✪✪

PLAIN ENGLISH ALTERNATIVES: very happy; delighted; ecstatic; overjoyed

CLICHÉD ALTERNATIVES: over the moon; well chuffed; made up; happy as Larry; pleased as Punch

■ *Origins* A sandboy was a youth who sold bags of sand in the street, proverbially happy because of spending the profits on drink.

happy as Larry ✪✪

PLAIN ENGLISH ALTERNATIVES: very happy; delighted; ecstatic; overjoyed

CLICHÉD ALTERNATIVES: over the moon; well chuffed; made up; happy as a sandboy

■ *Origins* If there was an original Larry particularly noted for happiness he has been forgotten. It's more likely that the name was arbitrarily chosen to make a snappy near-rhyme with happy.

hard and fast ✪✪

PLAIN ENGLISH ALTERNATIVES: fixed; unalterable; strict; inflexible; immutable; rigid; absolute

hard as nails

CLICHÉD ALTERNATIVES: unalterable as the law of the Medes and Persians

hard as nails   ✪✪

PLAIN ENGLISH ALTERNATIVES: tough; callous; hardy; doughty;
uncompromising

CLICHÉD ALTERNATIVES: hard-bitten; hard-boiled; case-hardened; well
hard

hard stuff, the   ✪✪

PLAIN ENGLISH ALTERNATIVES: alcohol; spirits; strong drink

CLICHÉD ALTERNATIVES: strong waters; firewater

have a bad hair day   ✪✪✪

PLAIN ENGLISH ALTERNATIVES: have a day when nothing goes right; have an
unlucky day; not have a good day; be out of sorts

CLICHÉD ALTERNATIVES: get out of bed on the wrong side; have just one of
those days

▪ *Origins* Originally American, this comes from the idea of a day when one
'can't do a thing with' one's hair, extended to mean a day when one can't do
anything right.

have a ball   ✪✪

PLAIN ENGLISH ALTERNATIVES: have great fun; have a great time; enjoy
oneself greatly

CLICHÉD ALTERNATIVES: have a blast; have a high old time

▪ *Origins* From the idea of staging a dance.

have a bone to pick with someone   ✪✪

PLAIN ENGLISH ALTERNATIVES: be in dispute with someone; have a quarrel
with someone; have cause to disagree with someone

CLICHÉD ALTERNATIVES: have issues with someone

■ *Origins* Like 'bone of contention', this originates in the idea of dogs disputing ownership of a tasty bone.

have a field day ✪✪✪

PLAIN ENGLISH ALTERNATIVES: have great success; have great fun; exploit one's opportunities to the full; make the most of one's opportunities

CLICHÉD ALTERNATIVES: go to town

■ *Origins* From military usage, meaning 'a day when troops are taken out into the field for manoeuvres or training', and thus an enjoyable break from routine.

have a fit ✪✪

PLAIN ENGLISH ALTERNATIVES: become very angry; lose one's temper; become enraged

CLICHÉD ALTERNATIVES: blow a fuse; blow up; get out of one's pram; go ballistic; go off at the deep end; hit the roof; lose one's rag; lose one's head; lose it

■ *Origins* From the idea of being so enraged that one loses control of oneself.

have a high old time ✪✪

PLAIN ENGLISH ALTERNATIVES: have great fun; have a great time; enjoy oneself greatly

CLICHÉD ALTERNATIVES: have a ball; have a blast

have a lot on one's plate ✪✪

PLAIN ENGLISH ALTERNATIVES: be very busy; be fully occupied; have a great deal to do

CLICHÉD ALTERNATIVES: be rushed off one's feet; have one's hands full

■ *Origins* Someone presented with a large plateful of food will take time to clear it.

have a lump in one's throat ✪✪

PLAIN ENGLISH ALTERNATIVES: be affected; be moved; be saddened; be touched

CLICHÉD ALTERNATIVES: be visibly moved; be moved to tears; have a tear in one's eye

■ *Origins* From the difficulty in swallowing experienced by those who are strongly moved.

have ants in one's pants ✪✪

PLAIN ENGLISH ALTERNATIVES: be restless; be impatient; be agitated; be fidgety; be wired; fidget

CLICHÉD ALTERNATIVES: be unable to sit still; be like a cat on a hot tin roof; be ill at ease

have had its or one's day ✪✪

PLAIN ENGLISH ALTERNATIVES: be worn out; be useless; be passé; be past its (or one's) prime

CLICHÉD ALTERNATIVES: be a thing of the past; be over the hill; be yesterday's man; have seen better days

have had it up to here ✪✪

PLAIN ENGLISH ALTERNATIVES: be fed up; be exasperated; have had (more than) enough

CLICHÉD ALTERNATIVES: be at the end of one's tether; be sick and tired of something; be brassed off; be hacked off

■ *Origins* People often indicate where 'here' is by putting a hand to their chin. This suggests that the idea is of having had as much as one can swallow, or perhaps of being in water up to the point of risking drowning.

have I got news for you ✪

PLAIN ENGLISH ALTERNATIVES: I've got something to tell you; there's something you ought to know; wait until you hear this; you're not going to like this

CLICHÉD ALTERNATIVES: you don't know the half of it; now hear this

have it in for someone ✪✪

PLAIN ENGLISH ALTERNATIVES: have a grudge against someone; bear malice against someone; wish someone harm; bear ill will towards someone

CLICHÉD ALTERNATIVES: have issues with someone; have a thing about someone

■ *Origins* It is not clear what 'it' is or where it is 'in'.

have one foot in the grave ✪✪

PLAIN ENGLISH ALTERNATIVES: be at the point of death; be dying; be near death; be moribund; be dangerously ill; be critically ill; be likely to die; be *in extremis* (*Latin*)

CLICHÉD ALTERNATIVES: be on one's deathbed; be at death's door; be not long for this world; be knocking on heaven's door; be on the way out; be about to meet one's maker; be heading for the last roundup

have one in stitches ✪✪

PLAIN ENGLISH ALTERNATIVES: have one helpless with laughter; convulse one with laughter

CLICHÉD ALTERNATIVES: have one rolling in the aisles; have one laughing one's head off; have one in knots; have one laughing like a drain

have one's hands full ✪✪

PLAIN ENGLISH ALTERNATIVES: be very busy; be fully occupied; have a great deal to do

CLICHÉD ALTERNATIVES: be rushed off one's feet; have a lot on one's plate

have one's heart in one's boots ⊕⊕

PLAIN ENGLISH ALTERNATIVES: be despondent; be in despair; be depressed

CLICHÉD ALTERNATIVES: be at a low ebb

have one's heart in one's mouth ⊕⊕

PLAIN ENGLISH ALTERNATIVES: be in trepidation; be anxious; be excited; be fearful

CLICHÉD ALTERNATIVES: be on tenterhooks

▪ *Origins* From the difficulty in swallowing experienced by those in the throes of great emotion.

have one's heart in the right place ⊕⊕

PLAIN ENGLISH ALTERNATIVES: be kind; be decent; be sympathetic

CLICHÉD ALTERNATIVES: be a decent sort

have one's heart set on something ⊕⊕

PLAIN ENGLISH ALTERNATIVES: desire something earnestly; want something above all else; be determined to have something

CLICHÉD ALTERNATIVES: give one's right arm for something

have one's name up in lights ⊕⊕

PLAIN ENGLISH ALTERNATIVES: be famous; be a star; get to the top

CLICHÉD ALTERNATIVES: make it; make one's mark; be a major player; be top of the bill

▪ *Origins* From the illuminated display of stars' names outside a theatre.

have other fish to fry ⊕⊕

PLAIN ENGLISH ALTERNATIVES: have other things to do; have something else to attend to; be otherwise engaged

CLICHÉD ALTERNATIVES: have other irons in the fire

have seen better days ✪✪

PLAIN ENGLISH ALTERNATIVES: be past its (or one's) prime; be worn out; be decrepit

CLICHÉD ALTERNATIVES: be over the hill; be past it

have something down to a fine art ✪✪

PLAIN ENGLISH ALTERNATIVES: be highly proficient; be very skilled; be a master/mistress of something

CLICHÉD ALTERNATIVES: be a wizard at something; be a dab hand at something; be a past master of something

have what it takes ✪✪

PLAIN ENGLISH ALTERNATIVES: be competent; be adequate; possess the requisite talents; have the skills needed

CLICHÉD ALTERNATIVES: be up to the job; cut the mustard

having said that ✪✪

PLAIN ENGLISH ALTERNATIVES: that said; furthermore; moreover; besides

CLICHÉD ALTERNATIVES: what is more

head and shoulders above ✪✪

PLAIN ENGLISH ALTERNATIVES: much better than; pre-eminent over; far superior to

CLICHÉD ALTERNATIVES: streets ahead of; in a different class from

head for the hills ✪✪

PLAIN ENGLISH ALTERNATIVES: leave; depart; decamp; flee; run away; scarper; take off

CLICHÉD ALTERNATIVES: make oneself scarce; run for it; beat it; make tracks; hit the road

headless chicken scenario

- *Origins* Probably from the phrase being used in lots of Westerns.

headless chicken scenario ✪✪✪✪✪

PLAIN ENGLISH ALTERNATIVES: panic; chaos; consternation; hysteria; bedlam; pandemonium

CLICHÉD ALTERNATIVES: scene of utter confusion

- *Origins* From the idea that a chicken that has just had its head cut off may run about aimlessly for a few moments.

head over heels ✪✪

PLAIN ENGLISH ALTERNATIVES: completely; utterly; totally

CLICHÉD ALTERNATIVES: hook, line and sinker; heart and soul; lock, stock and barrel

- *Origins* As in turning a somersault.

heads will roll ✪✪

PLAIN ENGLISH ALTERNATIVES: the guilty will be punished; severe punishment will ensue; people will lose their jobs

CLICHÉD ALTERNATIVES: there will be hell to pay

- *Origins* From execution by having one's head chopped off.

heap ridicule on ✪✪

PLAIN ENGLISH ALTERNATIVES: mock; deride; laugh at; lampoon; make fun of

CLICHÉD ALTERNATIVES: laugh out of court; laugh to scorn; send up rotten; make a laughing stock of

hear, hear! ✪✪

PLAIN ENGLISH ALTERNATIVES: that's absolutely right; that's true; I quite agree; I am in full agreement with you; I agree entirely

✪ mild ✪✪ highly unoriginal ✪✪✪ irritating

CLICHÉD ALTERNATIVES: well said

■ *Origins* Shortened from 'hear him, hear him!', an exclamation used in Parliament to draw attention to someone making a speech.

heart and soul ✪✪

PLAIN ENGLISH ALTERNATIVES: completely; utterly; totally; sincerely; devotedly

CLICHÉD ALTERNATIVES: hook, line and sinker; lock, stock and barrel

heart-to-heart ✪✪

PLAIN ENGLISH ALTERNATIVES: intimate; confidential; candid; unreserved

CLICHÉD ALTERNATIVES: full and frank

he/she couldn't organize a piss-up in a brewery ✪✪

PLAIN ENGLISH ALTERNATIVES: he/she is incompetent; he/she is not up to the job; he/she is inept; he/she is useless; he/she is no use; he/she is a living embodiment of the Peter Principle

CLICHÉD ALTERNATIVES: he/she couldn't find his/her backside with both hands

> **!** *Original alternative:* he/she couldn't run a flag up a pole

hell for leather ✪✪

PLAIN ENGLISH ALTERNATIVES: furiously; at a furious pace; like fury; as fast as possible; at top speed

CLICHÉD ALTERNATIVES: all out; like mad; at a rate of knots; like a bat out of hell; as if one's life depended on it

■ *Origins* Some suggest that the leather refers to the saddle of a horse, and that it is being given 'hell'; others feel that the phrase is a corruption of 'all of a lather'.

hell on wheels ✪✪

PLAIN ENGLISH ALTERNATIVES: a dreadful situation; an awful predicament; chaos; mayhem; murder

■ *Origins* Originally American, this has been said to spring from the drinking and gambling that went on in accommodation for 19th-century railway workers, but it may simply be a reference to going to hell quickly.

he/she would argue black was white ✪✪

PLAIN ENGLISH ALTERNATIVES: he/she is argumentative; he/she has a contrary nature; he/she is contradictory; he/she is contentious by nature

CLICHÉD ALTERNATIVES: he/she could start a fight in an empty room

he/she wouldn't hurt a fly ✪✪

PLAIN ENGLISH ALTERNATIVES: he/she is harmless; he/she has no malice in him/her; he/she would never do anyone the slightest injury

CLICHÉD ALTERNATIVES: he/she wouldn't say boo to a goose; he/she would never lay a finger on one; he/she wouldn't harm a hair of one's head

he/she wouldn't say boo to a goose ✪✪

PLAIN ENGLISH ALTERNATIVES: he/she is very shy; he/she is highly diffident; he/she is timorous; he/she is timid

CLICHÉD ALTERNATIVES: he/she is as quiet as a church mouse; he/she wouldn't dream of opening his/her mouth

hidden agenda ✪✪✪

PLAIN ENGLISH ALTERNATIVES: secret purposes; disguised purposes; concealed intentions; secret aims

CLICHÉD ALTERNATIVES: axe to grind

hide one's light under a bushel ✪

PLAIN ENGLISH ALTERNATIVES: be too modest; be self-effacing; conceal one's talents; belittle oneself

CLICHÉD ALTERNATIVES: cry stinking fish

■ *Origins* From the Bible (*Matthew* 5.15): 'Neither do men light a candle, and put it under a bushel, but on a candlestick.' The bushel referred to was a vessel large enough to contain a bushel of grain or some other commodity.

high and dry ✪✪

PLAIN ENGLISH ALTERNATIVES: stranded; helpless; marooned; abandoned; left out; left behind; sidelined

CLICHÉD ALTERNATIVES: on the beach; out in the cold; in the lurch

■ *Origins* A nautical phrase, describing a vessel run aground on a shore, too far from the water to regain it easily.

his/her name is mud ✪✪✪

PLAIN ENGLISH ALTERNATIVES: he/she is in disgrace; he/she is out of favour; he/she is unwelcome

CLICHÉD ALTERNATIVES: he/she is in the bad books; he/she has a black mark against his/her name; he/she is persona non grata; he/she is not flavour of the month; he/she is in the doghouse; he/she is under a cloud; he/she couldn't get arrested in this town

■ *Origins* In the late 18th and early 19th centuries, to call a person 'mud' was to label them as stupid.

hither and thither ✪✪

PLAIN ENGLISH ALTERNATIVES: here and there; to and fro; back and forth

CLICHÉD ALTERNATIVES: this way and that

hit or miss ✪✪

PLAIN ENGLISH ALTERNATIVES: haphazard; random; careless

hit pay dirt

Clichéd alternatives: hit and miss

hit pay dirt ✪✪

Plain English alternatives: succeed; win; find what one was looking for

Clichéd alternatives: strike it rich; strike it lucky; score; get a result; hit the jackpot

- *Origins* From mining, meaning 'ground that will yield something valuable'.

hit the hay or sack ✪✪

Plain English alternatives: go to bed; retire for the night; go to sleep

Clichéd alternatives: turn in; go up the wooden hill (to Bedfordshire)

- *Origins* From the idea of sleeping on hay in a barn or on a sack filled with this.

hit the nail on the head ✪✪

Plain English alternatives: be exact; be precise; arrive at the correct conclusion; say the right thing

Clichéd alternatives: be spot-on; get it in one

- *Origins* From the importance of being accurate with one's hammer in striking the nail and not one's fingers.

hit the road ✪✪

Plain English alternatives: leave; depart; decamp; get going; take off; be on one's way; set off

Clichéd alternatives: make oneself scarce; beat it; make tracks; head for the hills

hit the sack

See **hit the hay**.

✪ mild   ✪✪ highly unoriginal   ✪✪✪ irritating

hoist with one's own petard   ✪

PLAIN ENGLISH ALTERNATIVES: caught in one's own trap; defeated with one's own weapons

■ *Origins* A petard was an old weapon, basically a container filled with explosive, used chiefly for blowing in gates during a siege. As with many early explosive devices, it was quite likely to go off prematurely and blow up the person trying to set it off.

hold one's horses   ✪✪

PLAIN ENGLISH ALTERNATIVES: wait; hold on; whoa; be patient; don't be hasty

CLICHÉD ALTERNATIVES: hold on a minute; not so fast; take it slow; hold hard

hold one's own   ✪✪

PLAIN ENGLISH ALTERNATIVES: maintain one's position; hold out; do one's share

CLICHÉD ALTERNATIVES: keep one's end up; stand one's ground

hold out the olive branch   ✪✪

PLAIN ENGLISH ALTERNATIVES: offer peace; offer to end hostilities; propose a truce; propose a ceasefire; seek reconciliation

CLICHÉD ALTERNATIVES: make peaceful overtures; offer to kiss and make up

■ *Origins* The branch of an olive tree is an ancient symbol of peace.

hook, line and sinker   ✪✪

PLAIN ENGLISH ALTERNATIVES: completely; utterly; totally

CLICHÉD ALTERNATIVES: heart and soul; lock, stock and barrel

■ *Origins* From fishing, in which a fish that is very keen will swallow not only the baited hook but also the lead weight (sinker) and part of the fishing line.

horse of a different colour ✪✪

PLAIN ENGLISH ALTERNATIVES: something else again; something different altogether; a completely different matter; an entirely different affair; another thing

CLICHÉD ALTERNATIVES: something completely different; a different kettle of fish

■ *Origins* From the different colours of horses in a race. In the film *The Wizard of Oz* (1939) a joke was made of this by calling a horse that literally changed colour due to magic as 'A Horse of a Different Color'.

hotly contested ✪✪✪✪

PLAIN ENGLISH ALTERNATIVES: keenly fought; highly competitive; eagerly fought over

CLICHÉD ALTERNATIVES: fiercely disputed

hot potato ✪✪

PLAIN ENGLISH ALTERNATIVES: controversial issue; tricky problem

CLICHÉD ALTERNATIVES: bone of contention; vexed question

■ *Origins* Like a potato straight from the oven, something that one would rather avoid touching but which must be handled with care if one is obliged to do so.

hot to trot ✪✪

PLAIN ENGLISH ALTERNATIVES: impatient; agog; chafing; eager

CLICHÉD ALTERNATIVES: champing at the bit; like a cat on hot bricks; raring to go; good to go; straining at the leash; mad for it

■ *Origins* Probably from a horse impatient to be allowed to move.

hot under the collar ✪✪

PLAIN ENGLISH ALTERNATIVES: angry; indignant; irritated; enraged; upset; embarrassed; chagrined

CLICHÉD ALTERNATIVES: all het up

house of ill repute or ill fame ✪✪

PLAIN ENGLISH ALTERNATIVES: brothel; whorehouse; bagnio; bordello; knocking-shop; cathouse

CLICHÉD ALTERNATIVES: bawdy house; disorderly house; sporting house

how long is a piece of string? ✪✪

PLAIN ENGLISH ALTERNATIVES: who knows?; who can say?; who can tell?; there's no telling

CLICHÉD ALTERNATIVES: it's anybody's guess; your guess is as good as mine

hue and cry ✪✪

PLAIN ENGLISH ALTERNATIVES: fuss; uproar; clamour; commotion; disturbance; protest; ballyhoo; hullabaloo; to-do

■ *Origins* This originally meant a public outcry summoning all who heard to help in pursuing and detaining someone suspected of a crime.

hum and haw ✪✪

PLAIN ENGLISH ALTERNATIVES: delay; temporize; shilly-shally; hesitate; dither; be indecisive

■ *Origins* From the inarticulate noises made by someone who can't decide what to say.

I beg to differ   ✪✪

Plain English alternatives: I disagree; I cannot agree; I think you are wrong; on the contrary; that's not correct

Clichéd alternatives: you're on the wrong track

I couldn't believe it   ✪✪✪✪✪

Plain English alternatives: it was a surprise; what a surprise; it took me completely by surprise; it was surprising; it was unexpected; it was remarkable; I found it hard to believe; it was hard to take in

Clichéd alternatives: I was gobsmacked

I couldn't care less   ✪✪

Plain English alternatives: it doesn't matter to me; it doesn't bother me; I am indifferent; it doesn't affect me

Clichéd alternatives: it's no skin off my nose; I don't care one way or the other; it makes no difference (or odds) to me; whatever

I didn't see that one coming   ✪✪

Plain English alternatives: I wasn't expecting that; that was completely unexpected; that was a surprise; that took me by surprise

Clichéd alternatives: that came out of nowhere; that caught me napping; that just sneaked up on me; that was a bolt from the blue; what a turn-up for the books!

if it ain't not broke, don't fix it ✪✪✪

PLAIN ENGLISH ALTERNATIVES: don't interfere unnecessarily; don't tinker with something that's working well

CLICHÉD ALTERNATIVES: leave well enough alone; let sleeping dogs lie

if the worst comes to the worst ✪✪

PLAIN ENGLISH ALTERNATIVES: if the least desirable outcome results; if the most disadvantageous events occur

CLICHÉD ALTERNATIVES: if all else fails; in the worst-case scenario

if truth be told ✪✪

PLAIN ENGLISH ALTERNATIVES: to be frank; frankly speaking; if one may speak frankly; truly; putting it plainly

CLICHÉD ALTERNATIVES: to tell the truth; truth to tell; in all honesty; not to put too fine a point on it

if you've got it, flaunt it ✪✪✪✪

PLAIN ENGLISH ALTERNATIVES: make the most of what you've got; exploit your assets to the full

CLICHÉD ALTERNATIVES: don't hide your light under a bushel

if you've seen one, you've seen them all ✪✪

PLAIN ENGLISH ALTERNATIVES: I am not impressed; that's not particularly impressive

CLICHÉD ALTERNATIVES: so what?; big deal; ho-hum; I've seen them all

ignorance is bliss ✪✪

PLAIN ENGLISH ALTERNATIVES: it's better not to know; you're better off not knowing

I hear what you're saying

CLICHÉD ALTERNATIVES: you'll sleep easier if you don't know; don't ask!

■ *Origins* A quotation from *Ode on a Distant Prospect of Eton College* by Thomas Gray (1716–71): 'Thought would destroy their paradise. / No more; where ignorance is bliss, / 'Tis folly to be wise.'

I hear what you're saying   ✪✪✪✪

PLAIN ENGLISH ALTERNATIVES: I know what you mean; I understand; I get it; I see

CLICHÉD ALTERNATIVES: I know where you're coming from; I read you loud and clear; I get the picture

I know where you're coming from   ✪✪✪✪✪

PLAIN ENGLISH ALTERNATIVES: I know what you mean; I understand; I get it; I see; I know what you're trying to tell me

CLICHÉD ALTERNATIVES: I hear what you're saying

ill-gotten gains   ✪✪

PLAIN ENGLISH ALTERNATIVES: dishonestly-acquired money; illegal profits; immoral earnings; proceeds of crime

CLICHÉD ALTERNATIVES: dirty money

in a big way   ✪✪

PLAIN ENGLISH ALTERNATIVES: greatly; immensely; vastly; very much; to a large extent; vigorously; enthusiastically

CLICHÉD ALTERNATIVES: big-time; to the nth degree

in a cleft stick   ✪✪

PLAIN ENGLISH ALTERNATIVES: in a dilemma; faced with two undesirable alternatives

CLICHÉD ALTERNATIVES: between Scylla and Charybdis; between the devil and the deep blue sea; in a quandary; on the horns of a dilemma

■ *Origins* Probably an allusion to Shakespeare's *The Tempest* (Act I, Scene 2): '…
she did confine thee… Into a cloven pine; within which rift / Imprisoned, thou
didst painfully remain'.

in actual fact   ✪✪✪✪✪

PLAIN ENGLISH ALTERNATIVES: in fact, actually; in actuality

CLICHÉD ALTERNATIVES: in point of fact; it so happens; as it happens

Note: Not only a cliché but tautological: there's no such thing as a fact that is *not*
actual.

in all conscience   ✪✪

PLAIN ENGLISH ALTERNATIVES: by all that is right and fair; to be fair; with
an easy mind; justifiably

CLICHÉD ALTERNATIVES: by any reasonable standard; by all accepted
standards

in all honesty   ✪✪

PLAIN ENGLISH ALTERNATIVES: frankly; frankly speaking; truly

CLICHÉD ALTERNATIVES: if truth be told; to tell the truth; truth to tell

in a manner of speaking   ✪✪

PLAIN ENGLISH ALTERNATIVES: as it were; in a way; as one might put it; in a
sense; in some sense

CLICHÉD ALTERNATIVES: so to speak; to coin a phrase

in an ideal world   ✪✪

PLAIN ENGLISH ALTERNATIVES: ideally; if one had one's way; in ideal
circumstances

CLICHÉD ALTERNATIVES: in a perfect world; all things being equal

in a nutshell ✪✪

PLAIN ENGLISH ALTERNATIVES: briefly; concisely; in a few words; succinctly; in brief

CLICHÉD ALTERNATIVES: in a word

■ *Origins* A classical allusion: the Roman scholar and statesman Pliny (Gaius Plinius Secundus, AD 23–79) wrote that a version of Homer's *Iliad* existed that was copied in such small characters that it could be rolled up and fitted into a nutshell.

in any way, shape or form ✪✪✪✪

PLAIN ENGLISH ALTERNATIVES: at all; to any extent; in the least; in the slightest

CLICHÉD ALTERNATIVES: in any way whatsoever

in a very real sense ✪✪✪✪✪

PLAIN ENGLISH ALTERNATIVES: in an important way; truly; importantly; in a way that matters

Note: It could be argued that nothing should be substituted for this phrase as it is usually only padding and doesn't mean anything much at all.

in a word ✪✪

PLAIN ENGLISH ALTERNATIVES: briefly; concisely; in a few words; succinctly; in brief

CLICHÉD ALTERNATIVES: in a nutshell

in cahoots ✪✪

PLAIN ENGLISH ALTERNATIVES: in collusion; intimate; co-operating; in close association

CLICHÉD ALTERNATIVES: hand in glove

■ *Origins* No definitive etymology of this has been established, but one suggestion is that it relates to the French word *cahute* meaning 'cabin', and that the expression arose from North American pioneers sharing both cramped living quarters and unscrupulous plans.

in clover ✪✪

PLAIN ENGLISH ALTERNATIVES: in luxury; at one's ease; in luck; in great comfort; luxuriously

CLICHÉD ALTERNATIVES: on easy street; in the lap of luxury

■ *Origins* From the idea that cattle feeding in a field containing clover were in more luxury than those feeding only on grass.

in cold blood ✪✪

PLAIN ENGLISH ALTERNATIVES: cold-bloodedly; dispassionately; deliberately; without emotion

■ *Origins* From a traditional idea that the temperature of the blood altered according to the emotions being experienced.

in fine fettle ✪✪

PLAIN ENGLISH ALTERNATIVES: active; flourishing; healthy; vigorous

CLICHÉD ALTERNATIVES: in rude health; fighting fit; in good nick; in the best of health; in tip-top condition; in top form

■ *Origins* 'Fettle' comes from an Old English word meaning 'a belt'.

in fits and starts ✪✪

PLAIN ENGLISH ALTERNATIVES: spasmodically; irregularly; in bursts

CLICHÉD ALTERNATIVES: stop and go

in for a penny, in for a pound ✪✪

PLAIN ENGLISH ALTERNATIVES: there's no point in half-measures; there's no turning back

CLICHÉD ALTERNATIVES: it's all or nothing

in high dudgeon ✪✪✪

PLAIN ENGLISH ALTERNATIVES: in a huff; huffily; resentfully; peevishly; indignantly

▪ *Origins* The origin of 'dudgeon', an old word meaning 'resentment' or 'anger', is unknown.

in my book ✪✪

PLAIN ENGLISH ALTERNATIVES: in my opinion; in my view; as far as I am concerned; according to me; from my point of view

CLICHÉD ALTERNATIVES: to my mind; to my way of thinking

in no time ✪✪

PLAIN ENGLISH ALTERNATIVES: in a very short time; instantly; immediately; sharpish; right away

CLICHÉD ALTERNATIVES: in a tick; in two ticks; in two shakes; in a jiffy; before one knows it; before one can say Jack Robinson; in the twinkling of an eye

in no uncertain terms ✪✪✪

PLAIN ENGLISH ALTERNATIVES: frankly; clearly; plainly; candidly; bluntly; straight

CLICHÉD ALTERNATIVES: without mincing one's words; straight from the shoulder

in one's birthday suit ✪✪

PLAIN ENGLISH ALTERNATIVES: naked; nude; unclothed; undressed; stark naked; starkers; bare; sky-clad; bare-ass naked

CLICHÉD ALTERNATIVES: naked as the day one was born; in the altogether; in the buff; in the nuddy; in the nip (*Irish*); in the raw; without a stitch on

in point of fact ✪✪✪✪✪

PLAIN ENGLISH ALTERNATIVES: in fact; actually; in actuality

CLICHÉD ALTERNATIVES: as it happens; it so happens; in actual fact

in queer street ✪✪

PLAIN ENGLISH ALTERNATIVES: destitute; poverty-stricken; homeless; indigent; in debt; in a bad way financially

CLICHÉD ALTERNATIVES: on one's uppers; on the street; down and out; on the breadline

ins and outs ✪✪

PLAIN ENGLISH ALTERNATIVES: details; complexities; finer points; particulars; minutiae; niceties

CLICHÉD ALTERNATIVES: small print

in seventh heaven ✪✪

PLAIN ENGLISH ALTERNATIVES: delighted; ecstatic; enraptured; exalted; blissful; highly pleased; chuffed; overjoyed; thrilled; in ecstasies

CLICHÉD ALTERNATIVES: on cloud nine; pleased as Punch; over the moon; made up; well chuffed

■ *Origins* Believers in the mystic Jewish Cabbala held that there were seven levels of heaven, each more blissful than the one before, culminating in the seventh which was nearest to God.

in short supply ✪✪

PLAIN ENGLISH ALTERNATIVES: scarce; rare; at a premium

CLICHÉD ALTERNATIVES: few and far between; thin on the ground; scarce as hen's teeth

in stitches ✪✪

PLAIN ENGLISH ALTERNATIVES: laughing hysterically; laughing uncontrollably; collapsing with laughter

CLICHÉD ALTERNATIVES: falling about (laughing); rolling about laughing; rolling in the aisles; splitting one's sides; wetting oneself; laughing like a drain

in the bag ✪✪✪✪✪

PLAIN ENGLISH ALTERNATIVES: certain; as good as done; a virtual certainty; assured

CLICHÉD ALTERNATIVES: all over bar the shouting; a cert

- *Origins* From the stowing of shot creatures in a hunter's game bag.

in the cold light of day ✪✪

PLAIN ENGLISH ALTERNATIVES: with impartiality; with objectivity; after calm reflection; when all the facts are ascertained

CLICHÉD ALTERNATIVES: in the harsh glare of reality

in the dim and distant past ✪✪✪

PLAIN ENGLISH ALTERNATIVES: long ago; a long time ago

CLICHÉD ALTERNATIVES: in days gone by; in days of yore; in the old days; long ago and far away; when Adam was a lad; when one was knee-high to a grasshopper

in the doghouse ✪✪

PLAIN ENGLISH ALTERNATIVES: in disgrace; in disfavour

CLICHÉD ALTERNATIVES: in bad odour; in someone's bad books; persona non grata; not flavour of the month

- *Origins* Probably from the idea of a husband being exiled by an offended wife from the marital bed to the dog's kennel.

in the final analysis ✪✪✪✪✪

PLAIN ENGLISH ALTERNATIVES: finally; in the end; ultimately; when everything has been taken into consideration

CLICHÉD ALTERNATIVES: at the end of the day; in the final reckoning; when all is said and done; when you get right down to it

in the firing line ✪✪

PLAIN ENGLISH ALTERNATIVES: in an exposed (or vulnerable) position; open to attack; unprotected

CLICHÉD ALTERNATIVES: under siege; under attack; wide open

■ *Origins* The firing line is the most advanced place in a military position, in which one can be fired upon directly by the enemy, and, of course, fire back.

in the fullness of time ✪✪

PLAIN ENGLISH ALTERNATIVES: at the due time; eventually; finally; after a long delay

CLICHÉD ALTERNATIVES: at length; at long last; when the time is right

in the hot seat ✪✪

PLAIN ENGLISH ALTERNATIVES: under pressure; in a tricky situation; in an uncomfortable position

CLICHÉD ALTERNATIVES: on the spot

■ *Origins* Perhaps from the electric chair used to execute criminals in the USA being referred to in slang as 'the hot seat'.

in the land of Nod ✪✪

PLAIN ENGLISH ALTERNATIVES: asleep; fast asleep; sleeping

CLICHÉD ALTERNATIVES: in the arms of Morpheus; out for the count; dead to the world

■ *Origins* This is a pun on 'nodding off' and the land of Nod ('east of Eden') mentioned in the Bible (*Genesis* 4.16), to which Cain was exiled after killing Abel.

in the land of the living ✪✪

PLAIN ENGLISH ALTERNATIVES: alive; living; around

CLICHÉD ALTERNATIVES: to the fore; stalking the earth; alive and kicking; alive and well and living in …

in the lap of luxury ✪✪

PLAIN ENGLISH ALTERNATIVES: in luxury; in ease and comfort; with every comfort on hand; like royalty

CLICHÉD ALTERNATIVES: in clover; on easy street

in the lap of the gods ✪✪

PLAIN ENGLISH ALTERNATIVES: a matter of chance; a matter of luck; left to fortune; unpredictable; doubtful; out of one's control

CLICHÉD ALTERNATIVES: up in the air; anybody's guess

in the nick of time ✪✪

PLAIN ENGLISH ALTERNATIVES: at the latest possible time; as time runs out; just in time; at the critical moment

CLICHÉD ALTERNATIVES: at the last minute; at the eleventh hour

■ *Origins* From the practice of cutting nicks in a stick to record something such as a tally or the passage of time. Thus, 'in the nick of time' would be just as the nick was being cut to record that a certain time had passed.

in the pink ✪✪

PLAIN ENGLISH ALTERNATIVES: in good health; in perfect health; in fine condition; in prime condition; in good shape; physically fit

CLICHÉD ALTERNATIVES: fighting fit; fit as a fiddle; in tip-top condition; the picture of health

■ *Origins* Not, as one might assume, from being pink-cheeked and therefore healthy, but from the use of 'pink' to mean 'flower' and thus the prime or best condition.

in the pipeline ✪✪✪✪

PLAIN ENGLISH ALTERNATIVES: coming; on the way; under way; to be anticipated; in preparation

CLICHÉD ALTERNATIVES: on the cards

■ *Origins* From the idea of oil being transported down a pipe.

in the region of ✪✪

PLAIN ENGLISH ALTERNATIVES: approximately; around; about; roughly; circa

CLICHÉD ALTERNATIVES: in the neighbourhood of

in the same ballpark ✪✪✪✪

PLAIN ENGLISH ALTERNATIVES: reasonably close; not too far away; roughly similar

CLICHÉD ALTERNATIVES: not a million miles away

■ *Origins* See **ballpark figure**.

in the same boat ✪✪

PLAIN ENGLISH ALTERNATIVES: sharing the same predicament; in a similar situation; facing the same difficulties; affected by the same circumstances

in this day and age ✪✪

PLAIN ENGLISH ALTERNATIVES: at the present time; nowadays; these days; now; today

CLICHÉD ALTERNATIVES: at this point in time

in two shakes ✪✪

PLAIN ENGLISH ALTERNATIVES: in a very short time; instantly; immediately; sharpish; right away

CLICHÉD ALTERNATIVES: in a tick; in two ticks; in no time at all; in a jiffy; before one knows it; before one can say Jack Robinson; in the twinkling of an eye

■ *Origins* The fuller form is of course 'in two shakes of a lamb's tail', agitations of which member are somehow seen as being especially brief.

in words of one syllable ✪✪

PLAIN ENGLISH ALTERNATIVES: simply; basically; simply put; in a way that is easy to understand; in the simplest terms

CLICHÉD ALTERNATIVES: to spell it out; adapted to the meanest understanding

in your dreams ✪✪

PLAIN ENGLISH ALTERNATIVES: it's not going to happen; it'll never happen

CLICHÉD ALTERNATIVES: you'll be lucky; dream on; don't hold your breath; you're kidding yourself; never in a million years; don't count on it

in your face ✪✪✪✪

PLAIN ENGLISH ALTERNATIVES: provocative; confrontational; aggressive; direct; pushy; assertive

CLICHÉD ALTERNATIVES: with attitude

I read you loud and clear ✪✪✪

PLAIN ENGLISH ALTERNATIVES: I know what you mean; I understand; I get it; I see

CLICHÉD ALTERNATIVES: I know where you're coming from; I hear what you're saying; I get the picture; message received and understood

■ *Origins* Borrowed from radio communications, in which this would be a formula of response to the question 'How do you read me?'

I should be so lucky ✪✪✪

PLAIN ENGLISH ALTERNATIVES: there is not much hope of that; it'll never happen; it's unlikely I'll ever be given the opportunity

CLICHÉD ALTERNATIVES: I only wish I had the opportunity; chance would be a fine thing; that'll be the day

is the Pope a Catholic? ✪✪✪

PLAIN ENGLISH ALTERNATIVES: of course!; naturally!; obviously!; what do you think?

CLICHÉD ALTERNATIVES: you bet; do ducks fly south for the winter?; does a bear shit in the woods?

- *Origins* See **does a bear shit in the woods?**

it'll all come out in the wash ✪✪

PLAIN ENGLISH ALTERNATIVES: it'll become clear eventually; it'll work out in the end; things will be sorted out eventually

CLICHÉD ALTERNATIVES: time will tell

- *Origins* From the idea of a stain being removed by washing.

it'll all end in tears ✪✪

PLAIN ENGLISH ALTERNATIVES: there will be an unhappy outcome; nothing good will come of it; one will be sorry; one will regret it

CLICHÉD ALTERNATIVES: it is doomed to end in tears; there will be weeping and wailing and gnashing of teeth

it's a free country ✪✪

PLAIN ENGLISH ALTERNATIVES: you can do as you like; there's nothing to stop you; you have a free hand; do as you please

CLICHÉD ALTERNATIVES: feel free; there's no law against it; they can't touch you for it; if it feels good, do it

it's brass monkeys

it's brass monkeys

PLAIN ENGLISH ALTERNATIVES: it's very cold; it's freezing cold; it's bitterly cold; the weather is distinctly wintry; it's chilly out

> **!** *Original alternative:* it's as cold as a polar bear's nose

■ *Origins* Shortened from the phrase, 'It's cold enough to freeze the balls off a brass monkey.'

it's more than my job's worth

PLAIN ENGLISH ALTERNATIVES: I can't help you; it's beyond my power; there's nothing I can do; I can't afford to take the chance

CLICHÉD ALTERNATIVES: I'd be putting my job on the line

Note: So common is this cliché that it has even generated a noun for someone who uses it: a *jobsworth*, meaning a person who would rather stick to petty rules than be of help.

it's no big deal

PLAIN ENGLISH ALTERNATIVES: it doesn't really matter; it's not that important; it's unimportant; don't worry about it

CLICHÉD ALTERNATIVES: it's a mere detail; it's no biggie; it's nothing to write home about; not to worry

it's not over till the fat lady sings

PLAIN ENGLISH ALTERNATIVES: it's not over yet; there's still time; it's not the end; there's more to come; don't give up yet

CLICHÉD ALTERNATIVES: it's not over till it's over

■ *Origins* From a philistine's assessment, less than kind to sopranos, of opera.

it's not rocket science

PLAIN ENGLISH ALTERNATIVES: it's not that hard to grasp; it's not that intellectually demanding; it's easy enough to understand; it's quite simple really; it's elementary

CLICHÉD ALTERNATIVES: anyone with half a brain could understand it; you don't have to be Einstein to understand it; there's nothing to it

■ *Origins* From the US space programme, but, given that this is a relatively recent usage, it's odd that rocket science should be chosen, as opposed to, say, computer science, when rocket science is something that smacks of the 1960s and 1970s.

it's not the end of the world ✪✪

PLAIN ENGLISH ALTERNATIVES: it's not that serious; it's not critical; one can get over it

CLICHÉD ALTERNATIVES: it's no big deal; things could be a lot worse; one can live with it

it's only a formality ✪✪

PLAIN ENGLISH ALTERNATIVES: it's a matter of form; it's a case of going through the motions

CLICHÉD ALTERNATIVES: it's a foregone conclusion; it's nothing to worry about; it's all over bar the shouting

it speaks for itself ✪✪

PLAIN ENGLISH ALTERNATIVES: no further explanation is required; it's clear enough in itself; there's no need for further discussion

CLICHÉD ALTERNATIVES: it's as plain as the nose in your face; what more do you need?

it stands to reason ✪✪

PLAIN ENGLISH ALTERNATIVES: it's reasonable; it's logical; it's obvious; it makes sense; it's clear; it is logically manifest

CLICHÉD ALTERNATIVES: it goes without saying

it's your call ✪✪✪

PLAIN ENGLISH ALTERNATIVES: it's up to you; it's down to you; you must decide; whatever you think

CLICHÉD ALTERNATIVES: it's your pigeon

■ *Origins* Originally American, this probably comes from baseball, where an umpire's decision is known as a call. See also **close call**.

it's your funeral ✪✪

PLAIN ENGLISH ALTERNATIVES: it's your affair; it's your business; it's your responsibility

CLICHÉD ALTERNATIVES: it's your pigeon; it's your look-out

Note: This is slightly different in tone from the alternatives offered, as it carries the implication that the speaker thinks whatever the addressee is involved in will come to no good.

it's your pigeon ✪✪

PLAIN ENGLISH ALTERNATIVES: it's your affair; it's your business; it's your responsibility

CLICHÉD ALTERNATIVES: it's your funeral; it's your look-out

I've said it before and I'll say it again ✪✪✪✪

PLAIN ENGLISH ALTERNATIVES: I don't mind repeating myself; it bears repetition

CLICHÉD ALTERNATIVES: I've told you before; I don't mind telling you; what I always say is

J

jaundiced eye ✪✪

PLAIN ENGLISH ALTERNATIVES: cynical viewpoint; prejudiced eye; disapproving eye

■ *Origins* Referring to the traditional belief that to someone with jaundice everything looked yellow.

Jekyll and Hyde character ✪✪

PLAIN ENGLISH ALTERNATIVES: a person of contradictions; a person with different sides to them; a schizoid personality

CLICHÉD ALTERNATIVES: a split personality; a dual personality

■ *Origins* From *The Strange Case of Dr Jekyll and Mr Hyde* (1886), a novel by Robert Louis Stevenson in which a scientist attempts to separate the good and evil in his character into two distinct personalities.

jewel in the crown ✪✪

PLAIN ENGLISH ALTERNATIVES: the best; the cream; the pick; the flower

CLICHÉD ALTERNATIVES: the pièce de résistance; the crème de la crème

jockey for position ✪✪

PLAIN ENGLISH ALTERNATIVES: manoeuvre; jostle; contend

CLICHÉD ALTERNATIVES: try to get one over on the others

■ *Origins* From horse-racing.

Joe Public ✪✪✪✪

PLAIN ENGLISH ALTERNATIVES: the average person; the general public; the public at large

CLICHÉD ALTERNATIVES: the man in the street; the man on the Clapham omnibus; Joe Bloggs; Joe Sixpack (*US*)

join the choir invisible ✪✪

PLAIN ENGLISH ALTERNATIVES: die; perish; pass away; pass on; expire

CLICHÉD ALTERNATIVES: pop one's clogs; go the way of all flesh; shuffle off this mortal coil; buy it; kick the bucket; go belly up; peg out; join the majority

■ *Origins* From a poem, *O May I Join the Choir Invisible*, by George Eliot (1819–80): 'O may I join the choir invisible / Of those immortal dead who live again.'

judge a book by its cover

See **don't judge a book by its cover**.

jump on the bandwagon ✪✪

PLAIN ENGLISH ALTERNATIVES: join in

CLICHÉD ALTERNATIVES: go with the flow; follow suit

■ *Origins* From the old practice in the United States of parading a wagon carrying a band through the streets to draw attention to a political meeting. Those who climbed onto this wagon were simply demonstrating their support for the candidate or party sponsoring it.

jump the gun ✪✪

PLAIN ENGLISH ALTERNATIVES: anticipate; start too soon; act prematurely; act precipitately; make a false start

CLICHÉD ALTERNATIVES: go off at half-cock

■ *Origins* From the starting of a race by the firing of a gun and the unfair advantage, whether or not taken deliberately, of starting before the gun has gone off.

jury's still out, the ✪✪✪

PLAIN ENGLISH ALTERNATIVES: that has yet to be decided; a decision has still to be reached; people still have to make up their minds

CLICHÉD ALTERNATIVES: it's up in the air; it's a moot point

just deserts ✪✪

PLAIN ENGLISH ALTERNATIVES: what one deserves; deserved reward; merited punishment; comeuppance

CLICHÉD ALTERNATIVES: what is coming to one

just for the record ✪✪

PLAIN ENGLISH ALTERNATIVES: let it be noted; take note; to get the facts straight; so there can be no doubt

CLICHÉD ALTERNATIVES: don't get me wrong

just the ticket ✪✪

PLAIN ENGLISH ALTERNATIVES: exactly what's required; just right; ideal; spot-on; the very thing; exactly what's wanted

CLICHÉD ALTERNATIVES: just the job; just the thing; just what the doctor ordered

just what the doctor ordered ✪✪

PLAIN ENGLISH ALTERNATIVES: exactly what's required; just right; ideal; spot-on; the very thing; exactly what's wanted

CLICHÉD ALTERNATIVES: just the job; just the thing; just the ticket

■ *Origins* From the idea of something being as exactly the right thing to improve matters as a doctor's prescription would be to alleviate an illness.

K

keep a low profile ✪✪✪

PLAIN ENGLISH ALTERNATIVES: stay out of the public eye; stay out of the limelight; remain inconspicuous

CLICHÉD ALTERNATIVES: keep one's head down

keep a stiff upper lip ✪✪✪

PLAIN ENGLISH ALTERNATIVES: show resolution; control one's emotions; not give way; not let one's emotions get the better of one

CLICHÉD ALTERNATIVES: take it on the chin; take it like a man; tough it out

keep a straight face ✪✪

PLAIN ENGLISH ALTERNATIVES: refrain from laughing; be serious; avoid smiling

CLICHÉD ALTERNATIVES: keep one's face straight

keep one posted ✪✪✪

PLAIN ENGLISH ALTERNATIVES: keep one informed; keep one up to date; give one all the latest news; let one know all the latest developments

CLICHÉD ALTERNATIVES: keep one in the loop

■ *Origins* Originally American, probably from the posting (ie keeping up to date) of account books.

keep one's chin up ✪✪

PLAIN ENGLISH ALTERNATIVES: keep one's spirits up; not be downhearted; stay cheerful; stay hopeful

CLICHÉD ALTERNATIVES: keep smiling; keep one's pecker up; look on the bright side

keep one's ear to the ground   ✪✪

PLAIN ENGLISH ALTERNATIVES: keep well informed; be alert; keep up to date

CLICHÉD ALTERNATIVES: be alive to developments; keep one's eyes open

keep one's end up   ✪✪

PLAIN ENGLISH ALTERNATIVES: maintain one's position; do one's share

CLICHÉD ALTERNATIVES: hold one's own; hold one's ground; play one's part; do one's bit

keep one's eyes skinned or peeled   ✪✪

PLAIN ENGLISH ALTERNATIVES: be alert; keep a good lookout; be observant

CLICHÉD ALTERNATIVES: be on the lookout; be on the qui vive; keep one's eyes open

keep one's head above water   ✪✪

PLAIN ENGLISH ALTERNATIVES: keep solvent; keep going; get by

CLICHÉD ALTERNATIVES: stay afloat; keep body and soul together

■ *Origins* From the idea of a person in water struggling to keep from going under and drowning.

keep one's nose clean   ✪✪

PLAIN ENGLISH ALTERNATIVES: stay out of trouble; be good; behave oneself

CLICHÉD ALTERNATIVES: mind one's manners; not step out of line

keep one's nose to the grindstone   ✪✪

PLAIN ENGLISH ALTERNATIVES: apply oneself; work hard; be diligent

keep one's pecker up

CLICHÉD ALTERNATIVES: keep hard at it; slave away; put one's shoulder to the wheel; work one's fingers to the bone; knuckle down

keep one's pecker up ✪✪

PLAIN ENGLISH ALTERNATIVES: keep one's spirits up; not be downhearted; stay cheerful; stay hopeful

CLICHÉD ALTERNATIVES: keep smiling; keep one's chin up; look on the bright side

▪ *Origins* 'Pecker' here means nothing more rude than 'one's beak', as if one were a chicken.

keep the wolf from the door ✪✪

PLAIN ENGLISH ALTERNATIVES: make a living; stay solvent; stave off starvation

CLICHÉD ALTERNATIVES: make both ends meet

> **!** *Original alternative:* keep the missus from the pawnshop

▪ *Origins* From poverty imagined as a hungry wolf eager to devour one.

kick ass ✪✪✪

PLAIN ENGLISH ALTERNATIVES: do great things; be forceful; domineer; be aggressive; be dynamic

CLICHÉD ALTERNATIVES: show who's boss; lay about one

> **!** *Original alternative:* kick some bottoms

kick one's heels ✪✪

PLAIN ENGLISH ALTERNATIVES: have nothing to do; be idle; be unemployed; be unoccupied; hang about

CLICHÉD ALTERNATIVES: be at a loose end; twiddle one's thumbs

kill someone with kindness ✪✪

PLAIN ENGLISH ALTERNATIVES: overindulge someone; spoil someone; overwhelm someone with benevolence; coddle someone

CLICHÉD ALTERNATIVES: spoil someone rotten

■ *Origins* Perhaps from the story that in ancient Athens the magistrate Draco was smothered when the people threw hats and cloaks at him to express their approval.

kill the fatted calf ✪✪

PLAIN ENGLISH ALTERNATIVES: celebrate lavishly; prepare an extravagant reception

CLICHÉD ALTERNATIVES: push the boat out; lay on a wonderful spread; lay on a slap-up meal

■ *Origins* From the biblical parable of the prodigal son (*Luke* 15.30), in which the father welcoming home the son he thought was lost to him gives orders for a celebratory feast, including butchering the calf they had been fattening.

kill the goose that lays the golden eggs ✪✪

PLAIN ENGLISH ALTERNATIVES: be too greedy; over-exploit one's source; exhaust one's supply; sacrifice one's future for immediate gain

CLICHÉD ALTERNATIVES: cut off one's nose to spite one's face; mortgage the future

■ *Origins* From the fable in which a man who owns a goose that lays golden eggs kills it thinking, wrongly, that he will find more eggs inside.

kith and kin ✪✪

PLAIN ENGLISH ALTERNATIVES: friends and relations; friends and family

CLICHÉD ALTERNATIVES: one's own immediate circle

■ *Origins* Kith is an Old English word whose root is 'to know'.

knee-high to a grasshopper ✪✪

PLAIN ENGLISH ALTERNATIVES: very young; very small; very little; only a child; just a kid

CLICHÉD ALTERNATIVES: a twinkle in one's father's eye

knee-jerk reaction ✪✪✪

PLAIN ENGLISH ALTERNATIVES: automatic reaction; unthinking reaction; predictable reaction; reflex

■ *Origins* From the reflex reaction of the lower leg when one is tapped on the knee.

knock into a cocked hat ✪

PLAIN ENGLISH ALTERNATIVES: best; outclass; outdo; surpass; defeat easily; beat by a wide margin

CLICHÉD ALTERNATIVES: blow out of the water; knock spots off; leave standing; leave in the dust; leave for dead; put in the shade; wipe the floor with

■ *Origins* From the idea of a hat being knocked out of its normal shape.

knock spots off ✪✪

PLAIN ENGLISH ALTERNATIVES: best; outclass; outdo; surpass; defeat easily; beat by a wide margin; thrash; cuff

CLICHÉD ALTERNATIVES: leave standing; leave in the dust; leave for dead; put in the shade; wipe the floor with; give a good hiding

■ *Origins* Probably from target shooting at playing cards, aiming to hit the spots or pips.

know all the answers ✪✪

PLAIN ENGLISH ALTERNATIVES: be well informed; know everything; be extremely knowledgeable

CLICHÉD ALTERNATIVES: be right on the ball; be a wise guy; be too smart for one's own good; know one's onions

know a thing or two ✪✪

PLAIN ENGLISH ALTERNATIVES: have some idea; be well informed; be experienced; have the information

CLICHÉD ALTERNATIVES: be clued-up; know one's onions; know one's stuff; know the ropes; know the score; know one's way around; know a hawk from a handsaw

know how many beans make five ✪✪

PLAIN ENGLISH ALTERNATIVES: be sensible; be aware; be smart

CLICHÉD ALTERNATIVES: have one's wits about one; have one's head screwed on right; have the right idea; know what's what

know jack

See **you don't know jack.**

know on which side one's bread is buttered ✪✪

PLAIN ENGLISH ALTERNATIVES: be aware of one's own best interests; be mindful of one's own interests; look after one's own interests

CLICHÉD ALTERNATIVES: know what one's best look-out is

know the ropes ✪✪

PLAIN ENGLISH ALTERNATIVES: know what one is doing; be very familiar with something; be well informed; be knowledgeable; understand the details

CLICHÉD ALTERNATIVES: know one's onions; know one's stuff; be an old hand at something; know something inside out; know something like the back of one's hand

■ *Origins* A reference to the idea of an experienced sailor being able to identify all of the ropes in a ship's rigging and being familiar with their uses.

know the score ✪✪

PLAIN ENGLISH ALTERNATIVES: be well informed; be experienced; have the information; know the hard facts; know what to do; know what is necessary

CLICHÉD ALTERNATIVES: be clued-up; know what's what; know one's way around; know on which side one's bread is buttered

▪ *Origins* 'Score' here could refer to the points made in a game or to a tally of money owed.

know what I mean? ✪✪✪✪

PLAIN ENGLISH ALTERNATIVES: do you follow?; do you understand me?; do you see what I'm getting at?; is that clear?

CLICHÉD ALTERNATIVES: are you with me?; you know?

Note: While this is a perfectly reasonable way of checking that your listeners are taking in what you say, too often it is used as a mere verbal filler contributing nothing other than a pause for thought, know what I mean?

know where the bodies are buried ✪

PLAIN ENGLISH ALTERNATIVES: be well informed; have secret knowledge; possess incriminating information; know secrets

CLICHÉD ALTERNATIVES: have the lowdown; have the dirt on someone; know someone's guilty secret

▪ *Origins* From the knowledge possessed by a potential witness in a murder case.

knuckle under ✪✪

PLAIN ENGLISH ALTERNATIVES: acknowledge defeat; admit one is beaten; give in; give way; capitulate; yield; submit

CLICHÉD ALTERNATIVES: toe the line; throw in the towel; throw in one's hand; throw up the sponge

labour under a delusion ✪✪

PLAIN ENGLISH ALTERNATIVES: be fooling oneself; be misinformed; have the wrong idea

CLICHÉD ALTERNATIVES: be barking up the wrong tree; have the wrong end of the stick

lady of the night ✪✪

PLAIN ENGLISH ALTERNATIVES: prostitute; whore; tart; sex worker; call girl; streetwalker; brass; hooker

CLICHÉD ALTERNATIVES: fallen woman; working girl; white slave; fille de joie

lamb to the slaughter

See **like a lamb to the slaughter**.

land of the living

See **in the land of the living**.

lap of luxury

See **in the lap of luxury**.

large as life ✪✪

PLAIN ENGLISH ALTERNATIVES: in person; actually; in reality

CLICHÉD ALTERNATIVES: in the flesh; large as life and twice as ugly

larger than life ✪✪

PLAIN ENGLISH ALTERNATIVES: exaggerated; on a grand scale; extravagant; overblown

CLICHÉD ALTERNATIVES: over the top; highly coloured

lashings of ✪✪

PLAIN ENGLISH ALTERNATIVES: lots of; a large amount of; large portions of; an abundance of

CLICHÉD ALTERNATIVES: any amount of; stacks of; oodles of; bags of; heaps of

■ *Origins* Somewhat old-fashioned now, this probably derives from the idea of 'lashing out' in the sense of being extravagant.

last but not least ✪✪✪✪

PLAIN ENGLISH ALTERNATIVES: finally; lastly; to conclude

CLICHÉD ALTERNATIVES: bringing up the rear

last chance saloon

See **drinking in the last chance saloon**.

last legs

See **on its last legs**.

late in the day ✪✪

PLAIN ENGLISH ALTERNATIVES: unreasonably late; too late; overdue

late lamented ✪✪✪

PLAIN ENGLISH ALTERNATIVES: recently deceased; not long dead; much missed

laugh on the other side of one's face ✪✪

PLAIN ENGLISH ALTERNATIVES: be sorry; be bitterly disappointed; be filled with regret; suffer

CLICHÉD ALTERNATIVES: have cause to lament

law unto oneself, a ✪✪

PLAIN ENGLISH ALTERNATIVES: one who ignores convention; one who flouts the rules; no respecter of rules

CLICHÉD ALTERNATIVES: a fiercely independent person; a rugged individualist; a person of independent mind

lay it on the line ✪✪

PLAIN ENGLISH ALTERNATIVES: speak frankly; be firm; be straight; be candid; be blunt; make it clear; be utterly frank

CLICHÉD ALTERNATIVES: give it to someone straight (from the shoulder); tell it like it is; not mince one's words; be brutally frank

▪ *Origins* It's not clear which line is referred to here. Perhaps the idea comes from the US phrase 'lay one's money on the line', meaning 'to pay up when required'.

lay it on thick ✪✪

PLAIN ENGLISH ALTERNATIVES: be fulsome in one's praises; flatter extravagantly; exaggerate one's praise

CLICHÉD ALTERNATIVES: lay it on with a trowel

▪ *Origins* From the idea of laying on plaster in a good thick coat, especially using a trowel for a smooth finish.

lay one's cards on the table ✪✪

PLAIN ENGLISH ALTERNATIVES: declare one's plans openly; make one's position clear; be frank about one's motives

CLICHÉD ALTERNATIVES: come clean; cut to the chase; show one's hand

■ *Origins* From the point in a card game at which, to establish who has won, players must reveal the cards they hold.

leading light ✪✪

PLAIN ENGLISH ALTERNATIVES: person of influence; prominent person; principal; chief; star; luminary

CLICHÉD ALTERNATIVES: big gun

■ *Origins* From the lights fixed at harbour entrances, safe channels, etc to guide ships at night.

lead on Macduff ✪✪✪✪

PLAIN ENGLISH ALTERNATIVES: go ahead; lead the way; after you; let's go

CLICHÉD ALTERNATIVES: I'm right behind you

■ *Origins* Wrongly quoted from Shakespeare's *Macbeth* (Act V, Scene 8), in which Macbeth invites Macduff to fight him, actually saying, 'Lay on, Macduff; / And damn'd be him that first cries, "Hold, enough!"'

lead someone up the garden path ✪✪

PLAIN ENGLISH ALTERNATIVES: mislead someone; deceive someone; take someone in; make a fool of someone

CLICHÉD ALTERNATIVES: pull the wool over someone's eyes; take someone for a ride

■ *Origins* Why should something as seemingly innocent as a stroll along a garden path come to have overtones of deceit? Perhaps from the idea of a would-be seducer at a garden party enticing a young lady to a secluded spot.

lean over backwards

See **bend over backwards**.

leap in the dark ✪✪

PLAIN ENGLISH ALTERNATIVES: act whose consequences cannot be foreseen; risk; gamble; chance; speculative venture

CLICHÉD ALTERNATIVES: shot in the dark

■ *Origins* From the idea of being forced to jump when one cannot see where one is going to land. Perhaps the first recorded use of the phrase was in the last words attributed to the English philosopher Thomas Hobbes (1588–1679): 'I am about to take my last voyage, a great leap in the dark.'

least of one's worries ✪✪

PLAIN ENGLISH ALTERNATIVES: not the most important matter; not one's chief concern; of low priority

CLICHÉD ALTERNATIVES: not top of one's list; the last thing on one's mind; no big deal

leave much to be desired ✪✪

PLAIN ENGLISH ALTERNATIVES: be inadequate; be substandard; be unsatisfactory; fall short; fail to impress

CLICHÉD ALTERNATIVES: be found wanting; not come up to scratch; not cut the mustard; not make the grade

leave no stone unturned ✪✪✪

PLAIN ENGLISH ALTERNATIVES: do everything one can; be thorough; be exhaustive; make every effort; do one's utmost; try one's hardest; spare no effort; do all one can; search thoroughly; look everywhere

CLICHÉD ALTERNATIVES: pull out all the stops; carry out a fingertip search; go through something with a fine-tooth comb

■ *Origins* Apparently from an ancient Greek legend, in which a general searching for the abandoned treasure of a defeated Persian was advised by the Oracle of Delphi to 'leave no stone unturned'. So popular a phrase is this that it even generated a clichéd joke about a severe theatre critic refusing to leave a turn unstoned.

leave someone holding the baby ✪✪

PLAIN ENGLISH ALTERNATIVES: abandon someone; leave someone helpless; desert someone; let someone take the blame

CLICHÉD ALTERNATIVES: leave someone high and dry; leave someone to their fate; leave someone to their own devices; run out on someone; desert someone in their hour of need; leave someone in the lurch; leave someone to carry the can

leave someone in the lurch ✪✪

PLAIN ENGLISH ALTERNATIVES: abandon someone; leave someone helpless; desert someone

CLICHÉD ALTERNATIVES: leave someone high and dry; leave someone to their fate; leave someone to their own devices; run out on someone; desert someone in their hour of need; leave someone holding the baby; leave someone to stew in their own juice

■ *Origins* From card games in which 'the lurch' means a position in which one player or side is left far behind in scoring.

left, right and centre ✪✪

PLAIN ENGLISH ALTERNATIVES: everywhere; in all directions; from all directions; from every direction; all over

CLICHÉD ALTERNATIVES: all over the shop

legislate for

See **you can't legislate for ...**

let bygones be bygones ✪✪

PLAIN ENGLISH ALTERNATIVES: forget past quarrels; forget the past; bring a feud to an end

CLICHÉD ALTERNATIVES: achieve closure; bury the hatchet; forgive and forget; let the dead bury their dead

let it all hang out ✪✪✪

PLAIN ENGLISH ALTERNATIVES: relax; shake off one's inhibitions; be completely uninhibited; unwind; let oneself go

CLICHÉD ALTERNATIVES: let one's hair down; loosen up; get down; chill out; mellow out

let one's hair down ✪✪

PLAIN ENGLISH ALTERNATIVES: relax; shake off one's inhibitions; be completely uninhibited; unwind; let oneself go

CLICHÉD ALTERNATIVES: let it all hang out; loosen up; get down; chill out; mellow out

let's face it ✪✪✪✪

PLAIN ENGLISH ALTERNATIVES: one must accept the realities of the situation

CLICHÉD ALTERNATIVES: let's face the facts; let's face reality; let's be honest

Note: A much overused phrase, often uttered as a mere formula without there actually being a harsh reality that one's listeners are reluctant to confront.

let's get this show on the road ✪✪✪

PLAIN ENGLISH ALTERNATIVES: let's begin; let's get started; let's get going; stop wasting time; stop delaying

CLICHÉD ALTERNATIVES: let's head 'em up and move 'em out

■ *Origins* Originally American, this comes from travelling theatrical companies, circuses, etc.

let the cat out of the bag ✪✪

PLAIN ENGLISH ALTERNATIVES: disclose something secret; reveal a secret; reveal the truth; let the truth slip out

CLICHÉD ALTERNATIVES: spill the beans; give the game away

■ *Origins* Apparently from the sharp practice of traders who would entice the gullible to buy what they thought was a pig enclosed in a bag. When the bag was opened, the animal inside turned out to be merely a cat.

level playing field ✪✪✪✪

PLAIN ENGLISH ALTERNATIVES: equal terms; equal opportunity; position of equality; fair chance (or opportunity); even chance; fair play

CLICHÉD ALTERNATIVES: fair crack of the whip; sporting chance

■ *Origins* If a playing field has a slope there is likely to be an advantage to the team playing downhill.

lick one's lips ✪✪

PLAIN ENGLISH ALTERNATIVES: anticipate something with pleasure; look forward to something; salivate

CLICHÉD ALTERNATIVES: drool over something

life in the fast lane ✪✪✪

PLAIN ENGLISH ALTERNATIVES: a hectic life; an exciting life; a glamorous life

CLICHÉD ALTERNATIVES: life on the edge

■ *Origins* From the lane on a motorway used to overtake slower-moving vehicles.

life of Riley ✪✪

PLAIN ENGLISH ALTERNATIVES: a life of luxury; a life of ease; a life of wealth and indulgence

CLICHÉD ALTERNATIVES: la dolce vita

■ *Origins* Apparently from a 19th-century American comic song in which Riley, or Reilly, imagines how he'd live if he were wealthy.

like a bat out of hell ✪✪

PLAIN ENGLISH ALTERNATIVES: apace; at speed; at a furious pace; like fury; as fast as possible; at top speed

CLICHÉD ALTERNATIVES: all out; hell for leather; at a rate of knots; like the clappers; like greased lightning

■ *Origins* While bats are certainly nippy when flying about, and it's understandable why one would remove itself from the infernal regions as expeditiously as possible, it's not really clear why one would find itself there in the first place (unless it was being serenaded by Meat Loaf).

like a fish out of water ✪✪

PLAIN ENGLISH ALTERNATIVES: ill at ease; out of place; disoriented; uncomfortable; strange

CLICHÉD ALTERNATIVES: like a square peg in a round hole; out of one's element

like a house on fire ✪✪

PLAIN ENGLISH ALTERNATIVES: very well; splendidly; swimmingly; famously; brilliantly

CLICHÉD ALTERNATIVES: great guns; like nobody's business

like a lamb to the slaughter ✪✪

PLAIN ENGLISH ALTERNATIVES: meekly; innocently; without a struggle; without resistance; without putting up a fight

■ *Origins* A biblical reference (*Isaiah* 53.7): 'He is brought as a lamb to the slaughter.'

like a man possessed ✪✪

PLAIN ENGLISH ALTERNATIVES: vigorously; frenetically; enthusiastically; rapidly; frantically; hectically; wildly; furiously; feverishly

CLICHÉD ALTERNATIVES: like there's no tomorrow; like nobody's business; fast and furious; like one possessed

like a red rag to a bull ✪✪

PLAIN ENGLISH ALTERNATIVES: infuriating; maddening; exasperating; galling; highly provocative; intolerable

CLICHÉD ALTERNATIVES: enough to drive one mad

■ *Origins* The colour red is traditionally believed to infuriate bulls, although why this should be and how anyone found out remain mysterious.

like death warmed up ✪✪

PLAIN ENGLISH ALTERNATIVES: very unwell; ill; pale; half-dead

CLICHÉD ALTERNATIVES: green about the gills

like greased lightning ✪✪

PLAIN ENGLISH ALTERNATIVES: apace; at speed; at a furious pace; like fury; as fast as possible; at top speed

CLICHÉD ALTERNATIVES: all out; hell for leather; at a rate of knots; like the clappers; like a bat out of hell

■ *Origins* Lightning, already about as fast as you can get, would be even faster if you could get hold of some and coat it in grease.

like grim death ✪✪

PLAIN ENGLISH ALTERNATIVES: determinedly; as if to save one's life; desperately; urgently

CLICHÉD ALTERNATIVES: as if one's life depended on it; for dear life

like hot cakes

See **sell like hot cakes**.

like it was going out of fashion ✪✪✪

PLAIN ENGLISH ALTERNATIVES: vigorously; frenetically; enthusiastically; rapidly; extravagantly; hectically

CLICHÉD ALTERNATIVES: like there's no tomorrow; like nobody's business

like nobody's business ✪✪

PLAIN ENGLISH ALTERNATIVES: energetically; intensively; hectically; rapidly; vigorously; frenetically; eagerly

CLICHÉD ALTERNATIVES: fast and furious

like pulling teeth ✪✪

PLAIN ENGLISH ALTERNATIVES: arduous; very difficult; almost impossible; hard work; a thankless task; strenuous; laborious

CLICHÉD ALTERNATIVES: like getting blood out of a stone

like shooting fish in a barrel ✪✪

PLAIN ENGLISH ALTERNATIVES: easy; simple; child's play; ludicrously easy; no trouble at all

CLICHÉD ALTERNATIVES: a piece of cake; easy as pie; a doddle; easy-peasy; a pushover; like taking candy from a baby (*US*)

like something the cat dragged in ✪✪

PLAIN ENGLISH ALTERNATIVES: a mess; untidy; dishevelled; a state; bedraggled; scruffy; slovenly; unkempt; slatternly

CLICHÉD ALTERNATIVES: like an unmade bed

like the clappers ✪✪

PLAIN ENGLISH ALTERNATIVES: apace; at speed; at a furious pace; like fury; as fast as possible; at top speed

CLICHÉD ALTERNATIVES: all out; hell for leather; at a rate of knots; like a bat out of hell; like greased lightning

■ *Origins* A clapper is the tongue of a bell, that is, the part that strikes to make the noise.

like water off a duck's back ✪✪

PLAIN ENGLISH ALTERNATIVES: without effect; making no impression; pointless; ineffective

literary lion ✪✪

PLAIN ENGLISH ALTERNATIVES: famous writer; vogue writer; popular author

CLICHÉD ALTERNATIVES: one of the bug guns of literature

- *Origins* The idea of a celebrity as a lion comes from the London tradition of showing tourists the lions kept at the Tower of London, and thus 'lion' came to cover any of the must-see sights.

living on borrowed time ✪✪

PLAIN ENGLISH ALTERNATIVES: dying; moribund; alive despite the odds; desperately ill

CLICHÉD ALTERNATIVES: on the way out; having one's days numbered; not long for this world

- *Origins* The idea is that one has somehow been lent extra time by Death.

lock, stock and barrel ✪✪

PLAIN ENGLISH ALTERNATIVES: completely; utterly; totally; entirely; altogether; in entirety

CLICHÉD ALTERNATIVES: hook, line and sinker; root and branch

- *Origins* This literally means the whole of a rifle: its lock (firing mechanism), its stock (wooden part) and its barrel.

lone wolf ✪✪

PLAIN ENGLISH ALTERNATIVES: loner; individualist; maverick; outsider; solitary

CLICHÉD ALTERNATIVES: rugged individualist

- *Origins* As wolves hunt in packs, this term not only epitomizes singleness but carries overtones of danger.

long and the short of it, the ✪✪

Plain English alternatives: essence; upshot; sum; crux; gist

Clichéd alternatives: nub of the matter; sum and substance; heart of the matter

■ *Origins* This means the essence of the story, whether told in a comprehensive or digressive way or simply in a few words.

long in the tooth ✪✪

Plain English alternatives: old; elderly; superannuated; ancient

Clichéd alternatives: full of years; up in years; getting on; over the hill; past it

■ *Origins* From the teeth of an aging horse, which appear to grow longer as its gums recede.

long shot ✪✪

Plain English alternatives: remote chance; outside chance; speculation

Clichéd alternatives: slim chance

■ *Origins* From hunting, in which one's chances of hitting a target decrease as the distance from it increases.

lose one's bottle ✪✪✪✪

Plain English alternatives: be too scared to go through with it; lose one's nerve; lose courage

Clichéd alternatives: bottle it; bottle out; chicken out; crap out; show one's yellow streak

■ *Origins* In Cockney rhyming slang, 'bottle' is short for 'bottle and glass' meaning 'arse'. Presumably what is connoted here is not actual loss of one's arse but of control over it.

lose one's thread ✪✪

Plain English alternatives: forget what one is saying; lose one's train of thought; become confused; become distracted; stray from the point

CLICHÉD ALTERNATIVES: lose one's place; go astray; get sidetracked; go off at a tangent

■ *Origins* A reference to Greek mythology, in which Theseus was able to find his way back out of the Cretan labyrinth by following a thread which he had unrolled from a ball as he went in.

lost cause ✪✪

PLAIN ENGLISH ALTERNATIVES: foregone conclusion; losing battle; a fight that has already been lost

CLICHÉD ALTERNATIVES: no-win situation; lose-lose situation

love you and leave you ✪✪

PLAIN ENGLISH ALTERNATIVES: go; depart; leave; bid farewell

CLICHÉD ALTERNATIVES: take one's leave; make tracks

M

mad as a hatter ✪✪

PLAIN ENGLISH ALTERNATIVES: insane; crazy; loopy; mental; nuts; nutty; doolally; cracked; touched

CLICHÉD ALTERNATIVES: barking mad; daft as a brush; mad as a March hare; nutty as a fruitcake; not playing with a full deck; not the full shilling; off one's rocker; off one's trolley; out to lunch; round the bend; round the twist

■ *Origins* Lewis Carroll's *Alice's Adventures in Wonderland* (1865) introduced the reading public to the archetypal Mad Hatter, but the makers of hats were already known for eccentric behaviour, which was ascribed to over-exposure to chemicals such as mercury used in their trade.

mad as a March hare ✪✪

PLAIN ENGLISH ALTERNATIVES: insane; crazy; loopy; mental; nuts; nutty; doolally; cracked; touched

CLICHÉD ALTERNATIVES: barking mad; daft as a brush; mad as a hatter; nutty as a fruitcake; not playing with a full deck; not the full shilling; off one's rocker; off one's trolley; out to lunch

■ *Origins* March is the time of year when hares are in their mating season and are given to exuberant behaviour.

made of sterner stuff ✪✪

PLAIN ENGLISH ALTERNATIVES: stronger; more resolute; indomitable; determined; staunch; tough

mad for it

PLAIN ENGLISH ALTERNATIVES: ardent; avid; eager; enthusiastic; keen; voracious

CLICHÉD ALTERNATIVES: into it; up for it

magnum opus

PLAIN ENGLISH ALTERNATIVES: masterpiece; masterwork; pièce de résistance; great work; chef d'oeuvre

CLICHÉD ALTERNATIVES: crowning glory

- *Origins* A Latin phrase meaning literally 'great work'.

make a beeline for

PLAIN ENGLISH ALTERNATIVES: take the most direct way to; go straight to; head straight for; go directly to

- *Origins* From the belief that bees conserve energy when gathering pollen by taking the straightest possible route between the hive and the pollen source.

make a clean breast of it

PLAIN ENGLISH ALTERNATIVES: confess; tell the truth; make a frank admission

CLICHÉD ALTERNATIVES: come clean; make a full and frank confession; fess up; get it off one's chest

- *Origins* Like 'getting something off one's chest', this refers to the old idea that the breast – and particularly the heart – is the physical location of one's feelings. If you clear something from your breast, your conscience will be clean.

make a clean sweep

PLAIN ENGLISH ALTERNATIVES: win everything; win the lot; take all the prizes; clear everything out; make a clearance

CLICHÉD ALTERNATIVES: pocket all the stakes; sweep the board; carry all before one

- *Origins* From the idea of gathering up everything.

make all the right noises ✪✪✪

PLAIN ENGLISH ALTERNATIVES: say the right things; sound convincing; be agreeable; tell people what they want to hear

CLICHÉD ALTERNATIVES: look the part; hit the right note; press the right buttons

make a mountain out of a molehill ✪✪

PLAIN ENGLISH ALTERNATIVES: exaggerate the difficulties; magnify the problem; overdramatize things; make things sound worse than they are

CLICHÉD ALTERNATIVES: make a fuss about nothing

make a song and dance about ✪✪

PLAIN ENGLISH ALTERNATIVES: make an unnecessary fuss about; make too much of

CLICHÉD ALTERNATIVES: make a great to-do out of; make a big thing of; make a meal of; make a big production out of; make a performance out of; make a federal case out of (*US*)

make (both) ends meet ✪✪

PLAIN ENGLISH ALTERNATIVES: live within one's income; manage to get by; avoid getting into debt; scrape by

CLICHÉD ALTERNATIVES: balance the books; balance the budget

■ *Origins* Probably from a French expression meaning to join the two ends of the year, that is, to have enough money to last from the end of one year to the beginning of the next.

make hay while the sun shines ✪✪

PLAIN ENGLISH ALTERNATIVES: make the most of one's opportunities; seize the opportunity while it lasts; carpe diem

CLICHÉD ALTERNATIVES: strike while the iron is hot; grab the opportunity with both hands

make heavy weather of ✪✪

PLAIN ENGLISH ALTERNATIVES: find difficult; have trouble with; have problems with; find that something does not go smoothly; encounter difficulties in doing

■ *Origins* A nautical image, referring to a ship labouring to make progress during a storm at sea.

make no bones about it ✪✪

PLAIN ENGLISH ALTERNATIVES: be open; be frank; be candid; make no fuss; have no scruples about it; make no difficulties

CLICHÉD ALTERNATIVES: be up-front about it

■ *Origins* Perhaps from gambling, in which 'bones' is a slang term for 'dice', and the phrase means 'to throw the dice without making a fuss'.

make no mistake ✪✪

PLAIN ENGLISH ALTERNATIVES: be assured; be quite certain; be quite clear

CLICHÉD ALTERNATIVES: don't run away with the wrong idea; get it straight

make-or-break ✪✪✪

PLAIN ENGLISH ALTERNATIVES: critical; crucial; decisive; momentous; pivotal

CLICHÉD ALTERNATIVES: all-important; now-or-never

make short work of ✪✪

PLAIN ENGLISH ALTERNATIVES: accomplish quickly; dispatch hurriedly; carry out with dispatch; dispose of briskly; expedite

CLICHÉD ALTERNATIVES: zip through; race through

make someone an offer they can't refuse ✪✪✪✪

PLAIN ENGLISH ALTERNATIVES: convince someone; persuade someone; prevail upon someone; succeed in making someone agree

CLICHÉD ALTERNATIVES: make someone the offer of a lifetime; bring someone round; offer someone a sweetheart deal

■ *Origins* Made popular in the movie *The Godfather* (1972), in which the eponymous Mafia don played by Marlon Brando uses the expression to cover somewhat dubious methods of persuasion.

make someone's flesh creep ✪✪

PLAIN ENGLISH ALTERNATIVES: horrify someone; terrify someone; frighten someone; scare someone; make someone shudder

CLICHÉD ALTERNATIVES: make someone's hair stand on end; make someone's spine tingle; fill someone with fear and loathing; give someone the creeps; give someone the willies

make the supreme sacrifice ✪✪

PLAIN ENGLISH ALTERNATIVES: give up one's life; lay down one's life; die; sacrifice oneself

make tracks ✪✪

PLAIN ENGLISH ALTERNATIVES: leave; depart; decamp; get going; take off; be on one's way; set off

CLICHÉD ALTERNATIVES: make oneself scarce; beat it; head for the hills

■ *Origins* From the idea of literally making a track that can be followed as one travels.

make waves ✪✪

PLAIN ENGLISH ALTERNATIVES: cause trouble; make a fuss; make trouble; cause a disturbance

CLICHÉD ALTERNATIVES: rock the boat; stir it; give someone grief

■ *Origins* From the waves caused by a ship passing through a body of water that was previously still.

man and boy ✪✪

PLAIN ENGLISH ALTERNATIVES: from childhood; from birth; all of one's life

CLICHÉD ALTERNATIVES: all one's days; since one was knee-high to a grasshopper

Note: It's strange how the logical chronology is reversed here: surely it should be 'boy and man'? And why do you never come across 'girl and woman'?

man in the street ✪✪✪

PLAIN ENGLISH ALTERNATIVES: the average person; the general public; the public at large; the ordinary citizen

CLICHÉD ALTERNATIVES: Joe Public; the everyday Tom, Dick or Harry; the man on the Clapham omnibus; Joe Bloggs; Joe Sixpack (*US*)

mark my words ✪✪

PLAIN ENGLISH ALTERNATIVES: pay attention to what I say; remember these words; note what I say

matter of life and death ✪✪

PLAIN ENGLISH ALTERNATIVES: critical matter; vitally important matter; crisis; emergency

CLICHÉD ALTERNATIVES: big deal; the end of the world

meet one's Waterloo ✪✪

PLAIN ENGLISH ALTERNATIVES: meet with final defeat; be crushingly defeated

CLICHÉD ALTERNATIVES: meet one's Nemesis; fall at last; go down in flames

■ *Origins* Waterloo was, of course, the site in Belgium of the battle that marked Napoleon's final defeat, as evoked memorably in many great literary works, paintings and films, and also in a pop song by Abba.

meet someone halfway ✪✪

PLAIN ENGLISH ALTERNATIVES: compromise; make concessions; reach an agreement; strike a balance

CLICHÉD ALTERNATIVES: meet someone in the middle; give and take; go fifty-fifty

mend one's fences ✪✪

PLAIN ENGLISH ALTERNATIVES: make peace; improve one's relationships; re-establish good relations

■ *Origins* Presumably from the idea of doing maintenance work on one's relationships in the same way as one would on one's fences.

mend one's ways ✪✪

PLAIN ENGLISH ALTERNATIVES: reform; improve one's behaviour

CLICHÉD ALTERNATIVES: clean up one's act; get back on the straight and narrow; pull one's socks up; straighten up and fly right; turn over a new leaf

might and main

See **with might and main**.

millstone around one's neck ✪✪

PLAIN ENGLISH ALTERNATIVES: burden; imposition; heavy responsibility; encumbrance

CLICHÉD ALTERNATIVES: albatross around one's neck

■ *Origins* A millstone is a large heavy circular stone, one of a pair used in a mill to grind corn. The idea of having one hung around one's neck comes from the Bible (*Matthew* 18.6): 'Whoso shall offend one of these little ones which believe in me, it were better for him that a millstone were hanged about his neck, and that he were drowned in the depth of the sea.'

mind boggles

See **the mind boggles**.

mind one's p's and q's ✪✪

PLAIN ENGLISH ALTERNATIVES: be punctilious; be careful; be circumspect; be prudent

CLICHÉD ALTERNATIVES: mind one's manners; keep one's nose clean; watch oneself

■ *Origins* Various attempts have been made to identify the p's and q's in question, including the idea that they are abbreviations for pints and quarts, but the most likely explanation is that this is a reference to children learning to write and being told to make sure that the letter they inscribe is the right way round.

miss the boat ✪✪

PLAIN ENGLISH ALTERNATIVES: lose one's opportunity; squander one's chances; miss out; forfeit one's opportunity; be too late

CLICHÉD ALTERNATIVES: blow one's chance; blow it

Mitty, Walter

See **Walter Mitty**.

moan and groan ✪✪

PLAIN ENGLISH ALTERNATIVES: complain; grumble; gripe; carp; beef; bitch; grouse; kvetch; whine; whinge

CLICHÉD ALTERNATIVES: weep and wail; lament one's fate

Note: It is perfectly possible to moan *or* groan as an independent act of complaint, and the temptation to yoke these together is to be resisted.

money for old rope ✪✪

PLAIN ENGLISH ALTERNATIVES: easy money; easy profits; money for nothing; money made for little effort

CLICHÉD ALTERNATIVES: money for jam

■ *Origins* Another nautical reference. In the days of sail, crew-members could supplement their wages by unpicking lengths of old rope and selling the strands for use as oakum (material used to caulk a ship's seams).

monkey business ✪✪

PLAIN ENGLISH ALTERNATIVES: mischief; misbehaviour; roguery; underhandedness; double-dealing; shenanigans; carrying on; antics; messing about

CLICHÉD ALTERNATIVES: funny business; jiggery-pokery; dirty work at the crossroads

month of Sundays ✪✪

PLAIN ENGLISH ALTERNATIVES: a very long time; an interminable period; ages; forever; an age; an eternity

CLICHÉD ALTERNATIVES: donkey's years; till the cows come home; yonks

moot point ✪✪

PLAIN ENGLISH ALTERNATIVES: a matter of debate; a matter of argument; a debatable point; a disputed point; an undecided matter

CLICHÉD ALTERNATIVES: bone of contention; vexed question

■ *Origins* 'Moot' comes from Old English roots, with the basic meaning being 'to meet'. A moot point originally referred to a hypothetical question being debated by law students.

more honoured in the breach than the observance ✪✪✪✪

PLAIN ENGLISH ALTERNATIVES: rarely respected; hardly ever complied with; more often broken than kept; disregarded; ignored; not done; not observed in practice

CLICHÉD ALTERNATIVES: a dead letter; a thing of the past

■ *Origins* Based on a misinterpretation of a line from Shakespeare. In *Hamlet* (Act I, Scene 4), the eponymous prince, referring to the heavy drinking at the Danish court, says, 'It is a custom more honoured in the breach than the observance.' His meaning is that it is more honourable to disregard the custom than to comply with it, but somehow this has been transmogrified into 'more people breach this rule than observe it', and this has become the clichéd use.

more in sorrow than in anger   ✪✪✪✪

PLAIN ENGLISH ALTERNATIVES: with regret; regretfully; taking no pleasure in it; with a sense of disappointment

CLICHÉD ALTERNATIVES: with a heavy heart

Note: Generally used by people who are about to administer a punishment and want to increase the culprit's sense of guilt. Like 'this is going to hurt me more than it hurts you', this cliché rarely conveys the truth.

more power to your elbow   ✪✪✪

PLAIN ENGLISH ALTERNATIVES: good luck; I wish you every success

CLICHÉD ALTERNATIVES: go for it; I'm right behind you

more than my job's worth

See **it's more than my job's worth**.

more than one can shake a stick at   ✪✪✪

PLAIN ENGLISH ALTERNATIVES: an enormous amount of; a great deal of; an abundance of; an endless amount of

CLICHÉD ALTERNATIVES: oodles of; stacks of; heaps of; scads of

■ *Origins* It is not clear why an abundance of something should be acknowledged by shaking a stick at it.

more to it than meets the eye

See **there's more to it than meets the eye**.

more years than one cares to remember ✪✪

PLAIN ENGLISH ALTERNATIVES: a very long time; years and years; ages; an unconscionably long time; forever

CLICHÉD ALTERNATIVES: donkey's years; yonks

mother and father of ... ✪✪✪✪

PLAIN ENGLISH ALTERNATIVES: the ultimate; the greatest possible; the worst imaginable; the biggest ever

CLICHÉD ALTERNATIVES: the granddaddy of them all

mountain to climb ✪✪✪

PLAIN ENGLISH ALTERNATIVES: a great deal to do; an enormous task; much to achieve

CLICHÉD ALTERNATIVES: a job on one's hands; a hard row to hoe; one's work cut out

move heaven and earth ✪✪

PLAIN ENGLISH ALTERNATIVES: do everything possible; make every effort; do all one can; go to great trouble

CLICHÉD ALTERNATIVES: spare no effort; try with might and main

movers and shakers ✪✪✪

PLAIN ENGLISH ALTERNATIVES: powerful people; influential people; go-getters

CLICHÉD ALTERNATIVES: the powers that be; people that matter

■ *Origins* From the poem *Ode* by English poet Arthur O'Shaughnessy (1844–81): 'Yet we are the movers and shakers / Of the world for ever, it seems.'

much of a muchness   ✪✪

PLAIN ENGLISH ALTERNATIVES: much the same; all the same; very much alike; very similar

CLICHÉD ALTERNATIVES: six of one and half a dozen of the other

muddy the waters   ✪✪

PLAIN ENGLISH ALTERNATIVES: cause confusion; confuse matters; complicate matters; obfuscate

mumbo-jumbo   ✪✪

PLAIN ENGLISH ALTERNATIVES: jargon; gobbledegook; double talk; unintelligible language; nonsense

CLICHÉD ALTERNATIVES: double Dutch

■ *Origins* Probably a corrupted version of the name of a Mandingo god heard by 19th-century British explorers in Africa.

mum's the word   ✪✪

PLAIN ENGLISH ALTERNATIVES: keep quiet; say nothing; keep something secret; keep something to oneself; tell no-one; keep one's mouth shut

CLICHÉD ALTERNATIVES: keep it under one's hat; don't breathe a word; keep shtoom; keep it under wraps; don't noise it about

■ *Origins* 'Mum' in this case does not refer to one's mother but to the inarticulate sound made when trying to speak with one's lips tightly closed.

mystery man or woman   ✪✪✪

PLAIN ENGLISH ALTERNATIVES: unidentified person; unknown person; stranger

CLICHÉD ALTERNATIVES: person or persons unknown; mysterious stranger

N

nail-biting finish

PLAIN ENGLISH ALTERNATIVES: close finish; anxious finish; cliffhanger

CLICHÉD ALTERNATIVES: near thing; near-run thing; neck-and-neck finish

> **!** *Original alternative:* buttock-clencher

nail in one's coffin

PLAIN ENGLISH ALTERNATIVES: blow; body blow; reverse; setback; factor contributing to one's downfall

- **Origins** From the nails used to secure the lid of a coffin, each one contributing to the unlikelihood of the person so confined making a return appearance.

naked truth

PLAIN ENGLISH ALTERNATIVES: plain truth; simple truth

CLICHÉD ALTERNATIVES: the truth and nothing but the truth; unvarnished truth; plain and simple truth; plain unvarnished truth; simple fact

- **Origins** From the traditional fable in which Truth's garments were stolen by Falsehood but Truth preferred to go naked rather than wear the garments of Falsehood.

name and shame

PLAIN ENGLISH ALTERNATIVES: expose; denounce; accuse; stigmatize

CLICHÉD ALTERNATIVES: blow the whistle on; point the finger at

name is mud

See **his/her name is mud.**

name of the game ✪✪✪

PLAIN ENGLISH ALTERNATIVES: important thing; central theme; purpose; essence; what matters

CLICHÉD ALTERNATIVES: what it's all about; be-all and end-all; bottom line; crux of the matter; nub of the matter

▪ *Origins* Originally American, perhaps from playing cards for money, in which the dealer would have to specify the exact form of the game before dealing, eg 'The name of the game is five-card stud.'

name to conjure with ✪✪✪

PLAIN ENGLISH ALTERNATIVES: famous name; influential name; well-known name

CLICHÉD ALTERNATIVES: big name

▪ *Origins* From the old idea that naming a person would summon their spirit to appear.

nasty piece of work ✪✪

PLAIN ENGLISH ALTERNATIVES: unpleasant person; objectionable person; horrible character; odious individual; villain; scoundrel

CLICHÉD ALTERNATIVES: bad news; good-for-nothing

near the knuckle ✪✪

PLAIN ENGLISH ALTERNATIVES: risqué; indecent; blue; improper; naughty; coarse; dirty; raunchy; smutty; vulgar; off-colour

CLICHÉD ALTERNATIVES: near the bone; close to the bone

neck and neck ✪✪

PLAIN ENGLISH ALTERNATIVES: side by side; close together; equal

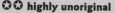

CLICHÉD ALTERNATIVES: nip and tuck; with nothing between them; evenly matched; level pegging

■ *Origins* From horse-racing, where the long neck of a horse may be the margin by which a race is won, and where two horses whose necks are close together are running at roughly the same pace.

neck of the woods ✪✪

PLAIN ENGLISH ALTERNATIVES: area; neighbourhood; territory; locality; turf; locale; vicinity

■ *Origins* Originally an American usage. 'Neck' here means a narrow cleared area in a forest.

needless to say ✪✪

PLAIN ENGLISH ALTERNATIVES: of course; evidently; obviously; clearly

CLICHÉD ALTERNATIVES: it goes without saying; one need hardly mention

Note: This is one of these expressions that seem to contradict themselves. Saying that something need not be said is invariably followed by making just that statement.

need something like a hole in the head ✪✪✪

PLAIN ENGLISH ALTERNATIVES: have no need for something; have no use for something; would rather not have something

CLICHÉD ALTERNATIVES: could do without something

neither fish, flesh nor fowl ✪✪

PLAIN ENGLISH ALTERNATIVES: neither one thing nor the other; uncategorizable; indefinite; undetermined

CLICHÉD ALTERNATIVES: neither fish, flesh nor good red herring

■ *Origins* Apparently from the idea that fish was food suitable for monks, flesh (ie meat) was for people in general, and fowl was the staple fare of the poor.

neither here nor there ✪✪

PLAIN ENGLISH ALTERNATIVES: irrelevant; unimportant; of no great importance; negligible; of no consequence; inconsequential; immaterial; insignificant

CLICHÉD ALTERNATIVES: not worth bothering about; not worth mentioning

new kid on the block ✪✪✪

PLAIN ENGLISH ALTERNATIVES: newcomer; beginner; late arrival

CLICHÉD ALTERNATIVES: Johnny-come-lately; new face

▪ *Origins* Originally American, meaning a youth whose family has just moved into a neighbourhood.

next to nothing ✪✪

PLAIN ENGLISH ALTERNATIVES: very little; almost nothing; hardly anything at all; an insignificant amount

CLICHÉD ALTERNATIVES: a paltry sum

nick of time

See **in the nick of time**.

nine times out of ten ✪✪

PLAIN ENGLISH ALTERNATIVES: usually; generally; in most cases; more often than not

CLICHÉD ALTERNATIVES: for the most part

no bones about it

See **make no bones about it**.

no can do ✪✪✪

PLAIN ENGLISH ALTERNATIVES: I can't do it; it cannot be done; I am unable to help; it's impossible; it's not doable

CLICHÉD ALTERNATIVES: no chance; nothing doing; no dice; no joy

no great shakes ✪✪

PLAIN ENGLISH ALTERNATIVES: not very good; of no account; poor; inferior; mediocre; second-rate

CLICHÉD ALTERNATIVES: not up to much; nothing to write home about; not much cop

no laughing matter ✪✪

PLAIN ENGLISH ALTERNATIVES: a serious matter; a grave matter; a matter of importance; something to be taken seriously

CLICHÉD ALTERNATIVES: no joke; nothing to laugh about

no mean ... ✪✪✪✪✪

PLAIN ENGLISH ALTERNATIVES: a formidable ...; an accomplished ...; a powerful ...; a serious ...

CLICHÉD ALTERNATIVES: a ... to be reckoned with

no more Mr Nice Guy ✪✪✪

PLAIN ENGLISH ALTERNATIVES: now the fight begins in earnest; there will be no more holding back; no mercy will be shown

CLICHÉD ALTERNATIVES: no punches will be pulled; no prisoners will be taken; the gloves are off

no oil painting ✪✪

PLAIN ENGLISH ALTERNATIVES: no great beauty; not particularly good-looking; homely; plain; unattractive; unprepossessing

CLICHÉD ALTERNATIVES: no honey; nothing much to look at; a minger

■ *Origins* From the idea that an artist painting a portrait in oils will tend to flatter the sitter.

no picnic ✪✪

PLAIN ENGLISH ALTERNATIVES: difficult; tough; arduous; a struggle; unpleasant; not easy; demanding; toilsome

CLICHÉD ALTERNATIVES: a hard row to hoe; no easy task

no problem ✪✪

PLAIN ENGLISH ALTERNATIVES: it's all right; that's easy; don't mention it

CLICHÉD ALTERNATIVES: it's no big deal; consider it done; no sweat; no worries; not a problem

nose to the grindstone

See **keep one's nose to the grindstone.**

no skin off my nose ✪✪

PLAIN ENGLISH ALTERNATIVES: it doesn't matter to me; it doesn't bother me; I am indifferent; it doesn't affect me

CLICHÉD ALTERNATIVES: I couldn't care less; I don't care one way or the other; it makes no difference (or odds) to me; whatever

no spring chicken ✪✪

PLAIN ENGLISH ALTERNATIVES: not young; mature; no longer young

CLICHÉD ALTERNATIVES: not in the first flush of youth; past one's sell-by date

■ *Origins* A spring chicken is a young chicken, making particularly tender eating.

no such luck ✪✪

PLAIN ENGLISH ALTERNATIVES: unfortunately not; I'm afraid not; it was not possible

CLICHÉD ALTERNATIVES: no dice; no joy; chance would be a fine thing; I should be so lucky

not a fit night out for man nor beast ✪✪

PLAIN ENGLISH ALTERNATIVES: a stormy night; a wild night; an inclement night; a blustery night; a night for staying indoors

CLICHÉD ALTERNATIVES: a dark and stormy night

not a happy bunny ✪✪✪

PLAIN ENGLISH ALTERNATIVES: displeased; discontented; unhappy; dissatisfied; annoyed; angry

CLICHÉD ALTERNATIVES: not in the best of moods; ticked off; fed up

■ *Origins* It's not clear why rabbits are singled out here as the standard of happiness. Perhaps it is an echo from a children's story.

not a pretty sight ✪✪

PLAIN ENGLISH ALTERNATIVES: distressing; disturbing; frightful; grim; horrible; repugnant; revolting; shocking; ugly

CLICHÉD ALTERNATIVES: stomach-turning

not as black as one is painted ✪✪

PLAIN ENGLISH ALTERNATIVES: not as bad as all that; not all bad; having redeeming features; having good points

■ *Origins* This is shortened from the phrase 'The Devil is not as black as he is painted.'

not a snowball's chance ✪✪

PLAIN ENGLISH ALTERNATIVES: no chance; not a chance; no possibility; not the slimmest of chances; not a hope

CLICHÉD ALTERNATIVES: fat chance; not a hope in hell; not a dog's chance; not the ghost of a chance; Buckley's chance (*Australian*)

■ *Origins* Shortened from 'a snowball's chance in hell'.

not born yesterday ✪✪

PLAIN ENGLISH ALTERNATIVES: not a fool; not an innocent; not gullible; not easily fooled; experienced; clued-up; wise; streetwise; smart; wily

CLICHÉD ALTERNATIVES: nobody's fool; not a mug; not wet behind the ears; wise in the ways of the world

not by a long chalk ✪✪

PLAIN ENGLISH ALTERNATIVES: by no means; not by any means; in no way; not in the slightest; not in the least; not at all

CLICHÉD ALTERNATIVES: not in anyone's book

▪ *Origins* Probably from the use of chalk to mark up players' scores in a game.

not cricket ✪✪✪

PLAIN ENGLISH ALTERNATIVES: not fair; unfair; not sporting; unsporting; unethical

CLICHÉD ALTERNATIVES: not playing the game; not the done thing; playing dirty; dirty pool

▪ *Origins* Strange how cricket retains its position as a shibboleth of sporting behaviour, as if 'sledging' didn't exist.

not for all the tea in China ✪✪✪✪

PLAIN ENGLISH ALTERNATIVES: under no circumstances; not for any reward; not for anything

CLICHÉD ALTERNATIVES: not for any money; not for a king's ransom; not if you handed it to one on a plate

not for turning ✪✪

PLAIN ENGLISH ALTERNATIVES: not to be dissuaded; steadfast; constant; unswerving; unfaltering; unwavering; immovable; resolute

CLICHÉD ALTERNATIVES: sticking to one's guns

▪ *Origins* From a speech made by Margaret Thatcher at the Conservative Party Conference in 1980: 'U-turn if you want to. The lady's not for turning.' This, in turn, is a pun on the title of a play by Christopher Fry, *The Lady's not for Burning* (1948).

not have a clue ✪✪

PLAIN ENGLISH ALTERNATIVES: have no idea; have no inkling; have no notion; lack the information; be ignorant; not know what to do; be baffled; be nonplussed

CLICHÉD ALTERNATIVES: be completely in the dark; not have the foggiest; not have the least idea

not have a leg to stand on ✪✪

PLAIN ENGLISH ALTERNATIVES: have no case; have no argument; have no excuse; have no defence

nothing if not ✪✪

PLAIN ENGLISH ALTERNATIVES: very; highly; above all; primarily; fundamentally; totally

nothing to write home about ✪✪✪

PLAIN ENGLISH ALTERNATIVES: not very good; unexciting; mediocre; second-rate; nothing out of the ordinary; unexceptional; uninteresting

CLICHÉD ALTERNATIVES: not up to much; no great shakes; not much cop; run of the mill; no big deal; nothing to get excited about

■ *Origins* From the days when letter-writing was a more important channel of communication than it is now, and a correspondent would recount anything interesting that had taken place.

nothing ventured, nothing gained ✪✪

PLAIN ENGLISH ALTERNATIVES: take a chance; take a risk; take courage; be bold; be brave; be daring

CLICHÉD ALTERNATIVES: go for it; get stuck in; have a go; faint heart never won fair maid

not in the same league ✪✪

PLAIN ENGLISH ALTERNATIVES: vastly inferior; not of the same calibre; much less important; on a much smaller scale

CLICHÉD ALTERNATIVES: not a patch on; not to be mentioned in the same breath

not know one's arse from one's elbow ✪✪

PLAIN ENGLISH ALTERNATIVES: have no idea; have no inkling; have no notion; be ignorant; know nothing

CLICHÉD ALTERNATIVES: not have the foggiest; not have the least idea; not know one's arse from a hole in the ground; not know whether one is Arthur or Martha (*Australian*)

not know someone from Adam ✪✪

PLAIN ENGLISH ALTERNATIVES: not know someone at all; have no idea who someone is; be utterly unfamiliar with someone; be unacquainted with someone

▪ *Origins* It is the Biblical Adam who is referred to here, but it is unlikely that anyone should ever come across him in an identity parade.

not one iota ✪✪

PLAIN ENGLISH ALTERNATIVES: not (by) the smallest amount; not the slightest bit; not the least bit

CLICHÉD ALTERNATIVES: not a jot; not one jot or tittle; not one bit

▪ *Origins* Iota is the smallest letter in the Greek alphabet.

not one's cup of tea ✪✪

PLAIN ENGLISH ALTERNATIVES: not to one's taste; not the sort of thing one likes; unacceptable; unappealing

CLICHÉD ALTERNATIVES: not to one's fancy; not one's idea of a good time

not to put too fine a point on it

not out of the woods ✪✪

PLAIN ENGLISH ALTERNATIVES: not out of danger; not safe; still at risk; still in a critical position

CLICHÉD ALTERNATIVES: not in the clear

not quite the thing ✪✪

PLAIN ENGLISH ALTERNATIVES: unconventional; unacceptable; improper; objectionable

CLICHÉD ALTERNATIVES: not the done thing; beyond the pale

not the only fish in the sea ✪✪

PLAIN ENGLISH ALTERNATIVES: not unique; not irreplaceable

CLICHÉD ALTERNATIVES: not the only pebble on the beach

not to be sneezed at ✪✪

PLAIN ENGLISH ALTERNATIVES: not to be despised; not to be dismissed; not to be underrated; not inconsiderable; worth considering

CLICHÉD ALTERNATIVES: not to be sniffed at; not to be scoffed at

not to mention ✪✪

PLAIN ENGLISH ALTERNATIVES: to say nothing of; not forgetting

CLICHÉD ALTERNATIVES: needless to say; one need hardly add

not to put too fine a point on it ✪✪✪

PLAIN ENGLISH ALTERNATIVES: to be frank; to be blunt; to speak frankly; to speak bluntly; frankly speaking; to put it plainly

CLICHÉD ALTERNATIVES: to come straight to the point; to call a spade a spade

not touch a drop ✪✪

PLAIN ENGLISH ALTERNATIVES: drink no alcohol; have nothing to drink; abstain; be abstemious

CLICHÉD ALTERNATIVES: be stone-cold sober

Note: This is quite an odd phrase to have become fixed in the language: it's not 'touching' a drop of alcohol that does the damage.

no two ways about it

See **there's no two ways about it.**

no way ✪✪✪✪

PLAIN ENGLISH ALTERNATIVES: that's not going to happen; absolutely not; definitely not; under no circumstances; I refuse; it's not possible

CLICHÉD ALTERNATIVES: no chance; no dice; forget it; no way, José

no-win situation ✪✪✪✪

PLAIN ENGLISH ALTERNATIVES: an impossible situation; a position in which one can't succeed; a situation in which one can't win

CLICHÉD ALTERNATIVES: a lose-lose situation; a hiding to nothing

now you're talking ✪✪

PLAIN ENGLISH ALTERNATIVES: that's better; that's more acceptable

CLICHÉD ALTERNATIVES: now you're making sense; that's more like it; that's what I like to hear

nuts and bolts ✪✪

PLAIN ENGLISH ALTERNATIVES: practical details; basic facts; minutiae

CLICHÉD ALTERNATIVES: brass tacks; nitty-gritty

O

odds and ends ✪✪

PLAIN ENGLISH ALTERNATIVES: miscellaneous things; remnants; oddments; fragments; sundry items

CLICHÉD ALTERNATIVES: odds and sods; bits and pieces; bits and bobs

off message ✪✪✪

PLAIN ENGLISH ALTERNATIVES: straying from the approved party line

CLICHÉD ALTERNATIVES: not message-focussed; not toeing the line; not singing from the same hymnsheet

off one's own bat ✪✪

PLAIN ENGLISH ALTERNATIVES: on one's own initiative; by one's own efforts; with no assistance; by oneself; unaided

CLICHÉD ALTERNATIVES: by dint of one's own efforts; by the sweat of one's brow

■ *Origins* From cricket, referring to runs scored by one's own batting as opposed to those scored by one's batting partner.

off the beaten track ✪✪

PLAIN ENGLISH ALTERNATIVES: remote; out of the way; outlying; isolated

CLICHÉD ALTERNATIVES: in the back of beyond; in the middle of nowhere; in the sticks; in the boondocks (*US*); beyond the black stump (*Australian*)

off the cuff ✪✪

PLAIN ENGLISH ALTERNATIVES: improvised; offhand; without preparation; unrehearsed; extemporaneously; extempore; extemporized; impromptu

CLICHÉD ALTERNATIVES: off the top of one's head

- *Origins* From an after-dinner speaker using an old-fashioned stiff cuff to write apposite ideas on as they occur during dinner, to be used as memory aids.

off the hook ✪✪

PLAIN ENGLISH ALTERNATIVES: out of danger; no longer in trouble; no longer under suspicion

- *Origins* From angling, in which a fish that manages to wriggle off the hook can make its escape.

off the wall ✪✪✪

PLAIN ENGLISH ALTERNATIVES: eccentric; unconventional; unorthodox; strange; weird; wacky; out-there; bizarre; way-out

CLICHÉD ALTERNATIVES: out of left field (*US*)

- *Origins* Unclear, but perhaps the reference is to an unpredictable rebound of a ball, ice hockey puck, etc off a wall.

of the first water ✪✪

PLAIN ENGLISH ALTERNATIVES: outstanding; extreme; unsurpassed; unequalled; unparalleled; first class

CLICHÉD ALTERNATIVES: of the first magnitude

- *Origins* A diamond of the first water is one of the highest degree of lustre.

oh my God! ✪✪✪✪✪

PLAIN ENGLISH ALTERNATIVES: what a surprise!; how unexpected!; how surprising!; how amazing!; how marvellous!; isn't that remarkable?

CLICHÉD ALTERNATIVES: well I never!; would you believe it?; would you Adam and Eve it?; I'm gobsmacked; stone the crows!; well I'll go to the foot of our stairs!

Note: Largely through overuse on American television programmes, this exclamation has become not only a cliché but greatly devalued. What was originally a fairly powerful oath has turned into an automatic reaction to the most minor of events. It is surprising that in a country as overtly religious as the USA what was once known as 'taking the Lord's name in vain' passes without comment in everyday speech.

old as the hills

See **as old as the hills**.

on a daily basis ✪✪✪

PLAIN ENGLISH ALTERNATIVES: daily; every day; each day; per diem
CLICHÉD ALTERNATIVES: day in, day out; day after day

on a hiding to nothing ✪✪

PLAIN ENGLISH ALTERNATIVES: bound to lose; facing impossible odds; in a position in which one can't succeed; in a situation in which one can't win
CLICHÉD ALTERNATIVES: in a no-win situation; in a lose-lose situation

▪ *Origins* Literally, to have no chance of escaping a beating.

on a roll ✪✪

PLAIN ENGLISH ALTERNATIVES: having a run of good luck; having continuing success; doing particularly well; performing well
CLICHÉD ALTERNATIVES: on a winning streak; on song; on the crest of a wave; riding one's luck

▪ *Origins* Perhaps from surfing, referring to riding a powerful wave.

once and for all ✪✪

PLAIN ENGLISH ALTERNATIVES: finally; decisively; emphatically; conclusively; for the last time
CLICHÉD ALTERNATIVES: for all time

once in a blue moon ✪✪

PLAIN ENGLISH ALTERNATIVES: very rarely; hardly ever; on rare occasions; almost never; scarcely ever; seldom

CLICHÉD ALTERNATIVES: once in a while; only now and then

▪ *Origins* The moon does sometimes appear blue because of the interference of dust particles with its reflected light.

on cloud nine ✪✪

PLAIN ENGLISH ALTERNATIVES: elated; exhilarated; transported; exultant

CLICHÉD ALTERNATIVES: walking on air; high as a kite; in a dream; over the moon; in seventh heaven

▪ *Origins* From a classification of clouds used by the US Weather Bureau, with cloud nine referring to cumulonimbus, a very high variety.

on easy street ✪✪

PLAIN ENGLISH ALTERNATIVES: in luxury; at one's ease; in luck; in great comfort; luxuriously; in affluence

CLICHÉD ALTERNATIVES: in clover; in the lap of luxury

one foot in the grave

See **have one foot in the grave**.

one for the record books ✪✪

PLAIN ENGLISH ALTERNATIVES: a memorable example; a noteworthy example; an outstanding example; a historic example; an unforgettable example

CLICHÉD ALTERNATIVES: one to remember; one for the ages; a textbook example

one in the eye for ... ✪✪

PLAIN ENGLISH ALTERNATIVES: a blow; a telling blow; a body blow; a reverse; a setback; a rebuff

CLICHÉD ALTERNATIVES: a stunning blow

- *Origins* From boxing, meaning 'a blow that will hurt'.

one man's meat is another man's poison ✪✪

PLAIN ENGLISH ALTERNATIVES: each to his/her own taste; we're not all the same

CLICHÉD ALTERNATIVES: different strokes for different folks; *chacun à son goût*

one of these days ✪✪

PLAIN ENGLISH ALTERNATIVES: one day; some day; sometime; at some point; on a suitable occasion

CLICHÉD ALTERNATIVES: one of these fine days

on its last legs ✪✪

PLAIN ENGLISH ALTERNATIVES: near the end; all but finished; moribund; obsolescent

CLICHÉD ALTERNATIVES: on the way out; about to give up the ghost; on its knees; under sentence of death

only time will tell ✪✪

PLAIN ENGLISH ALTERNATIVES: all will be revealed in time; one will know eventually; one won't find out for a while

CLICHÉD ALTERNATIVES: all will be revealed in the fullness of time

only too pleased ✪✪

PLAIN ENGLISH ALTERNATIVES: delighted; highly pleased; chuffed; overjoyed; thrilled

CLICHÉD ALTERNATIVES: pleased as Punch; over the moon; made up; well chuffed; in seventh heaven; tickled pink

on message ✪✪✪✪

PLAIN ENGLISH ALTERNATIVES: following the approved party line

CLICHÉD ALTERNATIVES: message-focussed; toeing the line; singing from the same hymnsheet

on song ✪✪✪

PLAIN ENGLISH ALTERNATIVES: in good form; working well; doing particularly well; performing well

CLICHÉD ALTERNATIVES: on a roll; on top form

on tenterhooks ✪✪

PLAIN ENGLISH ALTERNATIVES: in suspense; anxious; tense; apprehensive; nervous; on edge; uptight

CLICHÉD ALTERNATIVES: on pins and needles; a nervous wreck

- **Origins** A tenter is a frame on which new-woven cloth is stretched, and tenterhooks are the nails that attach the cloth to the frame. A person in a state of suspense might feel that their nerves were being stretched.

on the ball ✪✪

PLAIN ENGLISH ALTERNATIVES: alert; attentive; observant; on the alert; wide awake; up to date; *au courant*

CLICHÉD ALTERNATIVES: bright-eyed and bushy-tailed; in command of the situation; on one's toes; on the qui vive

- **Origins** From sport, where it is all-important to be in control of the ball or at least keep a close eye on it.

on the cards ✪✪

PLAIN ENGLISH ALTERNATIVES: probable; likely; likely to happen; not out of the question; to be expected

CLICHÉD ALTERNATIVES: in the wind

▪ *Origins* From the use of playing cards to tell fortunes.

on the dot ✪✪

PLAIN ENGLISH ALTERNATIVES: exactly; precisely; sharp; prompt

CLICHÉD ALTERNATIVES: on the button

▪ *Origins* From the dots used on some clocks to indicate the hours.

on the horns of a dilemma ✪✪✪

PLAIN ENGLISH ALTERNATIVES: in a dilemma; faced with two undesirable alternatives; in a quandary

CLICHÉD ALTERNATIVES: between Scylla and Charybdis; between the devil and the deep blue sea; in a cleft stick; between a rock and a hard place

▪ *Origins* From the horns of a bull, each equally able to injure.

on the line ✪✪✪

PLAIN ENGLISH ALTERNATIVES: at risk; in jeopardy; in danger; at stake

CLICHÉD ALTERNATIVES: up for grabs

▪ *Origins* Perhaps from gambling, in which stakes must be laid down where they can be seen.

on the money ✪✪✪

PLAIN ENGLISH ALTERNATIVES: exact; precise; accurate; just right; spot-on; perfect

CLICHÉD ALTERNATIVES: on the button

▪ *Origins* Originally US, this is probably another term from gambling, designating a winning score, etc.

on the same page ✪✪✪✪

PLAIN ENGLISH ALTERNATIVES: in accord; in broad agreement; in harmony; thinking along the same lines; following the approved party line

CLICHÉD ALTERNATIVES: message-focussed; on message; of the same way of thinking; singing from the same hymnsheet

on the same wavelength ✪✪✪

PLAIN ENGLISH ALTERNATIVES: thinking the same way; in tune; having a shared cast of mind; having a mutual understanding; in sympathy; sympathetic

CLICHÉD ALTERNATIVES: of the same way of thinking; thinking along the same lines; singing from the same hymnsheet

▪ *Origins* From radio communication, in which only people using the same wavelength can talk to one another.

on the skids ✪✪

PLAIN ENGLISH ALTERNATIVES: in decline; deteriorating; on a downward path; on the way down

CLICHÉD ALTERNATIVES: going to pot; going to the dogs

▪ *Origins* Skids here refers to lengths of wood down which heavy items could be slid or rolled when manhandling them.

on the spur of the moment ✪

PLAIN ENGLISH ALTERNATIVES: without thinking; impetuously; impulsively; spontaneously; suddenly; unpremeditatedly; on an impulse; instantly

CLICHÉD ALTERNATIVES: just like that; in the heat of the moment; at the drop of a hat

▪ *Origins* Perhaps from the idea of reacting suddenly as if pricked by a spur.

on the wagon ✪✪

PLAIN ENGLISH ALTERNATIVES: abstaining from alcohol; abstinent; sober; off the drink

CLICHÉD ALTERNATIVES: having signed the pledge

- *Origins* Shortened from 'on the water wagon', referring to a cart used to transport drinking water.

on the way out   ✪✪

PLAIN ENGLISH ALTERNATIVES: obsolescent; becoming unfashionable; becoming less popular; losing its appeal

CLICHÉD ALTERNATIVES: on the wane

on thin ice   ✪

PLAIN ENGLISH ALTERNATIVES: in a precarious situation; in a delicate position; in a risky situation

CLICHÉD ALTERNATIVES: on eggshells

on with the motley   ✪✪

PLAIN ENGLISH ALTERNATIVES: let's begin; let's get started; let's get going; one might as well get on with it

CLICHÉD ALTERNATIVES: let's get this show on the road

- *Origins* 'Motley' means the varicoloured clothes traditionally worn by a jester. The particular reference is to the opera *I Pagliacci* by Leoncavallo (1892), in which the clown Canio sings the tenor aria 'Vesti la giubba' (which does not literally mean 'on with the motley' but is often translated as such) when he knows he must perform to make people laugh even though his own sadness is so great that he cannot help but sob.

on your bike   ✪✪

PLAIN ENGLISH ALTERNATIVES: go away; get lost; beat it; scram; clear off; vamoose; off you go

CLICHÉD ALTERNATIVES: make yourself scarce; sling your hook; take yourself off

- *Origins* Although the phrase was in use beforehand, in most people's minds it is associated with the Conservative Employment Secretary Norman Tebbit who, in a speech in 1981, advised the jobless to do as his father had done in the Depression and get on their bikes to go and look for work.

open the door to ✪✪

PLAIN ENGLISH ALTERNATIVES: lead to; allow; facilitate; create an opportunity for; make possible; permit

CLICHÉD ALTERNATIVES: leave the door open for

other half ✪✪✪✪

PLAIN ENGLISH ALTERNATIVES: spouse; partner; wife; husband; mate; helpmate; helpmeet

CLICHÉD ALTERNATIVES: better half; significant other; her indoors; the missus; the old man; the old woman; the old lady; the little woman

OTT ✪✪✪

PLAIN ENGLISH ALTERNATIVES: excessive; gross; too much; exaggerated; overdone; exorbitant; immoderate; unreasonable

CLICHÉD ALTERNATIVES: over the top; a bit much

- **Origins** Short for *over the top*.

ours not to reason why ✪✪

PLAIN ENGLISH ALTERNATIVES: we have no choice but to do as we are told; we have to obey orders; it's not up to us; we just have to get on with it

CLICHÉD ALTERNATIVES: needs must when the devil drives

- **Origins** Altered from Tennyson's poem *The Charge of the Light Brigade* (1854): 'Theirs not to reason why, / Theirs but to do or die'.

out in the cold ✪✪

PLAIN ENGLISH ALTERNATIVES: spurned; ignored; neglected; sidelined; rejected; ostracized

CLICHÉD ALTERNATIVES: given the cold shoulder; watching from the sidelines

- *Origins* Not welcome to come indoors where it's warm.

out of order ✪✪✪

PLAIN ENGLISH ALTERNATIVES: inappropriate; unacceptable; uncontrolled; excessive; unsuitable

CLICHÉD ALTERNATIVES: bang out of order; not on; dead wrong; out of line; pushing one's luck

out of sorts ✪✪

PLAIN ENGLISH ALTERNATIVES: in poor health; slightly unwell; ailing; indisposed; in low spirits; poorly

CLICHÉD ALTERNATIVES: below par; under the weather; not up to snuff; off-colour; not feeling oneself

- *Origins* From playing cards, where the 'sorts' are the four suits. If the cards are out of sorts they are all mixed up and not in their usual order.

out of the ark ✪✪✪

PLAIN ENGLISH ALTERNATIVES: utterly old-fashioned; archaic; antiquated; antediluvian; outdated; outmoded

CLICHÉD ALTERNATIVES: as old as the hills; past its sell-by date; a thing of the past; from way back

- *Origins* This refers to things being so old as to have been around at the time of the Biblical Flood and to have been carried in Noah's Ark.

out of the blue ✪✪

PLAIN ENGLISH ALTERNATIVES: unexpectedly; suddenly; all of a sudden; without warning; abruptly

CLICHÉD ALTERNATIVES: out of a clear blue sky

- *Origins* Like something falling unexpectedly from a clear blue sky.

out of this world ✪✪

PLAIN ENGLISH ALTERNATIVES: wonderful; marvellous; delightful; amazing; extraordinary; fantastic; phenomenal; sensational

CLICHÉD ALTERNATIVES: absolutely fabulous; a dream come true

out on a limb ✪✪

PLAIN ENGLISH ALTERNATIVES: isolated; cut off; on one's own; stranded

CLICHÉD ALTERNATIVES: out in the cold

■ *Origins* Like a hunted animal that has sought safety by moving out as far as possible onto a tree branch.

over and done with ✪✪

PLAIN ENGLISH ALTERNATIVES: finished; over; ended; closed; concluded; in the past

CLICHÉD ALTERNATIVES: a thing of the past; done and dusted

over my dead body ✪✪

PLAIN ENGLISH ALTERNATIVES: not if I can help it; not if I have anything to do with it; not if I have any say in the matter; not if I am able to prevent it; I will do all I can to prevent it

■ *Origins* The suggestion is that one will give up one's life rather than acquiesce in whatever detestable scenario is being proposed.

over the hill ✪✪

PLAIN ENGLISH ALTERNATIVES: past one's prime; past one's best; past one's peak; too old; in decline; no longer at the height of one's powers

CLICHÉD ALTERNATIVES: past it; on the downward slope

■ *Origins* From the idea of having reached the top of the hill (one's peak) and now descending down the other side.

over the moon   ✪✪✪✪✪

PLAIN ENGLISH ALTERNATIVES: very happy; delighted; ecstatic; overjoyed; in ecstasies; thoroughly pleased

CLICHÉD ALTERNATIVES: happy as a sandboy; well chuffed; made up; happy as Larry; in seventh heaven; in hog heaven

■ *Origins* Probably borrowed from the nursery rhyme in which the cow jumps over the moon.

over the score   ✪✪

PLAIN ENGLISH ALTERNATIVES: beyond reasonable limits; excessive; too much; unfair; unreasonable

CLICHÉD ALTERNATIVES: a bit much

■ *Origins* Perhaps from 'score' in the sense of an amount of money owed at a tavern, and hence exceeding what is properly due.

over the top   ✪✪✪

PLAIN ENGLISH ALTERNATIVES: excessive; gross; too much; exaggerated; overdone; exorbitant; immoderate; unreasonable

CLICHÉD ALTERNATIVES: OTT; a bit much

■ *Origins* From World War I, in which going over the top meant climbing out of the trenches to attack the enemy, an extreme thing to do.

P

packed like sardines ✪✪

PLAIN ENGLISH ALTERNATIVES: crowded; overcrowded; crushed; crammed; congested; packed out

CLICHÉD ALTERNATIVES: jam-packed; chock-a-block; chocker; like the Black Hole of Calcutta

▪ *Origins* From a tin of sardines which, when opened, reveals a mass of tiny fishy bodies crammed close together.

paddle one's own canoe ✪✪

PLAIN ENGLISH ALTERNATIVES: act independently; make one's own way; be self-reliant

CLICHÉD ALTERNATIVES: do one's own thing; do it one's way; go one's own sweet way

page three stunner ✪✪✪✪✪

PLAIN ENGLISH ALTERNATIVES: topless model; pin-up; glamour model

CLICHÉD ALTERNATIVES: page three girl; glamour girl

▪ *Origins* From the tabloid press's predilection for illustrating the third page with a photograph of a naked woman in the attempt to induce people to open their product.

painfully thin ✪✪

PLAIN ENGLISH ALTERNATIVES: too thin; skinny; anorexic; emaciated; scrawny; skeletal; underweight

CLICHÉD ALTERNATIVES: thin as a rake; skin and bone

pain in the neck ✪✪

PLAIN ENGLISH ALTERNATIVES: pain; annoyance; nuisance; tiresome person; pest

CLICHÉD ALTERNATIVES: pain in the arse; thorn in one's flesh

pale into insignificance ✪✪

PLAIN ENGLISH ALTERNATIVES: appear unimportant; seem less important; seem trivial; seem minor; dwindle by comparison; look small

CLICHÉD ALTERNATIVES: get put into perspective

par for the course ✪✪

PLAIN ENGLISH ALTERNATIVES: to be expected; just what one would expect; normal; customary; routine; average

CLICHÉD ALTERNATIVES: the same old story

■ *Origins* From golf, 'par' meaning the average score that a competent player ought to make.

part and parcel ✪✪

PLAIN ENGLISH ALTERNATIVES: an essential part; integral; intrinsic

pass muster ✪✪

PLAIN ENGLISH ALTERNATIVES: be adequate; be suitable; be what's required; be what's needed; fulfil the purpose; meet the demand; meet the requirements

CLICHÉD ALTERNATIVES: fit the bill; bear examination

■ *Origins* From military usage, referring to troops being mustered for inspection.

pass the buck ✪✪✪

PLAIN ENGLISH ALTERNATIVES: shirk one's responsibilities; evade blame; evade responsibility; shift the blame; dodge the blame

CLICHÉD ALTERNATIVES: cop out

■ *Origins* From gambling at cards, particularly poker, in which a buck was the marker used to show whose turn it was to deal.

past its/one's sell-by date ✪✪✪

PLAIN ENGLISH ALTERNATIVES: outdated; antiquated; superannuated; superseded; finished; obsolete; antiquated

CLICHÉD ALTERNATIVES: over the hill; no spring chicken; on the way out; old hat; out of the ark; past it

■ *Origins* From the branding of perishable goods.

pat on the back ✪✪

PLAIN ENGLISH ALTERNATIVES: congratulations; approbation; approval; words of encouragement; commendation; praise; recognition; kudos

CLICHÉD ALTERNATIVES: Brownie points

pay through the nose ✪✪

PLAIN ENGLISH ALTERNATIVES: pay a great deal; pay dearly; pay more than something is worth; pay too much

CLICHÉD ALTERNATIVES: be done; be rooked; be milked; pay top dollar; pay a premium price; pay till it hurts; pay an arm and a leg; pay over the odds

■ *Origins* Probably from the apocryphal poll tax imposed by the Danes in 9th-century Ireland, those finding themselves unable to pay being punished by having their noses slit.

pecking order ✪✪

PLAIN ENGLISH ALTERNATIVES: social order; order of importance; order of prestige; order of rank; rank; grade; precedence

CLICHÉD ALTERNATIVES: chain of command

■ *Origins* From chickens, amongst whom the top bird can peck any other and the next rank down can peck any except the top bird and so on down.

pick and choose ✪✪

PLAIN ENGLISH ALTERNATIVES: select; take one's choice; have one's choice; have one's pick; cherry-pick

CLICHÉD ALTERNATIVES: take one's pick

pick up the threads ✪✪

PLAIN ENGLISH ALTERNATIVES: resume; carry on from where one left off

CLICHÉD ALTERNATIVES: get back into the way of things; pick up where one left off

- *Origins* From weaving, meaning 'resume work on an unfinished piece'.

pièce de résistance ✪✪

PLAIN ENGLISH ALTERNATIVES: masterpiece; masterwork; great work; chef d'oeuvre; best item; best piece

CLICHÉD ALTERNATIVES: crowning glory; magnum opus; main event

- *Origins* Altered from the French *plat de résistance*, meaning 'the main dish in a meal', ie the one which offers the toughest resistance to those determined to clean their plates. Oddly, the phrase *pièce de résistance* is not actually used in French.

piece of cake ✪✪

PLAIN ENGLISH ALTERNATIVES: doddle; easy task; no trouble; no bother

CLICHÉD ALTERNATIVES: walk in the park; like taking candy from a baby; as easy as falling off a log; plain sailing

pillar of the community ✪

PLAIN ENGLISH ALTERNATIVES: estimable person; admirable person; thoroughly respectable person; person of some standing

piss-up in a brewery

See **he/she couldn't organize a piss-up in a brewery.**

plain sailing ✪✪

PLAIN ENGLISH ALTERNATIVES: doddle; easy task; no trouble; no bother

CLICHÉD ALTERNATIVES: walk in the park; like taking candy from a baby; as easy as falling off a log; piece of cake

■ *Origins* From nautical usage, meaning 'sailing in open water with no hazards at hand'.

plain unvarnished truth ✪✪

PLAIN ENGLISH ALTERNATIVES: plain truth; simple truth; naked truth

CLICHÉD ALTERNATIVES: the truth and nothing but the truth; unvarnished truth; plain and simple truth; simple fact

play a blinder ✪✪✪✪

PLAIN ENGLISH ALTERNATIVES: play well; perform well; excel

CLICHÉD ALTERNATIVES: have a great game; turn in a sterling performance; play the game of one's life

■ *Origins* 'Blinder' here means a sporting performance so spectacularly good that it is dazzling to the eye.

play ball ✪✪✪✪

PLAIN ENGLISH ALTERNATIVES: co-operate; agree; go along with something; help

CLICHÉD ALTERNATIVES: lend a helping hand; pitch in

■ *Origins* From the idea that you can't have a ball game without at least two people agreeing to play.

play for time ✪✪

PLAIN ENGLISH ALTERNATIVES: delay; prevaricate; procrastinate; be cunctatory; stall

CLICHÉD ALTERNATIVES: drag one's feet

■ *Origins* From sport, especially cricket, in which playing cautiously towards the end of a game may secure a draw when defeat looks likely.

play (merry) hell with   ✪✪

PLAIN ENGLISH ALTERNATIVES: upset; disorganize; disrupt; disturb

CLICHÉD ALTERNATIVES: play the devil with; throw into disorder; throw into disarray; mess up; make a mess of

play Russian roulette   ✪✪

PLAIN ENGLISH ALTERNATIVES: gamble with one's life; risk one's life; put one's life at risk; risk everything; perform an act of bravado

CLICHÉD ALTERNATIVES: put one's life on the line

■ *Origins* From the game played in Tsarist Russia of putting a revolver loaded with one bullet to one's head and pulling the trigger, giving one a one-in-six chance of blowing one's brains out. One supposes they had to make their own entertainment in those days.

Note: This cliché is often used inaccurately to mean simply a risky undertaking, not one that would have a chance of ending in death.

play the game   ✪✪

PLAIN ENGLISH ALTERNATIVES: play fair; play fairly; be sporting; be sportsmanlike; act in a sportsmanlike manner

CLICHÉD ALTERNATIVES: be a sport; play by the rules

play with fire   ✪✪

PLAIN ENGLISH ALTERNATIVES: take great risks; meddle with something dangerous; court danger; expose oneself to unnecessary risk

CLICHÉD ALTERNATIVES: dice with death; skate on thin ice

pleased as Punch   ✪✪

PLAIN ENGLISH ALTERNATIVES: very happy; delighted; ecstatic; overjoyed

CLICHÉD ALTERNATIVES: over the moon; well chuffed; made up; happy as Larry; happy as a sandboy

- *Origins* Punch is of course the self-satisfied star of Punch and Judy shows.

point taken   ✪✪

PLAIN ENGLISH ALTERNATIVES: I take your point; I understand; I accept what you're saying; granted

CLICHÉD ALTERNATIVES: I hear what you're saying

poles apart   ✪✪

PLAIN ENGLISH ALTERNATIVES: widely dissimilar; at odds; at variance; wildly contrasting; having no common ground

CLICHÉD ALTERNATIVES: streets apart

- *Origins* From the idea of being as far apart as the north and south poles.

pop the question   ✪✪✪✪

PLAIN ENGLISH ALTERNATIVES: propose marriage; ask someone to marry one

CLICHÉD ALTERNATIVES: ask for someone's hand in marriage; ask someone to make one the happiest man in the world

- *Origins* 'Pop' here means 'to blurt something out unexpectedly or nervously'.

pour cold water on   ✪✪

PLAIN ENGLISH ALTERNATIVES: discourage; disparage; dismiss; deprecate

CLICHÉD ALTERNATIVES: talk down

precious little/precious few   ✪✪

PLAIN ENGLISH ALTERNATIVES: very little; very few; hardly any; hardly anything; next to nothing; a small amount; not many; scarcely any; a handful

press the panic button ✪✪

PLAIN ENGLISH ALTERNATIVES: panic; lose one's nerve; cause alarm

CLICHÉD ALTERNATIVES: sound the alarm; fire off distress signals; put the wind up someone; spread fear and alarm; go to pieces; lose it big time; lose one's bottle

■ *Origins* From the name for a button used to activate an alarm or emergency device.

pretty pass ✪✪

PLAIN ENGLISH ALTERNATIVES: a deplorable condition; a bad way; a terrible state; a dreadful condition

CLICHÉD ALTERNATIVES: a poor state of affairs

pretty penny ✪✪

PLAIN ENGLISH ALTERNATIVES: a sizeable sum; a fair amount; a fair sum; a considerable sum; a fortune; millions

CLICHÉD ALTERNATIVES: a packet; an arm and a leg; a king's ransom

primrose path ✪✪

PLAIN ENGLISH ALTERNATIVES: the life of pleasure; the path of self-indulgence; a life of pleasure-seeking; self-gratification

CLICHÉD ALTERNATIVES: la dolce vita

■ *Origins* From Shakespeare's *Hamlet* (Act I, Scene 3): 'Himself the primrose path of dalliance treads'.

Prince Charming ✪✪

PLAIN ENGLISH ALTERNATIVES: paragon; dreamboat; dream lover; beau; beau ideal

CLICHÉD ALTERNATIVES: man of one's dreams; knight in shining armour

■ *Origins* From the prince of that name in the fairy tale of Cinderella.

pull a fast one ✪✪

PLAIN ENGLISH ALTERNATIVES: trick; con; fool; dupe; hoax

CLICHÉD ALTERNATIVES: put one over on someone; pull the wool over someone's eyes; take someone in

■ *Origins* From cricket, meaning 'to suddenly unleash a fast ball at the batsman'.

pull one's finger out ✪✪✪

PLAIN ENGLISH ALTERNATIVES: start working harder; be more productive; get (oneself) organized; sort oneself out; get a grip on oneself; sort oneself out; show improvement

CLICHÉD ALTERNATIVES: get a move on; get a wiggle on; get one's arse into gear; pull one's socks up; smarten up one's act; get one's act together; roll up one's sleeves

■ *Origins* Unknown, but probably rude and best left to the imagination.

pull one's punches ✪✪

PLAIN ENGLISH ALTERNATIVES: hold back; be less hard-hitting than one can; mitigate one's criticism; be lenient; be moderate

CLICHÉD ALTERNATIVES: temper one's blows; soften the blow; not go in for the kill

■ *Origins* From boxing, in which to 'pull' a punch is to deliberately fail to follow through in order to avoid hurting one's opponent.

pull one's socks up ✪✪

PLAIN ENGLISH ALTERNATIVES: get (oneself) organized; sort oneself out; get a grip on oneself; sort oneself out; show improvement

CLICHÉD ALTERNATIVES: pull one's finger out; smarten up one's act; get one's act together

pull out all the stops ✪✪

PLAIN ENGLISH ALTERNATIVES: try one's hardest; make every effort; do one's best; do all one can; do one's utmost; make a supreme effort

CLICHÉD ALTERNATIVES: do one's damnedest; give one hundred and ten per cent; go for it; go for broke; go to town; go the whole hog; make an all-out effort; give it one's all; bend (or lean) over backwards

- *Origins* From organ playing, in which pulling out all of the stops will increase the power and volume to the maximum.

pull someone's leg ⊗⊗

PLAIN ENGLISH ALTERNATIVES: deceive someone; tease someone; make fun of someone; kid someone on

CLICHÉD ALTERNATIVES: wind someone up; have someone on; pull someone's chain

- *Origins* From the practical joke of tripping someone.

pull the other one ⊗⊗

PLAIN ENGLISH ALTERNATIVES: I don't believe you; I am not so easily fooled; do you expect me to swallow that?

CLICHÉD ALTERNATIVES: don't make me laugh; you must be joking; you're having a laugh; and the band played 'Believe it if you like' (*Scottish*)

- *Origins* An accusation that someone is pulling your leg, with the implication that, as this is not working, they might as well try pulling one's other leg, which, as some would add, 'has got bells on'.

pull the wool over someone's eyes ⊗⊗

PLAIN ENGLISH ALTERNATIVES: hoodwink someone; deceive someone; fool someone; dupe someone; mislead someone

CLICHÉD ALTERNATIVES: lead someone up the garden path; pull a fast one on someone; take someone for a ride

- *Origins* The wool referred to is the material of which wigs were once made, and thus the idea is one of temporarily blinding someone by pulling their wig over their eyes.

pure as the driven snow ✪✪

PLAIN ENGLISH ALTERNATIVES: utterly pure; virginal; vestal; pristine; undefiled; immaculate; impeccable; unsullied

CLICHÉD ALTERNATIVES: whiter than white; *sans peur et sans reproche*

pushing up the daisies ✪✪

PLAIN ENGLISH ALTERNATIVES: dead; dead and buried; deceased

CLICHÉD ALTERNATIVES: no longer with us; dead and gone; dead as a dodo; dead as a doornail; no more; history; gone to meet one's maker; gone to one's eternal reward

push the boat out ✪✪

PLAIN ENGLISH ALTERNATIVES: celebrate lavishly; treat someone lavishly; be generously hospitable; do everything one can for someone

CLICHÉD ALTERNATIVES: pull out the stops; kill the fatted calf; spare no expense

▪ *Origins* Probably from the idea of a farewell drink before launching a boat on a voyage.

push the envelope ✪✪✪✪

PLAIN ENGLISH ALTERNATIVES: attempt what has not been done before; extend the limits; go beyond the limits

CLICHÉD ALTERNATIVES: push back the boundaries of knowledge; take it to the next level

▪ *Origins* From aviation, referring to the parameters of an aircraft's performance as illustrated on a graph.

put a different complexion on the matter ✪✪

PLAIN ENGLISH ALTERNATIVES: change everything; alter the case entirely; make it a completely different matter; turn it into another thing entirely

put a spoke in someone's wheel ✪✪

PLAIN ENGLISH ALTERNATIVES: thwart someone; hinder someone; frustrate someone; obstruct someone

CLICHÉD ALTERNATIVES: mess up someone's plans; queer someone's pitch; rain on someone's parade

■ *Origins* The spoke here is not one of those which form part of a wheel but a length of wood used as a kind of primitive brake, thrust into a hole in an old-fashioned solid wheel to stop it from turning.

put one's foot in it ✪✪

PLAIN ENGLISH ALTERNATIVES: blunder; be indiscreet; be tactless; say the wrong thing

CLICHÉD ALTERNATIVES: drop a clanger; drop a brick; make a bloomer; make a gaffe; commit a faux pas

put one's hands up ✪✪✪

PLAIN ENGLISH ALTERNATIVES: take the blame; accept responsibility; admit responsibility; own up; confess

CLICHÉD ALTERNATIVES: take the rap

put one's shoulder to the wheel ✪✪

PLAIN ENGLISH ALTERNATIVES: apply oneself; set to work in earnest; work hard; be diligent

CLICHÉD ALTERNATIVES: keep hard at it; slave away; keep one's nose to the grindstone; knuckle down

put one's thinking cap on ✪✪✪✪

PLAIN ENGLISH ALTERNATIVES: consider; deliberate; ponder; cogitate; meditate

CLICHÉD ALTERNATIVES: give it some thought; mull it over

put our heads together ✪✪

PLAIN ENGLISH ALTERNATIVES: confer; consult; co-operate

CLICHÉD ALTERNATIVES: compare notes

■ *Origins* The image is of people conferring secretly, speaking so quietly that their heads are almost touching.

put someone in the picture ✪✪

PLAIN ENGLISH ALTERNATIVES: fully inform someone; bring someone up to date

CLICHÉD ALTERNATIVES: make someone aware of the full facts; bring someone up to speed; give someone the full SP

■ *Origins* The idea is to allow someone to become involved in what is going on, and become part of the picture.

put someone's nose out of joint ✪✪

PLAIN ENGLISH ALTERNATIVES: disconcert someone; offend someone; rebuff someone; make someone feel aggrieved; humiliate someone; thwart someone; cause offence to someone

CLICHÉD ALTERNATIVES: rub someone up the wrong way; hurt someone's feelings

■ *Origins* From the idea of breaking someone's nose.

put something on hold ✪✪✪

PLAIN ENGLISH ALTERNATIVES: delay the implementation of something; keep something in reserve; suspend something; postpone something; leave something in abeyance

CLICHÉD ALTERNATIVES: put something on the back burner

put something on the back burner ✪✪✪✪

PLAIN ENGLISH ALTERNATIVES: delay the implementation of something; keep something in reserve; suspend something; postpone something;

leave something in abeyance; set something aside; defer something

CLICHÉD ALTERNATIVES: put something on hold; put something to one side; deprioritize something

- *Origins* From the rear burner on a cooker, used to keep something simmering while dishes that require immediate attention are dealt with.

put the boot in ✪✪

PLAIN ENGLISH ALTERNATIVES: be brutal; show no mercy; be merciless; be pitiless; administer the coup de grâce

CLICHÉD ALTERNATIVES: kick someone when they're down; finish someone off

put the cat among the pigeons ✪✪

PLAIN ENGLISH ALTERNATIVES: cause trouble; stir up trouble; cause a fuss; cause alarm

CLICHÉD ALTERNATIVES: stir up a hornet's nest; get people all worked up

put two and two together ✪✪

PLAIN ENGLISH ALTERNATIVES: draw a conclusion; come to a conclusion; realize what is going on

CLICHÉD ALTERNATIVES: work it out

put up or shut up ✪✪✪

PLAIN ENGLISH ALTERNATIVES: the initiative lies with you; you must make the next move; the decision is up to you; back up what you say with something tangible

CLICHÉD ALTERNATIVES: it's your move; it's up to you; the ball is at your feet; piss or get off the pot; the ball's in your court; put your money where your mouth is

- *Origins* An invitation to fight (put up one's fists) or be quiet.

Q

quantum leap ✪✪✪✪✪

PLAIN ENGLISH ALTERNATIVES: dramatic advance; sudden advance; breakthrough; significant progress

CLICHÉD ALTERNATIVES: great leap forward

■ *Origins* From physics, meaning a sudden transition of an elementary particle to a different energy state.

queer someone's pitch ✪✪

PLAIN ENGLISH ALTERNATIVES: thwart someone; spoil someone's chances; make things difficult for someone; negate someone's efforts

CLICHÉD ALTERNATIVES: mess things up for someone; put a spoke in someone's wheel

■ *Origins* The pitch referred to is the place where a street trader sets up a stall. To queer a pitch is to interfere with such a trader's attempts to work.

queer street

See **in queer street**.

quick as a flash ✪✪

PLAIN ENGLISH ALTERNATIVES: rapidly; instantly; immediately; pronto; speedily

CLICHÉD ALTERNATIVES: before you can say Jack Robinson; like lightning; like greased lightning; pretty damn quick; pdq; quick as you like

quiet as a mouse ✪✪

PLAIN ENGLISH ALTERNATIVES: very quiet; totally quiet; silent; mum

CLICHÉD ALTERNATIVES: silent as the grave

> **!** *Original alternative:* like a Trappist monk playing charades

quite something ✪✪

PLAIN ENGLISH ALTERNATIVES: impressive; remarkable; excellent; wonderful; marvellous

CLICHÉD ALTERNATIVES: something to behold; something to see

R

rack and ruin

See **go to rack and ruin**.

rack one's brains ✪✪

PLAIN ENGLISH ALTERNATIVES: puzzle over something; think hard; search one's memory

CLICHÉD ALTERNATIVES: cudgel one's brains; delve deep in one's memory

▪ *Origins* The image is of torturing one's brains on a rack.

rain cats and dogs ✪✪

PLAIN ENGLISH ALTERNATIVES: pelt down; pour down; rain heavily; teem; sheet down; bucket down

CLICHÉD ALTERNATIVES: come down in buckets; come down in stair-rods

▪ *Origins* Uncertain, but perhaps the simplest explanation is that the sight of cats and dogs drowned in flooded gutters would suggest they had fallen from the sky as a particularly lumpy form of precipitation.

rain or shine

See **come rain or shine**.

raise Cain ✪✪

PLAIN ENGLISH ALTERNATIVES: cause trouble; cause a commotion; create a disturbance; make a fuss

CLICHÉD ALTERNATIVES: raise hell; raise the roof; kick up a fuss; kick up a stink

■ *Origins* In the Bible, Cain was the first murderer, who killed his brother Abel.

raw deal ✪✪

PLAIN ENGLISH ALTERNATIVES: injustice; unfair treatment; unfair bargain; harsh treatment; unjust treatment

CLICHÉD ALTERNATIVES: hard time

■ *Origins* The idea is that such treatment leaves one feeling 'raw' in the sense of 'tender'.

read my lips ✪✪✪✪

PLAIN ENGLISH ALTERNATIVES: listen carefully; pay attention to what I say; remember these words; note what I say

CLICHÉD ALTERNATIVES: mark my words

■ *Origins* Although he was not the first to use it, the person responsible for popularizing this rather condescending phrase was US President George Bush, who in 1988 employed it to emphasize his promise to levy no new taxes.

read you loud and clear

See **I read you loud and clear.**

real McCoy ✪✪✪✪✪

PLAIN ENGLISH ALTERNATIVES: real thing; genuine article; something of the highest quality

■ *Origins* Various explanations have been suggested but it appears that the phrase originated in Scotland as 'the real Mackay', referring to a brand of whisky.

red-letter day ✪✪

PLAIN ENGLISH ALTERNATIVES: special day; memorable day; day to remember; lucky day

- *Origins* From calendars in which, traditionally, holidays and saints' days would be marked in red ink.

red rag to a bull

See **like a red rag to a bull**.

rich beyond the dreams of avarice   ✪✪

PLAIN ENGLISH ALTERNATIVES: obscenely wealthy; affluent; loaded; minted

CLICHÉD ALTERNATIVES: filthy rich; stinking rich; rolling in it; made of money; having more money than one knows what to do with; having more money than one can shake a stick at

- *Origins* A quotation from a now little-known play, *The Gamester*, by British dramatist Edward Moore (1712–57): 'I am rich beyond the dreams of avarice.' So well known is the cliché that it has even been parodied as 'rich beyond the dreams of Elvis'.

ride roughshod over   ✪✪

PLAIN ENGLISH ALTERNATIVES: treat without consideration; treat arrogantly; domineer over; behave in a cavalier manner towards; disregard the feelings of

CLICHÉD ALTERNATIVES: lord it over

- *Origins* A horse is described as being 'roughshod' when its shoes have projecting nails for extra grip in icy conditions.

right as rain   ✪✪

PLAIN ENGLISH ALTERNATIVES: absolutely fine; just fine; perfectly in order; quite all right

CLICHÉD ALTERNATIVES: in tip-top condition; brand-new; in perfect nick

- *Origins* Perhaps from the idea of rain being just what's needed to grow crops.

ring a bell ✪✪

PLAIN ENGLISH ALTERNATIVES: evoke a memory; sound familiar; remind one of something; call someone or something to mind; bring back memories; awaken memories

CLICHÉD ALTERNATIVES: strike a chord; jog one's memory

■ *Origins* Perhaps from fairground test-your-strength machines, in which the participant strikes a surface with a hammer, thus sending a striker up a pole at the top of which is a bell that will ring if the striker makes it all the way up.

ring true ✪✪

PLAIN ENGLISH ALTERNATIVES: sound genuine; seem authentic; seem likely; add up; make sense; be convincing

CLICHÉD ALTERNATIVES: have the ring of truth; have a ring of authenticity

■ *Origins* From a traditional method of testing the authenticity of coins. When a coin was struck on a hard surface the sound made would tell a practised ear whether or not the coin contained precious metal.

rock the boat ✪✪

PLAIN ENGLISH ALTERNATIVES: cause trouble; make a fuss; make trouble; cause a disturbance; create difficulties; destabilize the situation; be disruptive

CLICHÉD ALTERNATIVES: make waves; stir it; give someone grief

■ *Origins* From the undesirability of moving around unnecessarily when in a boat.

rolling in the aisles ✪✪

PLAIN ENGLISH ALTERNATIVES: laughing hysterically; laughing uncontrollably; collapsing with laughter

CLICHÉD ALTERNATIVES: falling about (laughing); rolling about laughing; splitting one's sides; wetting oneself; laughing like a drain

roll one's sleeves up

See **roll up one's sleeves**.

roll something out ✪✪✪✪✪

PLAIN ENGLISH ALTERNATIVES: bring something in; introduce something; deploy something; phase something in; launch something; bring something into operation

CLICHÉD ALTERNATIVES: usher something in

roll up one's sleeves or roll one's sleeves up ✪✪

PLAIN ENGLISH ALTERNATIVES: get ready to start work; get ready for a fight; gird oneself; prepare for action; get (oneself) organized; sort oneself out

CLICHÉD ALTERNATIVES: gird up one's loins; get one's act together; pull one's finger out

root and branch ✪✪

PLAIN ENGLISH ALTERNATIVES: completely; utterly; totally; entirely; altogether; in entirety; without exception

CLICHÉD ALTERNATIVES: hook, line and sinker; lock, stock and barrel

- *Origins* This literally means all of the parts of a plant that is to be removed.

roses all the way ✪✪

PLAIN ENGLISH ALTERNATIVES: happy; pleasant; carefree; easy; trouble-free; without trouble; without problems; comfortable

CLICHÉD ALTERNATIVES: a bed of roses; all roses

rotten apple ✪✪

PLAIN ENGLISH ALTERNATIVES: corrupt person; dishonest person; crook; traitor; rogue; villain

CLICHÉD ALTERNATIVES: weak link

■ *Origins* From the proverbial statement that 'one rotten apple can spoil the barrel'.

rough and ready   ✪✪

PLAIN ENGLISH ALTERNATIVES: not perfect but useable; improvised; makeshift; make-do

round the bend   ✪✪

PLAIN ENGLISH ALTERNATIVES: insane; crazy; loopy; mental; nuts; nutty; doolally; cracked; touched

CLICHÉD ALTERNATIVES: barking mad; daft as a brush; mad as a hatter; mad as a March hare; nutty as a fruitcake; not playing with a full deck; not the full shilling; off one's rocker; off one's trolley; out to lunch; round the twist

■ *Origins* As in 'round the twist', the implication is of not being straight or true.

rub shoulders with   ✪✪

PLAIN ENGLISH ALTERNATIVES: come into social contact with; associate with; share the same milieu as; mix with; circulate among; be in the company of

CLICHÉD ALTERNATIVES: move in the same circles as

rub someone up the wrong way   ✪✪

PLAIN ENGLISH ALTERNATIVES: annoy someone; exasperate someone; irk someone; vex someone; rile someone; treat someone tactlessly

CLICHÉD ALTERNATIVES: get someone's goat; get on someone's nerves; get on someone's wick; get someone's back up; get someone's dander up; ruffle someone's feathers

■ *Origins* From the idea of annoying a cat by rubbing its fur against its natural pattern.

ruffle someone's feathers   ✪✪

PLAIN ENGLISH ALTERNATIVES: annoy someone; exasperate someone; irk someone; offend someone; vex someone; rile someone

CLICHÉD ALTERNATIVES: hurt someone's feelings; hurt someone's pride; get on someone's wick; get someone's back up; get someone's dander up; rub someone up the wrong way

- *Origins* From the idea of a bird looking undignified and resentful if its plumage is disarranged.

rule the roost   ✪✪

PLAIN ENGLISH ALTERNATIVES: predominate; be in authority; be in charge; be the boss; hold sway; predominate; lord it

CLICHÉD ALTERNATIVES: be number one; be king of the castle; be the big enchilada; be the daddy; wear the trousers

rumour has it   ✪✪✪

PLAIN ENGLISH ALTERNATIVES: they say; people are saying; it is rumoured; it is said; one hears

CLICHÉD ALTERNATIVES: a little bird tells one; the word on the streets is

run a tight ship   ✪✪

PLAIN ENGLISH ALTERNATIVES: exercise firm control; be a strict boss; be a disciplinarian; demand efficiency from one's staff

CLICHÉD ALTERNATIVES: rule with a rod of iron

- *Origins* As would seem obvious, this was originally a naval expression referring to a captain who demanded strict discipline from his crew.

run it up the flagpole and see who salutes   ✪✪✪✪✪

PLAIN ENGLISH ALTERNATIVES: try it out; see how people react to it; moot it; submit it

CLICHÉD ALTERNATIVES: put it on the table; sound people out about it

> **!** *Original alternative:* chuck her in the water and see if she floats

run off one's feet ✪✪

PLAIN ENGLISH ALTERNATIVES: very busy; overworked; exhausted; tired out

CLICHÉD ALTERNATIVES: rushed off one's feet; hard at it; up to the eyes; done in

run of the mill ✪✪

PLAIN ENGLISH ALTERNATIVES: ordinary; expected; unexciting; mediocre; nothing out of the ordinary; unexceptional

CLICHÉD ALTERNATIVES: no big deal; nothing to get excited about; nothing to write home about; vanilla

■ *Origins* The image is of a mill running smoothly and uninterruptedly, doing what it's supposed to do and nothing more.

run out of steam ✪✪

PLAIN ENGLISH ALTERNATIVES: lose impetus; lose energy; lose power; come to a standstill; run down

CLICHÉD ALTERNATIVES: grind to a halt

■ *Origins* From a steam engine being unable to keep working for lack of steam.

run rings round someone ✪✪

PLAIN ENGLISH ALTERNATIVES: beat someone with ease; outclass someone; be markedly superior to someone; make someone look bad

CLICHÉD ALTERNATIVES: beat someone hollow; leave someone standing; leave someone for dead; leave someone in the dust; take someone to the cleaners; put someone in the shade; wipe the floor with someone

■ *Origins* From football or rugby, meaning to have such speed and command of the ball that one's opponents are reduced to being spectators.

run something past someone ✪✪✪✪✪

PLAIN ENGLISH ALTERNATIVES: suggest something to someone; explain something to someone; tell someone about something; bring something to someone's attention; go through something with someone; go over something with someone

CLICHÉD ALTERNATIVES: put something in someone's in-tray

rushed off one's feet ✪✪

PLAIN ENGLISH ALTERNATIVES: very busy; overworked; exhausted; tired out

CLICHÉD ALTERNATIVES: run off one's feet; hard at it; up to the eyes; done in

Russian roulette

See **play Russian roulette**.

S

sad act ✪✪✪

PLAIN ENGLISH ALTERNATIVES: pitiable person; pathetic person; contemptible person; unfortunate individual; loser

CLICHÉD ALTERNATIVES: one of life's losers

safe and sound ✪✪

PLAIN ENGLISH ALTERNATIVES: unharmed; unhurt; uninjured; unscathed; whole; all right; okay

CLICHÉD ALTERNATIVES: alive and well; in one piece

▪ *Origins* 'Sound' here means 'in good condition'.

safe as houses ✪✪

PLAIN ENGLISH ALTERNATIVES: secure; firm; dependable; fast; immovable; steady; solid

CLICHÉD ALTERNATIVES: in safe hands; out of harm's way; safe as the Bank of England

▪ *Origins* From the idea of a house being something solid and reliable in an uncertain world (unless you're a pig building in straw and expecting a visit from a wolf).

safe bet ✪✪

PLAIN ENGLISH ALTERNATIVES: certainty; cert; guaranteed winner; someone or something to be relied on

CLICHÉD ALTERNATIVES: sure thing; sure-fire winner; dead cert

sail close to the wind ✪✪

PLAIN ENGLISH ALTERNATIVES: risk breaking the law; test the limits of the law; take great risks; flout the rules

CLICHÉD ALTERNATIVES: push one's luck; chance one's arm; play with fire

- *Origins* The literal meaning is 'to keep a sailing vessel's head pointed as much into the wind as possible', a practice requiring good judgement if one is to make progress.

salt of the earth ✪✪✪✪

PLAIN ENGLISH ALTERNATIVES: choice few; best; worthiest people

- *Origins* From the Bible, a description applied by Jesus to his disciples (*Matthew* 5.13): 'Ye are the salt of the earth.'

save someone's bacon ✪✪

PLAIN ENGLISH ALTERNATIVES: rescue someone; deliver someone; come to someone's aid; help someone out of a difficult situation

CLICHÉD ALTERNATIVES: bail someone out; pull someone's irons out of the fire; save someone's skin; save someone's neck

- *Origins* Not necessarily a cooking metaphor, as bacon here simply stands for anything one holds dear.

scream blue murder ✪✪

PLAIN ENGLISH ALTERNATIVES: shout loudly; cry out; screech; shriek; yell

CLICHÉD ALTERNATIVES: give a bloodcurdling scream; give an ear-splitting scream; shout and bawl; shout one's head off; shout oneself hoarse; scream at the top of one's voice; scream the walls down

- *Origins* A mistaken translation of the French oath *morbleu* as 'blue death'. It is actually a euphemism for *mort Dieu*, 'God's death'.

sea change ✪✪

PLAIN ENGLISH ALTERNATIVES: total transformation; complete change; marked change; metamorphosis; mutation

CLICHÉD ALTERNATIVES: complete makeover

■ *Origins* From Shakespeare's *The Tempest* (Act I, Scene 2): 'Nothing of him that doth fade, / But doth suffer a sea-change / Into something rich and strange.'

seal of approval ✪✪

PLAIN ENGLISH ALTERNATIVES: recommendation; commendation; ratification; endorsement; imprimatur; backing

CLICHÉD ALTERNATIVES: OK; green light

seal one's fate ✪✪

PLAIN ENGLISH ALTERNATIVES: finish one off; decide the issue; settle the matter; condemn one

CLICHÉD ALTERNATIVES: be the last nail in one's coffin

search high and low ✪✪

PLAIN ENGLISH ALTERNATIVES: look everywhere; search thoroughly; conduct an exhaustive search

CLICHÉD ALTERNATIVES: leave no stone unturned; turn the place upside down; scour the countryside

search me ✪✪

PLAIN ENGLISH ALTERNATIVES: I have no idea; I don't know; I couldn't say

CLICHÉD ALTERNATIVES: it beats me; I haven't a clue; I haven't the foggiest notion; how should I know?

second to none ✪✪

PLAIN ENGLISH ALTERNATIVES: the best; the greatest; unsurpassed; unequalled; unrivalled; peerless; the pick; the cream

CLICHÉD ALTERNATIVES: the leader of the pack; way out in front

see a man about a dog ✪✪✪✪

PLAIN ENGLISH ALTERNATIVES: go to the toilet; go to the bathroom; urinate

CLICHÉD ALTERNATIVES: inspect the plumbing; pay a visit; spend a penny

■ *Origins* Most likely this euphemism originally disguised itself as a wish to place a bet on a greyhound race.

see eye to eye ✪✪

PLAIN ENGLISH ALTERNATIVES: agree; concur; share the same opinion; think the same way; have a harmonious relationship

CLICHÉD ALTERNATIVES: be of the same mind

■ *Origins* From the Bible (*Isaiah* 52.8): 'For they shall see eye to eye, when the Lord shall bring again Zion.'

see how the land lies ✪✪

PLAIN ENGLISH ALTERNATIVES: reconnoitre; weigh up the circumstances; check out the situation; make a reconnaissance; have a recce; have a look round

CLICHÉD ALTERNATIVES: get the lie of the land; see what's what; see which way the wind blows

see red ✪✪

PLAIN ENGLISH ALTERNATIVES: lose one's temper; become exasperated; get angry; get mad; blow up; fire up

CLICHÉD ALTERNATIVES: fly off the handle; lose one's rag; lose the plot; go ballistic; lose it big time; go off at the deep end

■ *Origins* A reference to the idea that the colour red infuriates a bull. (See **like a red rag to a bull**.)

see stars ✪✪

PLAIN ENGLISH ALTERNATIVES: be dazed; be stunned; be reeling

CLICHÉD ALTERNATIVES: be knocked for six

■ *Origins* From the flashes of light often seen by someone dazed by a blow to the head.

see the light of day ✪✪

PLAIN ENGLISH ALTERNATIVES: come out; emerge; appear; become public; come to public notice; be published; be discovered; be born

CLICHÉD ALTERNATIVES: come to light; come into the world; crop up; make an entrance

self-starter ✪✪✪✪✪

PLAIN ENGLISH ALTERNATIVES: dynamic person; enterprising person; person able to act on their own initiative; go-getter; livewire

CLICHÉD ALTERNATIVES: proactive person

sell like hot cakes ✪✪✪

PLAIN ENGLISH ALTERNATIVES: sell quickly; sell promptly; prove very popular

CLICHÉD ALTERNATIVES: fly off the shelves; fly out of the shops; go down a bomb

sell someone down the river ✪✪

PLAIN ENGLISH ALTERNATIVES: betray someone; deceive someone; behave treacherously towards someone

CLICHÉD ALTERNATIVES: sell someone out; double-cross someone; stab someone in the back

■ *Origins* From the days of slavery in America. The river is the Mississippi, and for slave-owners to sell their slaves to plantations further south was almost certainly to condemn them to a much harsher environment.

send someone to Coventry ✪✪

PLAIN ENGLISH ALTERNATIVES: ostracize someone; ignore someone; shun someone; refuse to speak to someone; blackball someone; boycott someone; cold-shoulder someone

CLICHÉD ALTERNATIVES: give someone the cold shoulder; freeze someone out

■ *Origins* It is not clear why the proverbial place of exile should be this Midlands city. One theory is that it was a Parliamentarian stronghold in the English Civil War and Royalist prisoners were often sent there.

serious money ✪✪✪

PLAIN ENGLISH ALTERNATIVES: a considerable amount of money; a substantial sum; large sums

CLICHÉD ALTERNATIVES: big bucks; pots of money; oodles of cash

set someone's teeth on edge ✪✪

PLAIN ENGLISH ALTERNATIVES: annoy someone; exasperate someone; irk someone; irritate someone

CLICHÉD ALTERNATIVES: drive someone up the wall; get on someone's nerves; get on someone's wick; get someone's back up; get someone's dander up; get up someone's nose; rub someone up the wrong way

sex something up ✪✪✪✪✪

PLAIN ENGLISH ALTERNATIVES: add interest to something; make something more interesting; make something more exciting; make something more attractive

CLICHÉD ALTERNATIVES: add relish to something; add spice to something; give something some oomph; jazz something up; spice something up

■ *Origins* From the use of 'sexy' to mean 'interesting' or 'exciting'.

shake a leg ✪✪

PLAIN ENGLISH ALTERNATIVES: hurry up; make haste; rush

CLICHÉD ALTERNATIVES: get a move on; get weaving; get a wiggle on; get one's skates on

shake one's booty ✪✪✪

PLAIN ENGLISH ALTERNATIVES: dance; swing; jig; boogie; jive

CLICHÉD ALTERNATIVES: trip the light fantastic; get down; boogie on down; strut one's stuff; cut a rug

- *Origins* One's 'booty' here means one's bottom, and clearly denotes the variety of dancing in which this is slung about with some abandon.

shape up or ship out ✪✪

PLAIN ENGLISH ALTERNATIVES: get (oneself) organized; sort oneself out; show some improvement; mend one's ways

CLICHÉD ALTERNATIVES: get it together; get on the ball; get one's act together; get a grip on oneself; pull oneself together; pull one's finger out; clean up one's act; pull one's socks up; snap out of it; straighten up and fly right

- *Origins* Originally a US military threat meaning, 'Improve your behaviour or you'll be sent somewhere more unpleasant.'

shed light on ✪✪

PLAIN ENGLISH ALTERNATIVES: clarify; elucidate; explain; clear up; illuminate

shipshape (and Bristol fashion) ✪✪

PLAIN ENGLISH ALTERNATIVES: orderly; tidy; neat and tidy; in order; trim; proper; organized

CLICHÉD ALTERNATIVES: in apple-pie order; spick and span

- *Origins* 'Shipshape' of course means 'in the condition a ship ought to be'; the nautical flavour is continued in the reference to Bristol, a famous port.

shock horror ✪✪

PLAIN ENGLISH ALTERNATIVES: how dreadful!; isn't it awful?; how shocking!

CLICHÉD ALTERNATIVES: heaven help us!; saints preserve us!; heavens forfend!

shoot oneself in the foot ✪✪

PLAIN ENGLISH ALTERNATIVES: blunder; harm one's own interests; make a costly mistake; be self-destructive

CLICHÉD ALTERNATIVES: score an own goal; be hoist with one's own petard

■ *Origins* The image here is not of deliberate self-harm but of being so inept that in trying to fire a weapon at an enemy or quarry one hits oneself.

shoot someone down in flames ✪✪

PLAIN ENGLISH ALTERNATIVES: destroy someone's argument; utterly refute someone's argument

CLICHÉD ALTERNATIVES: blow someone out of the water; leave someone without a leg to stand on; pull the rug from under someone

shot in the dark ✪✪

PLAIN ENGLISH ALTERNATIVES: random guess; wild speculation; wild guess; random conjecture; utter guesswork

■ *Origins* A shot taken when it is too dark to see what one is aiming at will be very lucky to hit the target.

should be so lucky

See **I should be so lucky**.

shoulder the blame ✪✪

PLAIN ENGLISH ALTERNATIVES: be blamed; take the blame; accept responsibility

CLICHÉD ALTERNATIVES: carry the can; take the rap; put one's hands up

show must go on, the ✪✪✪

PLAIN ENGLISH ALTERNATIVES: it's too late to stop now; there's no turning back; one must carry on regardless

CLICHÉD ALTERNATIVES: on with the motley

■ *Origins* From show business, where it is every trouper's duty to give a performance no matter what happens.

show one's face ✪✪

PLAIN ENGLISH ALTERNATIVES: appear; attend; be present; show; turn up

CLICHÉD ALTERNATIVES: put in an appearance; show up

show one's hand ✪✪

PLAIN ENGLISH ALTERNATIVES: reveal one's intentions; expose one's purpose

CLICHÉD ALTERNATIVES: give the game away; give the show away

■ *Origins* From card playing.

show one's teeth ✪✪

PLAIN ENGLISH ALTERNATIVES: adopt a threatening posture; be aggressive; be belligerent; be menacing; demonstrate one's power; threaten violence

CLICHÉD ALTERNATIVES: rattle one's sabre

■ *Origins* From dogs, who show their teeth when they growl.

show someone the ropes ✪✪

PLAIN ENGLISH ALTERNATIVES: train someone; teach someone; coach someone; tutor someone; show someone what to do

CLICHÉD ALTERNATIVES: give someone an induction course; show someone their way round

■ *Origins* A nautical term. See **know the ropes**.

shrinking violet ✪✪

PLAIN ENGLISH ALTERNATIVES: shy person; modest person; diffident person; self-effacing person; mouse

CLICHÉD ALTERNATIVES: wallflower

■ *Origins* The violet is traditionally associated with modesty, perhaps because its flowers are said to recoil from being touched.

shuffle off this mortal coil ✪✪

PLAIN ENGLISH ALTERNATIVES: die; decease; perish; lose one's life

CLICHÉD ALTERNATIVES: bite the dust; come to a sticky end; pop one's clogs; give up the ghost; buy it; go the way of all flesh; kick the bucket; go belly up; peg out; join the choir invisible; join the majority

■ *Origins* Slightly adapted from Shakespeare, where 'mortal coil' means 'the troubles of human existence': 'For in that sleep of death what dreams may come, / When we have shuffled off this mortal coil, / Must give us pause.' (*Hamlet* Act III, Scene 1)

sick and tired ✪✪✪

PLAIN ENGLISH ALTERNATIVES: disgusted; weary; fed up; having had enough; browned off; ticked off; brassed off; hacked off; bored

CLICHÉD ALTERNATIVES: having had it up to here; fed up to the back teeth

sick as a parrot ✪✪✪✪✪

PLAIN ENGLISH ALTERNATIVES: very disappointed; deflated; unhappy; downcast; despondent; let down; dismayed; saddened; chagrined; feeling low

CLICHÉD ALTERNATIVES: in the slough of despond

> **!** *Original alternative:* like someone who stopped doing the lottery the week before their numbers came up

■ *Origins* Popularly seen as the opposite of 'over the moon', this phrase may have various explanations. Some would argue that the root of it psittacosis, a disease of parrots that can be contracted by humans; others that the essential meaning is 'as melancholy as a parrot', given that caged birds often seem given to introspection. Yet another theory is that it was popularized in the 1970s when a well-known comedian called Freddy 'Parrotface' Davis was using the catchphrase, 'I'm sick, sick, sick up to here!'

sight for sore eyes ✪✪

PLAIN ENGLISH ALTERNATIVES: pleasant sight; welcome sight; pleasing sight; delightful sight

CLICHÉD ALTERNATIVES: something to see

■ *Origins* The idea is that it is so pleasurable to see this person or thing that aching eyes will immediately feel soothed.

signed, sealed and delivered ✪✪✪

PLAIN ENGLISH ALTERNATIVES: concluded; finished; settled; sorted; rounded off; clinched; fixed; accomplished

CLICHÉD ALTERNATIVES: all wrapped up; all tied up; on a plate

■ *Origins* From legal documents that are validated by having both a signature and a seal on them. No doubt the phrase's popularity was furthered by its use by Stevie Wonder in his 1970 hit single 'Signed, Sealed, Delivered, I'm Yours'.

significant other ✪✪✪✪✪

PLAIN ENGLISH ALTERNATIVES: lover; partner; husband; wife; girlfriend; boyfriend

CLICHÉD ALTERNATIVES: other half

■ *Origins* Originally American, this represents a politically correct attempt not to specify the sex or marital status of the person in question.

singing from the same hymnsheet ✪✪✪✪✪

PLAIN ENGLISH ALTERNATIVES: in accord; in broad agreement; in harmony;

thinking along the same lines; following the approved party line

CLICHÉD ALTERNATIVES: message-focussed; on message; on the same page; of the same way of thinking; speaking the same language

sing the praises of

PLAIN ENGLISH ALTERNATIVES: commend; extol; praise; talk up; acclaim; applaud; cry up; laud

CLICHÉD ALTERNATIVES: pay tribute to; give a glowing recommendation to; give top marks to

- *Origins* From hymns, used to sing the praises of God.

sit on the fence

PLAIN ENGLISH ALTERNATIVES: hedge; refuse to commit oneself; not take sides; remain neutral; be noncommittal; not come down on one side or the other

CLICHÉD ALTERNATIVES: play both ends against the middle

- *Origins* From the idea of straddling a dividing line between two opposing camps.

sitting duck

PLAIN ENGLISH ALTERNATIVES: easy target; helpless victim; sitter

CLICHÉD ALTERNATIVES: fish in a barrel

- *Origins* It is far easier to shoot a duck on the water than in the air.

sit up and take notice

PLAIN ENGLISH ALTERNATIVES: pay attention; give one's attention; become alert; focus; take heed

sixes and sevens

See **at sixes and sevens**.

six of one and half a dozen of the other ✪✪

PLAIN ENGLISH ALTERNATIVES: much the same; all the same; very much alike; very similar; having nothing much to choose between them

CLICHÉD ALTERNATIVES: much of a muchness

sixty-four thousand dollar question ✪✪✪✪✪

PLAIN ENGLISH ALTERNATIVES: a hard one to answer; a difficult question; an impossible question; the decisive point; the decisive question; the crucial question

CLICHÉD ALTERNATIVES: a good question; the crux of the matter

▪ *Origins* From a US television quiz show in which answering the final question could win that sum of money. The show developed from a radio version in which the equivalent question was the 'sixty-four dollar question'. Thus are shown the effects of inflation even on the language we speak.

skating on thin ice ✪✪

PLAIN ENGLISH ALTERNATIVES: behaving rashly; being reckless; taking great (or unnecessary) risks; exposing oneself to danger

CLICHÉD ALTERNATIVES: living dangerously; flirting with danger; playing with fire; going in harm's way; risking life and limb

slap on the wrist ✪✪

PLAIN ENGLISH ALTERNATIVES: rebuke; reprimand; reproof; talking-to; dressing-down; stern word; admonition

CLICHÉD ALTERNATIVES: an admonitory word

slap-up meal ✪✪✪✪

PLAIN ENGLISH ALTERNATIVES: feast; sumptuous meal; lavish spread; first-rate meal; beanfeast; blowout

CLICHÉD ALTERNATIVES: quite a spread; a dinner fit for kings

▪ *Origins* One would be forgiven for thinking this had something to do with patting one's belly after a satisfying meal. However, it was only in the 20th century that 'slap-up' became irretrievably fixed to 'meal'. Before that it meant simply 'first-rate' and could be applied to all sorts of things. In fact, 'slap' here means 'precisely' and has nothing to do with the patting of well-filled stomachs.

slave over a hot stove ✪✪

PLAIN ENGLISH ALTERNATIVES: cook; do the cooking; make the dinner

CLICHÉD ALTERNATIVES: slave away in the kitchen; cook up a storm

smell a rat ✪✪

PLAIN ENGLISH ALTERNATIVES: become suspicious; suspect that something underhand is going on; detect something suspicious; perceive treachery; suspect that all is not well

CLICHÉD ALTERNATIVES: suspect foul play; think there's something fishy going on; believe there is more to it than meets the eye

- *Origins* It is, of course, a dead rat rather than a live one that offends the nose.

smoke and mirrors ✪✪✪

PLAIN ENGLISH ALTERNATIVES: deceit; deception; trickery; hocus-pocus; conjuring tricks

- *Origins* From the use of these items by stage illusionists.

smoking gun ✪✪

PLAIN ENGLISH ALTERNATIVES: conclusive proof; irrefutable proof; incriminating evidence

- *Origins* From the idea that possession of a recently fired gun is a pretty good indication of whodunnit.

snowball's chance

See **not a snowball's chance**.

snowed under with ✪✪

PLAIN ENGLISH ALTERNATIVES: overwhelmed with; buried under; inundated with; deluged with; flooded with; swamped with

CLICHÉD ALTERNATIVES: up to the eyes in

- *Origins* From being covered by a heavy fall of snow.

softly-softly approach ✪✪

PLAIN ENGLISH ALTERNATIVES: cautious line; delicate treatment; careful method; sensitive attitude; circumspection

CLICHÉD ALTERNATIVES: kid-glove treatment; gently-does-it attitude

- *Origins* From the mock pidgin English proverb 'softly softly catchee monkey'.

something is rotten in the state of Denmark ✪✪✪✪

PLAIN ENGLISH ALTERNATIVES: all is not well; there's something wrong; there is something suspicious afoot; I am suspicious

CLICHÉD ALTERNATIVES: there's something funny going on; I smell a rat

- *Origins* A quotation from Shakespeare's *Hamlet* (Act I, Scene 4). How cliché addicts love it when they can use this phrase in actually referring to Denmark!

something nasty in the woodshed ✪✪

PLAIN ENGLISH ALTERNATIVES: an unpleasant sight; a traumatic sight; a horrible sight; a disturbing sight; a shocking sight

- *Origins* From the novel *Cold Comfort Farm* (1932) by Stella Gibbons, in which a character is traumatized by seeing this.

some you win, some you lose

See **you can't win them all**.

song and dance ✪✪

PLAIN ENGLISH ALTERNATIVES: fuss; commotion; agitation; bustle; palaver; hullabaloo; brouhaha; kerfuffle

CLICHÉD ALTERNATIVES: great to-do

spare me the gory details ✪✪✪

PLAIN ENGLISH ALTERNATIVES: there's no need to go into detail; no further details are required; don't go any further; I don't want to hear any more

CLICHÉD ALTERNATIVES: leave it out; less is more; too much information!

speak the same language ✪✪✪✪

PLAIN ENGLISH ALTERNATIVES: be in accord; be in broad agreement; be in harmony; hold the same views; think along the same lines; understand one another perfectly

CLICHÉD ALTERNATIVES: be on the same page; be of the same way of thinking; sing from the same hymnsheet

spend a penny ✪✪

PLAIN ENGLISH ALTERNATIVES: go to the toilet; go to the bathroom; go to the loo; go to the WC; urinate

CLICHÉD ALTERNATIVES: inspect the plumbing; pay a visit; see a man about a dog

■ *Origins* From the cubicles in British public conveniences which, before decimalization, could only be opened by inserting a penny in the lock mechanism.

spick and span ✪✪

PLAIN ENGLISH ALTERNATIVES: orderly; tidy; neat and tidy; in order; trim; proper; organized

CLICHÉD ALTERNATIVES: in apple-pie order; all shipshape and Bristol-fashion

■ *Origins* Another nautical reference. A 'spick' was a wooden spike and a 'span' was a split wooden chip, and on a well-tended ship these would be clean and new.

spill the beans ✪✪

PLAIN ENGLISH ALTERNATIVES: disclose something secret; reveal a secret; reveal the truth; divulge information

CLICHÉD ALTERNATIVES: give the game away; let the cat out of the bag

■ *Origins* There are various explanations. One is that the phrase originally meant to vomit. Another relates it to the fairground attraction of guessing how many beans were in a jar, the answer only being revealed when the jar was emptied.

spitting image ✪✪

PLAIN ENGLISH ALTERNATIVES: double; image; exact copy; exact likeness; duplicate; twin; clone; doppelgänger

CLICHÉD ALTERNATIVES: spit and image; dead ringer; dead spit

■ *Origins* A corruption of 'spit and image'.

squeaky clean ✪✪✪✪

PLAIN ENGLISH ALTERNATIVES: spotless; spotlessly clean; completely clean; immaculate; impeccable

CLICHÉD ALTERNATIVES: clean as a whistle; not a mark on it; so clean one could eat one's dinner off it

■ *Origins* Some say that freshly washed hair squeaks if it is brushed, others maintain the squeak is that of a newly polished floor.

stand to reason

See **it stands to reason**.

start the ball rolling ✪✪

PLAIN ENGLISH ALTERNATIVES: begin; initiate the action; get things going;

make the first move; get things under way

CLICHÉD ALTERNATIVES: kick things off; open the ball; get the show on the road

■ *Origins* Perhaps from beginning a ball game by rolling the ball between the sides.

state-of-the-art ✪✪✪

PLAIN ENGLISH ALTERNATIVES: best available; unsurpassed; finest in its field; first-class

CLICHÉD ALTERNATIVES: top-of-the-range; top-end

stick-in-the-mud ✪✪

PLAIN ENGLISH ALTERNATIVES: fogey; conservative; old-fashioned person; dinosaur; fossil; fuddy-duddy; relic; square

CLICHÉD ALTERNATIVES: back number

■ *Origins* Someone who gets stuck in the mud is not progressing.

stick one's oar in ✪✪

PLAIN ENGLISH ALTERNATIVES: interfere; interpose; intrude; butt in; meddle

CLICHÉD ALTERNATIVES: poke one's nose in where it's not wanted

stick out like a sore thumb ✪✪

PLAIN ENGLISH ALTERNATIVES: be painfully obvious; be incongruous; be blatant; obtrude

CLICHÉD ALTERNATIVES: hit one in the eye; stick out a mile

sticky wicket ✪✪✪

PLAIN ENGLISH ALTERNATIVES: difficult situation; predicament; awkward position; corner; fix; hole; jam; pickle

CLICHÉD ALTERNATIVES: tight spot; hot water

■ *Origins* From cricket, referring to the days when rain could leave an uncovered wicket with a wet surface, which was likely to cause problems for the batsmen.

stiff upper lip

See **keep a stiff upper lip**.

straight face

See **keep a straight face**.

straight from the shoulder   ✪✪

PLAIN ENGLISH ALTERNATIVES: frankly; clearly; plainly; candidly; bluntly; straight

CLICHÉD ALTERNATIVES: in no uncertain terms; without mincing one's words; no punches pulled

■ *Origins* From boxing, in which a punch delivered straight from the shoulder is one given full force.

strain every nerve and sinew   ✪✪

PLAIN ENGLISH ALTERNATIVES: make every effort; do one's utmost; try one's hardest; spare no effort; do all one can

CLICHÉD ALTERNATIVES: try with all one's might and main; knock oneself out

strange as it may seem   ✪✪

PLAIN ENGLISH ALTERNATIVES: oddly enough; funnily enough; surprisingly enough; strangely enough; ironically enough; you might be surprised to find that

CLICHÉD ALTERNATIVES: believe it or not

stretch one's legs ✪✪

PLAIN ENGLISH ALTERNATIVES: go for a walk; take some exercise; have a stroll; walk about a bit

CLICHÉD ALTERNATIVES: take one's constitutional; take a turn

strike a chord ✪✪

PLAIN ENGLISH ALTERNATIVES: evoke a memory; sound familiar; remind one of something; call someone or something to mind; bring back memories; awaken memories

CLICHÉD ALTERNATIVES: ring a bell; jog one's memory

strike while the iron is hot ✪✪

PLAIN ENGLISH ALTERNATIVES: act promptly; seize the opportunity; take one's chance; carpe diem

CLICHÉD ALTERNATIVES: make hay while the sun shines; grab the opportunity with both hands

■ *Origins* From the work of a blacksmith, who must hammer metal into shape while it is still hot enough to be malleable.

stroll down memory lane ✪✪✪✪

PLAIN ENGLISH ALTERNATIVES: reminiscence; fond memories; nostalgia; remembrance

CLICHÉD ALTERNATIVES: blast from the past

strut one's stuff ✪✪✪

PLAIN ENGLISH ALTERNATIVES: show off; put on a performance; grandstand; swagger; hot-dog (*US*)

CLICHÉD ALTERNATIVES: show what one can do

suffer in silence ✪✪

PLAIN ENGLISH ALTERNATIVES: make no complaint; be uncomplaining; put up with it

CLICHÉD ALTERNATIVES: be long-suffering; soldier on; not kick against the pricks

swear blind ✪✪

PLAIN ENGLISH ALTERNATIVES: assert emphatically; affirm; assert; asseverate; avow

CLICHÉD ALTERNATIVES: swear on one's mother's grave

■ *Origins* From an oath wishing one may go blind if what one asserts is not true, along the same lines as 'gorblimey', which is a corruption of 'God blind me'.

sweep one off one's feet ✪✪

PLAIN ENGLISH ALTERNATIVES: carry away; overwhelm; transport; captivate; enchant; enrapture

CLICHÉD ALTERNATIVES: blow one away; take one's breath away; turn one's head around

sweep something under the carpet ✪✪

PLAIN ENGLISH ALTERNATIVES: hide; conceal; bury; cover up; conceal; keep out of sight; suppress

CLICHÉD ALTERNATIVES: draw a veil over; hush up; keep dark

■ *Origins* From sweeping up household dust and, rather than putting it in a bin, brushing it under the lifted edge of a rug.

sweep the board ✪✪

PLAIN ENGLISH ALTERNATIVES: win everything; win the lot; take all the prizes

CLICHÉD ALTERNATIVES: pocket all the stakes; make a clean sweep; scoop the pool

■ *Origins* A gambling term, from the action of gathering up all the stakes that have been placed.

sweetness and light ✪✪

PLAIN ENGLISH ALTERNATIVES: harmony; pleasantness; peace; peacefulness; co-operation; amity; friendliness; goodwill

■ *Origins* Although he was not the first to join these two terms, the phrase was popularized by the Victorian sage Matthew Arnold in *Culture and Anarchy* (1869): 'The pursuit of perfection, then, is the pursuit of sweetness and light. He who works for sweetness and light united, works to make reason and the will of God prevail.' (Chapter 1)

swing the lead ✪✪

PLAIN ENGLISH ALTERNATIVES: malinger; dodge one's responsibilities; shirk; evade work; skive; slack; skrimshank; loaf

CLICHÉD ALTERNATIVES: lie down on the job

■ *Origins* From the nautical practice of sounding the depth of water by dropping a lead weight on a line. Someone who was swinging the lead was merely making a show of doing this so as not to be assigned other duties.

take a back seat ✪✪

PLAIN ENGLISH ALTERNATIVES: be subordinate; play a secondary role; relinquish control; leave it to others to take the lead

CLICHÉD ALTERNATIVES: play second fiddle; stay in the background; watch from the wings

- *Origins* From sitting in the rear of a car rather than in the driver's seat.

take a leaf out of someone's book ✪✪

PLAIN ENGLISH ALTERNATIVES: follow someone's lead; follow someone's example; do the same as someone; imitate someone

CLICHÉD ALTERNATIVES: follow suit; follow in someone's footsteps; profit by someone's example

- *Origins* From plagiarizing someone by taking one of their written pages to copy.

take a shine to ✪✪

PLAIN ENGLISH ALTERNATIVES: take a liking to; develop a liking for; be attracted to; be charmed by

CLICHÉD ALTERNATIVES: take a fancy to; develop a crush on

- *Origins* Unclear.

take it from me ✪✪✪✪

PLAIN ENGLISH ALTERNATIVES: I assure you; believe me when I tell you; you can believe me

CLICHÉD ALTERNATIVES: let me tell you; I'm here to tell you; take my word for it

take it lying down   ✪✪

PLAIN ENGLISH ALTERNATIVES: submit without a struggle; give up without a fight; make no protest; not put up a fight; be supine

CLICHÉD ALTERNATIVES: let someone walk all over one; sit still for it

- *Origins* From the idea of a dog cowering on its belly.

take no prisoners   ✪✪

PLAIN ENGLISH ALTERNATIVES: show no mercy; be merciless; be harsh; take no half measures

CLICHÉD ALTERNATIVES: pull no punches; not suffer fools gladly

take one's eye off the ball   ✪✪

PLAIN ENGLISH ALTERNATIVES: lose concentration; lose focus; let one's attention slip; slip up; tune out; drift off

CLICHÉD ALTERNATIVES: let one's mind wander

- *Origins* From ball games, especially football.

take one's hat off to someone   ✪✪

PLAIN ENGLISH ALTERNATIVES: express one's admiration for someone; salute someone; praise someone; acknowledge someone's achievement; pay tribute to someone

CLICHÉD ALTERNATIVES: hand it to someone

- *Origins* From the old-fashioned act of doffing or raising one's hat as a salute.

take one's life in one's hands   ✪✪

PLAIN ENGLISH ALTERNATIVES: take great risks; meddle with something dangerous; court danger; expose oneself to unnecessary risk

CLICHÉD ALTERNATIVES: dice with death; skate on thin ice; play with fire

take someone down a peg or two ✪✪

PLAIN ENGLISH ALTERNATIVES: humble someone; humiliate someone; deflate someone; lower someone's self-esteem; put someone down

CLICHÉD ALTERNATIVES: make someone eat humble pie; put someone in their place; take the wind from someone's sails

■ *Origins* Another nautical allusion. A ship's colours could be hoisted at different levels by means of pegs, the higher the peg indicating the greater honour.

take someone to the cleaners ✪✪

PLAIN ENGLISH ALTERNATIVES: take all of someone's money; beat someone with ease; outclass someone; be markedly superior to someone; make someone look bad

CLICHÉD ALTERNATIVES: clean someone out; beat someone hollow; put someone in the shade; wipe the floor with someone

■ *Origins* From the idea of robbing someone's house so completely that it is cleaned out.

take something on board ✪✪✪✪

PLAIN ENGLISH ALTERNATIVES: accept; accommodate; understand; take into account; take into consideration; take note of; recognize

■ *Origins* From the idea of allowing something to be carried as cargo on a voyage.

take the cake or biscuit ✪✪

PLAIN ENGLISH ALTERNATIVES: surpass all; beat everything; exceed all others; be the ultimate; win the prize

CLICHÉD ALTERNATIVES: carry off the honours; leave everything else in the shade; top it all

■ *Origins* From the idea of a cake being awarded as a prize, probably for a dance competition whether among 19th-century black Americans (known as a 'cakewalk') or Irish dancers.

tale of woe ✪✪

PLAIN ENGLISH ALTERNATIVES: plea for sympathy; pitiful tale; complaint

CLICHÉD ALTERNATIVES: sob story

talk nineteen to the dozen ✪✪

PLAIN ENGLISH ALTERNATIVES: talk incessantly; talk rapidly; not stop talking; prattle on; rabbit on; witter on; be talkative; be garrulous; be long-winded

CLICHÉD ALTERNATIVES: run off at the mouth

■ *Origins* From the idea of a talkative person saying nineteen words in the time that anyone else would only manage twelve.

talk turkey ✪✪

PLAIN ENGLISH ALTERNATIVES: be frank; speak plainly; be direct; talk bluntly; talk business

CLICHÉD ALTERNATIVES: call a spade a spade; not mince one's words; talk turkey; give it to one straight from the shoulder; get right down to business

■ *Origins* No perfectly convincing explanation exists, but perhaps the least unlikely involves turkey hunters imitating the birds' gobbling cries to attract them.

tall order ✪✪

PLAIN ENGLISH ALTERNATIVES: unreasonable request; difficult assignment; stiff challenge; task that won't be easy; no easy task; no straightforward task

CLICHÉD ALTERNATIVES: hard nut to crack; no picnic; quite a job

tall story ✪✪

PLAIN ENGLISH ALTERNATIVES: unlikely tale; unbelievable story; exaggerated account; incredible story; lie; whopper

CLICHÉD ALTERNATIVES: fairy tale

- *Origins* 'Tall' here means 'exaggerated' or 'pretentious'.

tarred with the same brush ✪✪

PLAIN ENGLISH ALTERNATIVES: having the same faults; all the same; as bad as each other; equally to blame

CLICHÉD ALTERNATIVES: much of a muchness

- *Origins* From the practice of dabbing tar onto sheep to treat sores.

tell it like it is ✪✪✪✪

PLAIN ENGLISH ALTERNATIVES: speak frankly; be firm; be straight; be candid; be blunt; make it clear; be utterly frank

CLICHÉD ALTERNATIVES: give it to someone straight (from the shoulder); not mince one's words; lay it on the line

tell me about it! ✪✪✪

PLAIN ENGLISH ALTERNATIVES: don't I just know it!; I know exactly what you mean; you are absolutely right

CLICHÉD ALTERNATIVES: you're telling me!

terra firma ✪✪

PLAIN ENGLISH ALTERNATIVES: land; dry land; firm ground; the earth; solid earth

- *Origins* Latin, meaning 'firm ground'.

that'll be the day ✪✪

PLAIN ENGLISH ALTERNATIVES: there is not much hope of that; it'll never happen; it's unlikely

CLICHÉD ALTERNATIVES: I should be so lucky; I should live so long; chance would be a fine thing

that makes two of us ✪✪

PLAIN ENGLISH ALTERNATIVES: I'm with you; I'm in the same position; my case is the same; I'm the same as you; neither do I

CLICHÉD ALTERNATIVES: me too; me neither; same here; join the club

that's about the size of it ✪✪

PLAIN ENGLISH ALTERNATIVES: that's how it is; that's the way things are; that's how matters stand; that sums it up; that's the present state of affairs; that's how it's looking

CLICHÉD ALTERNATIVES: that's the way of it

that's all she wrote ✪✪✪

PLAIN ENGLISH ALTERNATIVES: it's all over; that's it; it's finished; there is no more to be said; that's the end; that's all there is

CLICHÉD ALTERNATIVES: that's the end of that

▪ *Origins* Originally and still predominantly American, this is thought to have come from the lament of a World War II serviceman reading a 'Dear John' letter.

that's the ticket ✪✪

PLAIN ENGLISH ALTERNATIVES: that's what's required; that's right; that's what to do; that's exactly right; that's the right thing to do

CLICHÉD ALTERNATIVES: that's the way; that's the stuff; way to go

▪ *Origins* The ticket here refers to tickets for food and clothing issued to the poor by 19th-century charities.

that's the way the cookie crumbles ✪✪✪

PLAIN ENGLISH ALTERNATIVES: that's how it goes; that's the way it is; that's what usually happens; it's to be expected

CLICHÉD ALTERNATIVES: that's life; that's the way the ball bounces; them's the breaks; these things happen; what can you do?

▪ *Origins* Originally American, as the word 'cookie' shows.

the jury's still out ✪✪✪

PLAIN ENGLISH ALTERNATIVES: it remains to be seen; no decision has been reached; it's still to be decided; it's still under discussion; a final judgement has not been made; people haven't made up their minds yet

CLICHÉD ALTERNATIVES: a verdict has still to be reached

- **Origins** From a trial jury retiring from the court until they reach a verdict.

the mind boggles ✪✪✪✪

PLAIN ENGLISH ALTERNATIVES: that is absurd; that is unbelievable; that defies belief; that is unreal; that is astonishing; one wouldn't believe it was possible

CLICHÉD ALTERNATIVES: that is beyond belief; would you believe it?

- **Origins** 'Boggle' seems to derive from *bogle*, meaning 'a goblin, ghost or some other scary supernatural being', and suggests the act of shying away in fright. The expression was given wider exposure by being a regular catchphrase in *The Perishers*, a cartoon strip in the *Daily Mirror* from the late 1950s on.

there's more to it than meets the eye ✪✪

PLAIN ENGLISH ALTERNATIVES: it's not as clear cut as it seems; it's not straightforward; it's complicated; there is something suspicious about it

CLICHÉD ALTERNATIVES: you don't know the half of it; there's something fishy going on

there's no two ways about it ✪✪

PLAIN ENGLISH ALTERNATIVES: there will be no discussion on the matter; there's no alternative; it's certain; this is what's going to happen; be assured

CLICHÉD ALTERNATIVES: it's cut and dried

there's the rub ✪✪✪

PLAIN ENGLISH ALTERNATIVES: that's the problem; that's the difficulty; that's the snag; that's the impediment; that's the hitch

the worse for wear

CLICHÉD ALTERNATIVES: that's the fly in the ointment

■ *Origins* From Shakespeare's *Hamlet* (Act III, Scene 1): 'To sleep: perchance to dream: ay, there's the rub; / For in that sleep of death what dreams may come'. The image here is from bowls, where 'rub' means an impediment or uneven place on the green.

the worse for wear ✪✪

PLAIN ENGLISH ALTERNATIVES: worn; battered; distressed; tired; run-down; tattered; tatty; exhausted; drunk

CLICHÉD ALTERNATIVES: under the weather; showing signs of wear; ragged round the edges

thick and fast ✪✪

PLAIN ENGLISH ALTERNATIVES: abundantly; frequently; in large numbers; steadily and rapidly; in quick succession

CLICHÉD ALTERNATIVES: hand over fist; by the barrowload; like nobody's business

■ *Origins* Probably from hails of arrows fired in a battle.

thing of the past

See **be a thing of the past**.

think outside the box ✪✪✪✪

PLAIN ENGLISH ALTERNATIVES: find an original solution; disregard conventional thinking; approach things in a new way; think creatively; use one's imagination

CLICHÉD ALTERNATIVES: look for answers in left field

■ *Origins* Unclear, perhaps from the idea of being unconstrained by limitations, or of refusing merely to tick boxes.

thin on the ground ✪✪

PLAIN ENGLISH ALTERNATIVES: scarce; rare; seldom met with

CLICHÉD ALTERNATIVES: few and far between; scarce as hen's teeth; in short supply

thin on top ✪✪

PLAIN ENGLISH ALTERNATIVES: going bald; balding; thinning; receding; losing one's hair

third degree

See **give someone the third degree**.

thorn in the flesh or side ✪✪

PLAIN ENGLISH ALTERNATIVES: irritant; source of irritation; pain; annoyance; nuisance; tiresome person; pest

CLICHÉD ALTERNATIVES: pain in the arse; pain in the neck

■ *Origins* From the Bible (II *Corinthians* 12.7): 'There was given to me a thorn in the flesh, the messenger of Satan to buffet me, lest I should be exalted beyond measure.'

those and such as those ✪✪

PLAIN ENGLISH ALTERNATIVES: the elite; one's superiors; one's betters; toffs

CLICHÉD ALTERNATIVES: the privileged few; the favoured few

three sheets in or to the wind ✪✪

PLAIN ENGLISH ALTERNATIVES: drunk; tipsy; merry; tight

CLICHÉD ALTERNATIVES: feeling no pain; tired and emotional; half seas over; rather the worse for drink; under the influence; off one's face

■ *Origins* Another nautical reference. A 'sheet' here means a rope used to secure a sail. If there's a sheet in the wind this means that one of these ropes has come untied and is blowing free. If three sheets are in the wind the sail will be flapping about without control.

through thick and thin ⊙⊗

PLAIN ENGLISH ALTERNATIVES: no matter what; in spite of all difficulties; under all conditions; whatever the difficulties

CLICHÉD ALTERNATIVES: in good times and bad; no matter what life throws at one

throw down the gauntlet ⊙⊗

PLAIN ENGLISH ALTERNATIVES: give a challenge; issue a challenge; dare someone

CLICHÉD ALTERNATIVES: tell someone to put their money where their mouth is

■ *Origins* From the medieval custom amongst knights of throwing a gauntlet to the ground to issue a challenge. Accepting the challenge would be indicated by picking up the gauntlet.

throw in the towel ⊙⊗

PLAIN ENGLISH ALTERNATIVES: acknowledge defeat; admit defeat; concede defeat; admit one is beaten; give in; give way; capitulate; yield; submit

CLICHÉD ALTERNATIVES: throw in one's hand; throw up the sponge

■ *Origins* From boxing, in which a trainer would indicate that his fighter had had enough by literally throwing a towel into the ring. The same was indicated by the trainer tossing a sponge into the air, hence 'throw up the sponge'.

throw the book at someone ⊙⊗

PLAIN ENGLISH ALTERNATIVES: administer severe punishment; punish someone severely; chastise someone

CLICHÉD ALTERNATIVES: give someone a hard time; give someone the works; lock someone up and throw away the key

■ *Origins* 'The book' refers to a real or imaginary volume of laws.

thumbs down ✪✪

PLAIN ENGLISH ALTERNATIVES: refusal; discouragement; knockback; no; rebuff; rejection

CLICHÉD ALTERNATIVES: no go

■ *Origins* From gladiatorial combats in ancient Rome, in which the crowd could decide whether or not a defeated fighter should live or die by either pointing their thumbs upward (for life) or downward (for death).

thumbs up ✪✪

PLAIN ENGLISH ALTERNATIVES: permission to proceed; consent; encouragement; assent; authorization; yes

CLICHÉD ALTERNATIVES: go-ahead; green light

tick all the boxes ✪✪✪✪

PLAIN ENGLISH ALTERNATIVES: meet all requirements; satisfy all conditions; come up to the required standard

CLICHÉD ALTERNATIVES: fill the bill; push all the right buttons; say all the right things; make all the right noises; pass muster

■ *Origins* From the idea of putting a tick in a box on a printed form.

tickled pink ✪✪

PLAIN ENGLISH ALTERNATIVES: delighted; highly amused; highly pleased; chuffed; overjoyed; thrilled

CLICHÉD ALTERNATIVES: pleased as Punch; over the moon; made up; well chuffed; in seventh heaven

■ *Origins* From a tickled person going red in the face from laughter.

tie the knot ✪✪

PLAIN ENGLISH ALTERNATIVES: marry; get married; wed; become husband and wife

tighten one's belt

CLICHÉD ALTERNATIVES: get spliced; get hitched; walk down the aisle

■ *Origins* There are various explanations. One derives this from the ancient custom of symbolizing marriage by tying the hems of the spouses' garments; another relates it to handfasting, a marriage ceremony in which the bride and groom's right hands would be tied together.

tighten one's belt ✪✪

PLAIN ENGLISH ALTERNATIVES: economize; make economies; reduce one's consumption; be economical; be frugal; cut back; retrench

CLICHÉD ALTERNATIVES: pull one's horns in; scrimp and save

■ *Origins* From the literal tightening of one's belt, whether to make one feel less hungry or to stop one's trousers falling down because one has lost weight.

till the cows come home ✪✪

PLAIN ENGLISH ALTERNATIVES: for a very long time; for an indefinite period; indefinitely; forever

CLICHÉD ALTERNATIVES: till all hours; till hell freezes over; till one is blue in the face

■ *Origins* From the idea of cows being left in the pasture until they are brought in to be milked.

time after time/time and time again ✪✪

PLAIN ENGLISH ALTERNATIVES: repeatedly; again and again; over and over; often; frequently

CLICHÉD ALTERNATIVES: many a time and oft; till one is blue in the face

tired and emotional ✪✪

PLAIN ENGLISH ALTERNATIVES: drunk; tipsy; merry; tight

CLICHÉD ALTERNATIVES: feeling no pain; three sheets in the wind; half seas over; rather the worse for drink; under the influence; off one's face

to all intents and purposes ✪✪

PLAIN ENGLISH ALTERNATIVES: in all that matters; in all important details; in practical terms; for all practical purposes; practically; virtually

CLICHÉD ALTERNATIVES: as near as makes no difference; in all but name

to a T ✪✪

PLAIN ENGLISH ALTERNATIVES: exactly; perfectly; accurately; precisely; absolutely

CLICHÉD ALTERNATIVES: right down to the ground; to the letter

- *Origins* From the use of a T-square in precision drawing.

to be perfectly honest ✪✪

PLAIN ENGLISH ALTERNATIVES: in all truth; in all honesty; in all sincerity; candidly; to be frank; frankly speaking; if one may speak frankly; truly; putting it plainly

CLICHÉD ALTERNATIVES: if you want my honest opinion; truth to tell; not to put too fine a point on it

to be reckoned with ✪✪

PLAIN ENGLISH ALTERNATIVES: formidable; accomplished; powerful; dangerous; serious; daunting; considerable

CLICHÉD ALTERNATIVES: no mean …

- *Origins* The meaning here is of being obliged to take account of something or someone.

to coin a phrase ✪✪✪✪✪

PLAIN ENGLISH ALTERNATIVES: in other words; in a way; as one might put it; in a sense

CLICHÉD ALTERNATIVES: as it were; so to speak; in a manner of speaking

- *Origins* The literal meaning is 'to invent a new expression', but most people merely use this cliché to accompany an existing one.

to cut a long story short ✪✪

PLAIN ENGLISH ALTERNATIVES: to come straight to the point; to be succinct; to sum up the matter in a few words

CLICHÉD ALTERNATIVES: to cut to the chase; not to beat about the bush; in a word

to die for ✪✪✪

PLAIN ENGLISH ALTERNATIVES: wonderful; marvellous; delightful; amazing; extraordinary; fantastic; phenomenal; sensational

CLICHÉD ALTERNATIVES: absolutely fabulous; out of this world

■ *Origins* From the idea that it would be worth surrendering one's life to obtain the item in question.

toe the line ✪✪

PLAIN ENGLISH ALTERNATIVES: submit; submit to authority; do as one is told; obey; follow orders; conform; acquiesce; fall in with someone's wishes

CLICHÉD ALTERNATIVES: come into line; bend the knee; bow the knee; knuckle under

■ *Origins* From the start of a running race, with competitors being obliged to place their toes no further forward than a marked line.

token of one's esteem ✪✪

PLAIN ENGLISH ALTERNATIVES: gift; present; gratuity; offering

CLICHÉD ALTERNATIVES: humble offering

Tom, Dick and Harry

See **every Tom, Dick and Harry**.

too awful to contemplate ✪✪

PLAIN ENGLISH ALTERNATIVES: dreadful; horrifying; horrendous; frightful; unbearable; appalling

CLICHÉD ALTERNATIVES: something that doesn't bear thinking about

too big for one's boots ✪✪

PLAIN ENGLISH ALTERNATIVES: cocksure; cocky; overconfident; bumptious; conceited; arrogant; self-important

CLICHÉD ALTERNATIVES: having too high an opinion of oneself; full of oneself; too big for one's breeches

to one's dying day ✪✪

PLAIN ENGLISH ALTERNATIVES: all one's life; until one dies; for the rest of one's life; as long as one lives; forever; always

CLICHÉD ALTERNATIVES: till the end of time; till Doomsday; forever and a day

too numerous to mention ✪✪✪

PLAIN ENGLISH ALTERNATIVES: innumerable; many; copious; countless; myriad

CLICHÉD ALTERNATIVES: many and varied

to put it mildly ✪✪

PLAIN ENGLISH ALTERNATIVES: not to exaggerate; to understate the case; without exaggeration; without overstating the case

touch and go ✪✪

PLAIN ENGLISH ALTERNATIVES: precarious; risky; uncertain; a narrow escape; a near thing

CLICHÉD ALTERNATIVES: a close call; a close-run thing; a near-run thing

touch base with

■ *Origins* There are various explanations, one being that it comes from a ship being in shallow enough water to touch bottom briefly but without running aground; another refers to a near-collision, in which two vehicles may brush against one another but are not halted in their movement.

touch base with ✪✪✪✪

PLAIN ENGLISH ALTERNATIVES: make contact with; get in touch with; keep in touch with; look up; say hello to; call; reach

CLICHÉD ALTERNATIVES: check in with

■ *Origins* The American origin of this phrase is shown by the fact that it is a baseball metaphor. A player attempting to score a run is required to touch each of the four bases on the way round.

tower of strength ✪✪

PLAIN ENGLISH ALTERNATIVES: reliable person; stable person; dependable person; someone one can depend on; stalwart

CLICHÉD ALTERNATIVES: tried and true supporter

track record ✪✪✪

PLAIN ENGLISH ALTERNATIVES: history; experience; career; past; record of one's past performance; CV; curriculum vitae

■ *Origins* From the record of the past performances of a racehorse or an athlete.

traumatic experience ✪✪✪✪

PLAIN ENGLISH ALTERNATIVES: ordeal; nightmare; bad time; hard time; suffering; torture; unpleasant experience

tread on someone's toes ✪✪

PLAIN ENGLISH ALTERNATIVES: encroach on someone's territory; encroach on someone's area of responsibility; infringe; offend someone

CLICHÉD ALTERNATIVES: get someone's goat; get in someone's face

tread the boards ✪✪

PLAIN ENGLISH ALTERNATIVES: act; be an actor; be a thespian; be a dramatic artist; follow the acting profession

CLICHÉD ALTERNATIVES: be on the stage; be a luvvie; strut and fret one's hour upon the stage

■ *Origins* The boards here are those making up a stage, and thus, strictly, this phrase should not be applied to cinema actors.

trials and tribulations ✪✪

PLAIN ENGLISH ALTERNATIVES: vicissitudes; difficulties; troubles; afflictions; hardships; griefs; woes

CLICHÉD ALTERNATIVES: slings and arrows; crosses to bear

tried and tested (or true) ✪✪

PLAIN ENGLISH ALTERNATIVES: reliable; dependable; sound; stalwart; proven; trusty; unfailing

trip the light fantastic ✪✪✪

PLAIN ENGLISH ALTERNATIVES: dance; swing; jig; boogie; jive

CLICHÉD ALTERNATIVES: shake one's booty; get down; boogie on down; strut one's stuff; cut a rug

■ *Origins* Adapted from Milton's poem *L'Allegro* (lines 33–4): 'Come, and trip it as you go / On the light fantastic toe.'

trouble at t'mill ✪✪✪✪

PLAIN ENGLISH ALTERNATIVES: trouble; disturbance; bother; agitation; hassle; ructions; unrest

CLICHÉD ALTERNATIVES: hell to pay

trump card

- *Origins* A mock Northern English catchphrase popularized especially in the 1960s by novels, plays and films set in the industrial North which often featured strikes and other forms of industrial unrest.

trump card   ✪✪

PLAIN ENGLISH ALTERNATIVES: advantageous move; successful expedient; decisive stroke; winning ploy; winning manoeuvre

CLICHÉD ALTERNATIVES: secret weapon; ace up one's sleeve

- *Origins* From card games in which cards of one particular suit may be designated as 'trumps' and as such rank higher than other cards.

tug at the heartstrings   ✪✪

PLAIN ENGLISH ALTERNATIVES: move one; affect one; touch one; be touching; be poignant; make one emotional; engage one's sympathy

CLICHÉD ALTERNATIVES: bring a tear to one's eye; make one gulp back a tear

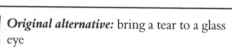

> **!** *Original alternative:* bring a tear to a glass eye

turn a blind eye to   ✪✪

PLAIN ENGLISH ALTERNATIVES: ignore; pretend not to see; overlook; take no notice of

CLICHÉD ALTERNATIVES: look the other way; shut one's eyes to; wink at

- *Origins* Popularly believed to have originated in connection with Lord Nelson's behaviour at the Battle of Copenhagen in 1801. Nelson disregarded a signal ordering him to disengage and pressed on to victory, and was said to have put the telescope to his blind eye, saying: 'I have only one eye: I have a right to be blind sometimes: I really do not see the signal.'

turn a deaf ear to ✪✪

PLAIN ENGLISH ALTERNATIVES: ignore; refuse to listen to; take no notice of; disregard

CLICHÉD ALTERNATIVES: turn one's back on

■ *Origins* Can't blame Nelson for this one; he sacrificed various limbs and faculties for his country but his hearing was not impaired.

turn on the waterworks ✪✪

PLAIN ENGLISH ALTERNATIVES: start crying; start bawling; begin to weep; burst into tears; burst out crying; shed tears

CLICHÉD ALTERNATIVES: dissolve in tears; dab one's eye; be visibly moved

turn over a new leaf ✪✪

PLAIN ENGLISH ALTERNATIVES: change one's ways; start afresh; start again; ameliorate one's behaviour; begin a new and better course of action

CLICHÉD ALTERNATIVES: make a fresh start; mend one's ways; straighten up and fly right; clean up one's act

■ *Origins* The idea is of turning to a clean page in a book.

turn the corner ✪✪

PLAIN ENGLISH ALTERNATIVES: begin to improve; start getting better; get past the difficult part; begin to pick up; begin to gain ground

CLICHÉD ALTERNATIVES: be on the mend; be over the worst; take a turn for the better

■ *Origins* Apparently a nautical allusion meaning 'to succeed in rounding a dangerous cape', such as Cape Horn, and thus to have accomplished the most difficult part of a voyage.

turn-up for the books ✪✪

PLAIN ENGLISH ALTERNATIVES: surprise; surprising development; unlooked-for event; shock; unexpected result; bombshell

CLICHÉD ALTERNATIVES: bolt from the blue; eye-opener; stroke of luck

- *Origins* From horse-racing, in which a surprise result would greatly affect the books (ie the records of bets taken by bookmakers).

twenty-four seven   ✪✪✪✪

PLAIN ENGLISH ALTERNATIVES: always; constantly; continually; all the time; round the clock

CLICHÉD ALTERNATIVES: day in, day out; morning, noon and night; night and day

- *Origins* From 'twenty-fours a day for seven days a week'.

twiddle one's thumbs   ✪✪

PLAIN ENGLISH ALTERNATIVES: be idle; be inactive; be unemployed; have nothing to do

CLICHÉD ALTERNATIVES: kick one's heels; be at a loose end

- *Origins* From people's almost unconscious tendency to play with their fingers when sitting waiting for something.

twilight years   ✪✪

PLAIN ENGLISH ALTERNATIVES: old age; senescence; dotage; Third Age

CLICHÉD ALTERNATIVES: declining years; autumn of one's life; evening of one's life

twist someone's arm   ✪✪

PLAIN ENGLISH ALTERNATIVES: coerce someone; force someone; persuade someone; railroad someone; bulldoze someone; prevail upon someone

CLICHÉD ALTERNATIVES: talk someone into something; make someone an offer they can't refuse

u

Uncle Sam

PLAIN ENGLISH ALTERNATIVES: the United States of America; the USA; the US; the US of A; the US government; America; the Americans; the Yanks

CLICHÉD ALTERNATIVES: Yankee Doodle

■ *Origins* From an early 19th-century American jocular explanation of the ubiquitous initials 'US'.

under a cloud

PLAIN ENGLISH ALTERNATIVES: in disgrace; in disfavour; out of favour; under suspicion

CLICHÉD ALTERNATIVES: in someone's bad books; having a black mark against one's name; persona non grata; not flavour of the month; in the doghouse

under fire

PLAIN ENGLISH ALTERNATIVES: subject to criticism; exposed to criticism; being criticized; being slated; under attack

CLICHÉD ALTERNATIVES: being given a bad press

under one's own steam

PLAIN ENGLISH ALTERNATIVES: unaided; unassisted; alone; autonomously; without help; by one's own efforts; on one's own; solo

CLICHÉD ALTERNATIVES: by the sweat of one's brow

under someone's thumb ✪✪

PLAIN ENGLISH ALTERNATIVES: under someone's influence; under someone's control; under someone's domination; dominated by someone; subservient to someone

CLICHÉD ALTERNATIVES: in someone's pocket

under the influence ✪✪

PLAIN ENGLISH ALTERNATIVES: drunk; tipsy; merry; tight

CLICHÉD ALTERNATIVES: tired and emotional; half seas over; rather the worse for drink; feeling no pain; three sheets in the wind

▪ *Origins* Shortened from 'under the influence of alcohol'.

under the sun ✪✪

PLAIN ENGLISH ALTERNATIVES: anywhere; on earth; in the world; in life; to be found

CLICHÉD ALTERNATIVES: in this world

under the weather ✪✪

PLAIN ENGLISH ALTERNATIVES: in poor health; slightly unwell; ailing; indisposed; in low spirits; poorly

CLICHÉD ALTERNATIVES: below par; out of sorts; not up to snuff; off-colour; not feeling oneself

▪ *Origins* From the idea of unpleasant or oppressive weather affecting one's spirits.

unequal to the task ✪✪

PLAIN ENGLISH ALTERNATIVES: overmatched; incompetent; incapable; inadequate

CLICHÉD ALTERNATIVES: not up to the job; unfitted to the task; tried and found wanting

untold wealth ✪✪

PLAIN ENGLISH ALTERNATIVES: great wealth; riches; vast wealth; fortune; uncountable wealth

CLICHÉD ALTERNATIVES: a king's ransom

■ *Origins* 'Untold' here means 'uncounted', from the old sense of 'tell', meaning 'to count'.

up a gum tree ✪✪✪

PLAIN ENGLISH ALTERNATIVES: in trouble; in an awkward situation; in an uncomfortable position

CLICHÉD ALTERNATIVES: in shtook; up the creek without a paddle; behind the eight ball

■ *Origins* Originally Australian, this refers to the gum trees up which a hunted opossum might try to hide.

up and running ✪✪✪✪

PLAIN ENGLISH ALTERNATIVES: in action; in operation; working; functioning; fully functional; under way

CLICHÉD ALTERNATIVES: rolled out

up for grabs ✪✪✪

PLAIN ENGLISH ALTERNATIVES: attainable; available; there for the taking; at stake

CLICHÉD ALTERNATIVES: on the line

up for it ✪✪✪✪✪

PLAIN ENGLISH ALTERNATIVES: ardent; avid; eager; enthusiastic; keen; voracious

CLICHÉD ALTERNATIVES: into it; mad for it

up in arms ✪✪

PLAIN ENGLISH ALTERNATIVES: angry; aroused; furious; indignant; protesting hotly; complaining furiously

CLICHÉD ALTERNATIVES: on the warpath

up in the air ✪✪

PLAIN ENGLISH ALTERNATIVES: undecided; to be decided; open; unsettled; vague; moot; pending

CLICHÉD ALTERNATIVES: in the balance

up one's street ✪✪✪

PLAIN ENGLISH ALTERNATIVES: to one's taste; in one's area of expertise; familiar to one

CLICHÉD ALTERNATIVES: in one's line; one's kind of thing; one's cup of tea; on one's home ground

upper crust ✪✪

PLAIN ENGLISH ALTERNATIVES: upper class; aristocracy; toffs; gentry; nobility; ruling class

CLICHÉD ALTERNATIVES: cream of society; high society

■ *Origins* Perhaps from the idea of the upper crust of a loaf of bread being 'on top'.

upset the apple-cart ✪

PLAIN ENGLISH ALTERNATIVES: cause confusion; spoil one's plans; throw things into confusion; throw one's plans into disorder; ruin things

CLICHÉD ALTERNATIVES: make a dog's breakfast of the whole thing; put the kibosh on one's plans

up the creek without a paddle ✪✪✪✪

PLAIN ENGLISH ALTERNATIVES: in trouble; in an awkward situation; in an uncomfortable position

CLICHÉD ALTERNATIVES: in shtook; up a gum tree; behind the eight ball

up to scratch ✪✪

PLAIN ENGLISH ALTERNATIVES: adequate; satisfactory; acceptable; of an acceptable standard; what's required; up to the required standard; good enough

CLICHÉD ALTERNATIVES: up to snuff; up to the mark

■ *Origins* From prizefighting, in which a fighter was said to 'come up to scratch' if, at the beginning of each round, he was able to walk from his corner and stand at a line scratched on the ground.

up to speed

See **bring someone up to speed**.

user-friendly ✪✪✪✪

PLAIN ENGLISH ALTERNATIVES: easy to use; easy to operate; easy to understand; straightforward; not unnecessarily complicated

CLICHÉD ALTERNATIVES: adapted to the meanest intelligence; simplicity itself

U-turn

See **do a U-turn**.

vanish into thin air

PLAIN ENGLISH ALTERNATIVES: disappear completely; become invisible; become lost to sight; evanesce; evaporate; fade into nothingness

CLICHÉD ALTERNATIVES: disappear without a trace; disappear from the face of the earth

vast majority ✪✪✪✪

PLAIN ENGLISH ALTERNATIVES: most; best part; greater part; preponderance; majority; bulk

Note: The temptation to yoke 'vast' to 'majority' in every circumstance should be resisted, especially on those occasions when the majority is far from vast.

vexed question ✪✪

PLAIN ENGLISH ALTERNATIVES: matter of great debate; argument; issue; point of dispute; disputed point

CLICHÉD ALTERNATIVES: bone of contention; bone to pick; moot point; political football; sore point

- *Origins* 'Vex' here means 'to discuss something excessively'.

villain of the piece ✪✪

PLAIN ENGLISH ALTERNATIVES: culprit; one responsible; one to blame; cause of all the trouble

CLICHÉD ALTERNATIVES: guilty party; fly in the ointment

- *Origins* 'Piece' here means a piece of drama, a play.

visibly moved ✪✪

PLAIN ENGLISH ALTERNATIVES: obviously affected; on the point of weeping; ready to burst into tears; in tears; weeping; crying

CLICHÉD ALTERNATIVES: blinking back the tears; on the brink of tears; moved to tears; with a tear in one's eye; with eyes brimming

▪ *Origins* Popular, especially formerly, as a journalistic euphemism to avoid reporting that someone was crying their eyes out.

voracious reader ✪✪

PLAIN ENGLISH ALTERNATIVES: someone who enjoys reading; enthusiastic reader

CLICHÉD ALTERNATIVES: avid reader; bookworm; a great one for books

vote with one's feet ✪✪

PLAIN ENGLISH ALTERNATIVES: leave; depart; take off

CLICHÉD ALTERNATIVES: make oneself scarce; beat it; make tracks; head for the hills; hit the road; stay away in droves

W

waiting in the wings   ✪✪

PLAIN ENGLISH ALTERNATIVES: holding oneself in readiness; awaiting one's opportunity; ready to take over; ready to take someone's place; on hand

■ *Origins* From the theatre, referring to an actor at the side of the stage listening for his cue to come on.

wait on someone hand and foot   ✪✪

PLAIN ENGLISH ALTERNATIVES: serve someone assiduously; carry out someone's every wish; pay assiduous attention to someone's needs

CLICHÉD ALTERNATIVES: cater to someone's every whim; be at someone's beck and call; be unable to do enough for someone; dance attendance on someone

wake up and smell the coffee   ✪✪✪✪✪

PLAIN ENGLISH ALTERNATIVES: confront reality; face the facts; stop dreaming

CLICHÉD ALTERNATIVES: get real; wake up to the facts; wake up to reality; come back down to earth; have a reality check

wake-up call   ✪✪✪✪

PLAIN ENGLISH ALTERNATIVES: alarm; alert; warning; notification

CLICHÉD ALTERNATIVES: danger sign; danger signal; word to the wise

■ *Origins* This originally and literally meant a phone-call one arranged with a hotel reception or other service to wake one up in the morning.

walking on air ✪✪

PLAIN ENGLISH ALTERNATIVES: elated; exhilarated; transported; exultant

CLICHÉD ALTERNATIVES: on cloud nine; high as a kite; in a dream; over the moon

■ *Origins* This phrase may have been coined by Robert Louis Stevenson, whose use of it in *Memories and Portraits* (1887) seems to be the first in print: 'I went home that morning walking upon air.'

walk the walk ✪✪✪✪✪

PLAIN ENGLISH ALTERNATIVES: carry out one's promises; do what one said one could; make good on one's boasts; fulfil one's claims; put one's ideas into practice

CLICHÉD ALTERNATIVES: put one's money where one's mouth is

■ *Origins* From the longer phrase, 'You can talk the talk, but can you walk the walk?'

wall-to-wall ✪✪✪

PLAIN ENGLISH ALTERNATIVES: ubiquitous; omnipresent; endless; limitless; uninterrupted; constant

CLICHÉD ALTERNATIVES: hot and cold running …

■ *Origins* The image is of wall-to-wall carpeting covering an entire floor.

Walter Mitty ✪✪

PLAIN ENGLISH ALTERNATIVES: daydreamer; dreamer; fantasist; escapist

CLICHÉD ALTERNATIVES: someone with their head in the clouds

■ *Origins* From the short story *The Secret Life of Walter Mitty* (1939) by the US humorist James Thurber (1894–1961), the hero of which escapes from his humdrum life into daydreams of being successful and powerful. Further popularized by the film of the same name (1947), starring Danny Kaye.

warts and all ✪✪✪

PLAIN ENGLISH ALTERNATIVES: candid; uncensored; unvarnished; unidealized; realistic; true-to-life; showing all defects and blemishes; concealing no shortcomings; without airbrushing

CLICHÉD ALTERNATIVES: with no punches pulled

■ *Origins* From remarks made by Oliver Cromwell (1599–1658) to Sir Peter Lely, who was to paint his portrait: 'Mr Lely, I desire you would use all your skill to paint my picture truly like me, and not flatter me at all; but remark all these roughnesses, pimples, warts, and everything as you see me, otherwise I will never pay a farthing for it.'

wash one's hands of ✪✪

PLAIN ENGLISH ALTERNATIVES: disclaim responsibility for; refuse to have anything further to do with; abandon; drop; renounce; withdraw from

CLICHÉD ALTERNATIVES: leave someone to their own devices; leave someone to stew in their own juice

■ *Origins* From the Bible, in which Pilate is described as refusing to condemn Jesus, leaving his fate to the mob (*Matthew* 27.24): '… he took water, and washed his hands before the multitude, saying, I am innocent of the blood of this just person: see ye to it'.

watering hole ✪✪

PLAIN ENGLISH ALTERNATIVES: pub; bar; hostelry; inn; boozer

■ *Origins* This literally means a place where wild animals come to drink water.

water off a duck's back

See **like water off a duck's back**.

watery grave ✪✪

PLAIN ENGLISH ALTERNATIVES: death by drowning; drowning; burial at sea

CLICHÉD ALTERNATIVES: Davy Jones's locker

wax lyrical ✪✪✪

PLAIN ENGLISH ALTERNATIVES: become effusive; gush; versify; poeticize; use flowery language

■ *Origins* 'Wax' here means 'become'.

ways and means ✪✪

PLAIN ENGLISH ALTERNATIVES: methods; facilities; resources; strategies; procedures; systems

way to go ✪✪✪✪✪

PLAIN ENGLISH ALTERNATIVES: that's what's required; that's right; that's what to do; that's exactly right; that's the right thing to do

CLICHÉD ALTERNATIVES: that's the way; that's the stuff; that's the ticket

■ *Origins* This exclamation of encouragement was originally American.

wear one's heart on one's sleeve ✪✪

PLAIN ENGLISH ALTERNATIVES: show one's feelings; make no secret of one's feelings; reveal one's feelings openly; let the world see how one feels

CLICHÉD ALTERNATIVES: cry one's feelings from the rooftops

■ *Origins* From the old custom of tying a lady's ribbon or other love-token on one's arm to show where one's affections lay.

wear the trousers ✪✪

PLAIN ENGLISH ALTERNATIVES: be the boss; be in charge; dominate; predominate; be the dominant partner

CLICHÉD ALTERNATIVES: wear the pants (*US*); rule the roost

■ *Origins* This was originally applied to wives who dominated their husbands (in the days when women didn't actually wear trousers).

weasel words ✪✪✪

PLAIN ENGLISH ALTERNATIVES: evasive language; misleading remarks; ambiguous language; meaningless words

▪ *Origins* From the idea that the meaning of the words has been extracted, in the same way as a weasel sucks out the content of an egg, leaving only an empty shell.

weather the storm ✪✪

PLAIN ENGLISH ALTERNATIVES: survive; make it through; win through; come safely through; hold out; pull through

CLICHÉD ALTERNATIVES: turn the corner

▪ *Origins* From the idea of a ship riding out a storm at sea.

wedded bliss ✪✪✪✪✪

PLAIN ENGLISH ALTERNATIVES: marriage; matrimony; wedlock; coupledom

CLICHÉD ALTERNATIVES: the estate of matrimony; blissful union

weeping and wailing (and gnashing of teeth) ✪✪✪

PLAIN ENGLISH ALTERNATIVES: lamentation; mourning; grief; sorrow

CLICHÉD ALTERNATIVES: tears before bedtime

▪ *Origins* Elaborated from the Bible (*Matthew* 8.12): 'But the children of the kingdom shall be cast out into outer darkness: there shall be weeping and gnashing of teeth.'

welcome with open arms ✪✪

PLAIN ENGLISH ALTERNATIVES: welcome heartily; be overjoyed to see; be glad about; make thoroughly welcome; greet warmly; receive with gratitude; embrace

CLICHÉD ALTERNATIVES: roll out the red carpet for

well and truly ✪✪

PLAIN ENGLISH ALTERNATIVES: completely; utterly; thoroughly; downright; unreservedly; beyond all doubt

CLICHÉD ALTERNATIVES: completely and utterly

well hard ✪✪✪✪✪

PLAIN ENGLISH ALTERNATIVES: tough; hard-bitten; hard-boiled; callous

CLICHÉD ALTERNATIVES: hard as nails; a bit tasty

 Original alternative: as hard as Henderson's arse *(an expression from Aberdeen that surely deserves to be used more widely)*

Note: The use of 'well' as a simple intensifier is becoming ever more widespread; one looks forward to the day when someone who has fully recovered from illness will be described as 'well well'.

well I never! ✪✪

PLAIN ENGLISH ALTERNATIVES: what a surprise!; how unexpected!; how surprising!; how amazing!; how marvellous!; isn't that remarkable?

CLICHÉD ALTERNATIVES: wonders will never cease!; would you believe it?; would you Adam and Eve it?; I'm gobsmacked; I never saw that one coming

- *Origins* Shortened from expressions such as 'Well I never heard the like!'

well-nigh ✪✪

PLAIN ENGLISH ALTERNATIVES: almost; all but; nearly; next to; virtually; practically

CLICHÉD ALTERNATIVES: more or less; just about

well said ✪✪

PLAIN ENGLISH ALTERNATIVES: that's absolutely right; that's true; I quite agree; I am in full agreement with you; I agree entirely

CLICHÉD ALTERNATIVES: hear, hear!

wend one's way ✪✪

PLAIN ENGLISH ALTERNATIVES: go; proceed; journey; travel; fare; progress

CLICHÉD ALTERNATIVES: make one's way; follow the road

wet behind the ears ✪✪✪

PLAIN ENGLISH ALTERNATIVES: innocent; gullible; easily fooled; inexperienced; naïve; green; unworldly; credulous

CLICHÉD ALTERNATIVES: innocent as a newborn child; not wise in the ways of the world

▪ *Origins* From the idea that the hollow behind the ears of a newborn child or animal is one of the last places to dry.

what else is new? ✪✪

PLAIN ENGLISH ALTERNATIVES: I'm not impressed; so what?; there's nothing new about that; that's hardly news to me

CLICHÉD ALTERNATIVES: big deal; tell me something I don't know; heard it!

whatever turns you on ✪✪✪✪

PLAIN ENGLISH ALTERNATIVES: each to his/her own taste; we're not all the same; it makes no difference to me

CLICHÉD ALTERNATIVES: each to his own; it takes all kinds; whatever gets you through the night

what makes one tick   ✪✪

PLAIN ENGLISH ALTERNATIVES: one's motivation; one's driving force; one's ruling passion; one's inspiration; one's beliefs; one's interests

CLICHÉD ALTERNATIVES: what one is all about; what one is into

■ *Origins* From the idea of comparing a person to a clock, whose mechanism of course makes it tick.

what's the damage?   ✪✪✪

PLAIN ENGLISH ALTERNATIVES: how much?; how much do I owe you?; what's the cost?

CLICHÉD ALTERNATIVES: give me the bad news

what's your poison?   ✪✪

PLAIN ENGLISH ALTERNATIVES: what would you like to drink?; what are you drinking?; what will you have?; what can I get you to drink?

CLICHÉD ALTERNATIVES: name your poison

when Adam was a lad   ✪✪

PLAIN ENGLISH ALTERNATIVES: a long time ago; long ago

CLICHÉD ALTERNATIVES: beyond the mists of time; in the dim and distant past; in days gone by; in days of yore; in the old days; long ago and far away; when one was knee-high to a grasshopper; way back when

■ *Origins* It is the Biblical Adam who is referred to, but somewhat inaccurately for the sake of exaggeration, as Adam was created as a man and never was a lad.

when all is said and done   ✪✪✪✪✪

PLAIN ENGLISH ALTERNATIVES: finally; in the end; ultimately; when everything has been taken into consideration

CLICHÉD ALTERNATIVES: in the final analysis; in the final reckoning; at the end of the day

when it comes to the crunch ✪✪✪

PLAIN ENGLISH ALTERNATIVES: when a crisis is reached; when decisive action must be taken; when it's time to make decisions; when things become difficult; at a critically important moment

CLICHÉD ALTERNATIVES: when push comes to shove; when it comes to the bit (*Scottish*); when the chips are down; when the going gets tough; when the shit hits the fan

whiter than white ✪✪✪

PLAIN ENGLISH ALTERNATIVES: utterly pure; untainted; immaculate; spotless; unsullied; without a blemish

CLICHÉD ALTERNATIVES: beyond reproach; pure as the driven snow

whole different ball game

See **whole new ball game**.

whole kit and caboodle, the ✪✪✪

PLAIN ENGLISH ALTERNATIVES: absolutely everything; every conceivable thing; the whole lot; the entirety

CLICHÉD ALTERNATIVES: everything but the kitchen sink; the full monty; the lot; the whole nine yards; the whole shooting match; the whole ball of wax

■ *Origins* 'Caboodle' is a word of unknown origin meaning 'a collection'.

whole new or different ball game ✪✪✪✪✪

PLAIN ENGLISH ALTERNATIVES: something else again; something different altogether; a completely different matter; an entirely different affair; another thing entirely

CLICHÉD ALTERNATIVES: something completely different; a different kettle of fish; a horse of a different colour

■ *Origins* Originally American, as 'ball game' here refers to a baseball match.

whys and wherefores ✪✪

PLAIN ENGLISH ALTERNATIVES: reasons; details; purposes; motives

CLICHÉD ALTERNATIVES: reasons why; ins and outs

wine and dine ✪✪

PLAIN ENGLISH ALTERNATIVES: entertain; treat; provide with food and drink; regale

CLICHÉD ALTERNATIVES: show someone a good time; shower hospitality on

wine, women and song ✪✪

PLAIN ENGLISH ALTERNATIVES: a life of hedonism; self-indulgence; loose living; dissipation; debauchery; intemperance; wantonness

CLICHÉD ALTERNATIVES: cigarettes, whisky and wild, wild women

■ *Origins* Perhaps from a remark attributed to Martin Luther (1483–1546): 'Who loves not wine, women and song, / Remains a fool his whole life long.'

win hands down ✪✪

PLAIN ENGLISH ALTERNATIVES: win easily; win by a wide margin; crush one's opponent

CLICHÉD ALTERNATIVES: win by a mile; run away with it; stroll through it

■ *Origins* From horse-racing, in which a jockey riding with his hands down is not having to put much effort into driving his horse on.

wipe the floor with ✪✪

PLAIN ENGLISH ALTERNATIVES: utterly outclass; completely surpass; defeat easily; beat by a wide margin; demolish; floor

CLICHÉD ALTERNATIVES: inflict a humiliating defeat on; blow out of the water; knock spots off; leave standing; leave in the dust; leave for dead; put in the shade

with all due respect ✪✪✪

PLAIN ENGLISH ALTERNATIVES: respectfully; with no wish to cause offence

CLICHÉD ALTERNATIVES: with all due deference; with the greatest of respect; if one may make so bold

with attitude ✪✪✪✪✪

PLAIN ENGLISH ALTERNATIVES: provocative; confrontational; aggressive; direct; pushy; assertive

CLICHÉD ALTERNATIVES: in-your-face

with bated breath ✪✪✪✪

PLAIN ENGLISH ALTERNATIVES: breathlessly; holding one's breath in suspense; holding one's breath through fear

CLICHÉD ALTERNATIVES: hardly daring to breathe; on tenterhooks; with one's heart in one's mouth

- *Origins* 'Bated' here is a shortened form of 'abated'.

with flying colours ✪✪

PLAIN ENGLISH ALTERNATIVES: easily; triumphantly; brilliantly; gloriously; with distinction

CLICHÉD ALTERNATIVES: in a breeze

- *Origins* From the colours flown by naval ships, which would still be at the masthead of a vessel that had been victorious in battle.

within an ace of ✪✪

PLAIN ENGLISH ALTERNATIVES: on the point of; on the verge of

CLICHÉD ALTERNATIVES: within a hair's-breadth of; a kick in the arse away from

- *Origins* From card games, suggesting one needs only one ace to win.

within the realms or bounds of possibility ✪✪

PLAIN ENGLISH ALTERNATIVES: possible; just possible; conceivable; likely; not out of the question

with might and main ✪✪

PLAIN ENGLISH ALTERNATIVES: with all one's strength; with utmost strength; manfully; powerfully; determinedly

CLICHÉD ALTERNATIVES: with everything one has; like a Trojan

with no or without fear of contradiction ✪✪

PLAIN ENGLISH ALTERNATIVES: confident that everyone will agree; sure that no-one will disagree; sure that one speaks for everyone

with one's tail between one's legs ✪✪

PLAIN ENGLISH ALTERNATIVES: downcast; dejected; humiliated; crestfallen; disheartened

CLICHÉD ALTERNATIVES: like a whipped cur

- *Origins* Refers to the cowering attitude of a dog that has been punished.

with one's tongue in one's cheek ✪✪

PLAIN ENGLISH ALTERNATIVES: ironically; humorously; insincerely; as a joke; sarcastically; mockingly

CLICHÉD ALTERNATIVES: for laughs; without really meaning it

- *Origins* Derives from the old custom of sticking one's tongue into one's cheek as a sign that one disbelieved what one was being told.

without fear of contradiction

See **with no fear of contradiction**.

without more or further ado ✪✪

PLAIN ENGLISH ALTERNATIVES: at once; without delay; straight away; right away; forthwith; directly; without prevarication

CLICHÉD ALTERNATIVES: with no further delay; without any more faffing about; with no more beating about the bush

woefully inadequate ✪✪

PLAIN ENGLISH ALTERNATIVES: no good at all; hopeless; pathetic; rubbish; lousy; pitiful; pitiable; wretched; shocking; well below the required standard

CLICHÉD ALTERNATIVES: worse than useless; a waste of time; piss-poor; pants

wonders will never cease ✪✪

PLAIN ENGLISH ALTERNATIVES: what a surprise!; how unexpected!; how surprising!; how amazing!; how marvellous!; isn't that remarkable?

CLICHÉD ALTERNATIVES: well I never!; would you believe it?; would you Adam and Eve it?; I'm gobsmacked; I never saw that one coming

woods are full of them, the ✪✪✪

PLAIN ENGLISH ALTERNATIVES: there are plenty of them about; they are easily found; there is no shortage of them; they are abundant; they are quite common

CLICHÉD ALTERNATIVES: the place is infested with them; they are two a penny

■ *Origins* A hunting allusion, meaning that the particular quarry in question is easily located.

word in one's ear ✪✪

PLAIN ENGLISH ALTERNATIVES: word of advice; piece of good advice; discreet warning; confidential remark

CLICHÉD ALTERNATIVES: word in one's shell-like; word to the wise

words fail me ✪✪

PLAIN ENGLISH ALTERNATIVES: I am speechless; I am dumbfounded; I don't know what to say; I don't know how to react

CLICHÉD ALTERNATIVES: I'm at a loss for words; I'm lost for words; I'm gobsmacked

work one's fingers to the bone ✪✪

PLAIN ENGLISH ALTERNATIVES: wear oneself out; slave away; work hard; work tirelessly; drudge; toil; sweat

CLICHÉD ALTERNATIVES: labour long and hard; work till one drops

world and his wife or brother, the ✪✪✪

PLAIN ENGLISH ALTERNATIVES: everybody; everyone; every single one; each one; one and all

CLICHÉD ALTERNATIVES: all and sundry; every man Jack; every Tom, Dick and Harry; the whole world

worth its weight in gold ✪✪

PLAIN ENGLISH ALTERNATIVES: valuable; invaluable; of great value; priceless; prized; highly useful

CLICHÉD ALTERNATIVES: worth a king's ransom

worth one's salt ✪✪

PLAIN ENGLISH ALTERNATIVES: valuable; useful; efficient; earning one's pay; proficient; productive; prized

CLICHÉD ALTERNATIVES: worth every penny of one's pay

■ *Origins* From the idea of salt being a valuable and necessary commodity. Some say the expression dates back to Roman times, either from the practice of paying the legionaries in salt or from their wages being considered as money for buying salt.

wouldn't hurt a fly

See **he/she wouldn't hurt a fly**.

wouldn't say boo to a goose

See **he/she wouldn't say boo to a goose**.

writing is on the wall, the ✪✪✪

PLAIN ENGLISH ALTERNATIVES: one will not survive much longer; one does not have long to live; one is obsolescent; the end is coming; disaster is inevitable

CLICHÉD ALTERNATIVES: one's days are numbered; one is on the way out; the end is nigh; the signs are there for all to see

- *Origins* See **days are numbered, one's**.

wrong end of the stick ✪✪

PLAIN ENGLISH ALTERNATIVES: wrong impression; mistaken impression; false impression; misapprehension; misunderstanding

CLICHÉD ALTERNATIVES: wrong idea

- *Origins* Probably from grasping the wrong end of a walking-stick, which could very well be dirty.

wrong side of the tracks ✪✪

PLAIN ENGLISH ALTERNATIVES: slum; poor area; disadvantaged area; ghetto; socially inferior neighbourhood

CLICHÉD ALTERNATIVES: the gutter

- *Origins* Originally American, this phrase refers to the common practice of locating industrial areas on the other side of the railway line from the more residential areas, allowing any pollution to be carried away by the prevailing wind.

XYZ

X-rated ✪

PLAIN ENGLISH ALTERNATIVES: obscene; pornographic; dirty; filthy; blue; indecent; smutty; offensive; gross

CLICHÉD ALTERNATIVES: near the knuckle; liable to deprave and corrupt

▪ *Origins* From the former classification of cinema films in which X indicated that a film was suitable for adults only, because of its depiction of explicit sexual activity or graphic violence.

yawning gap ✪✪

PLAIN ENGLISH ALTERNATIVES: wide gap; wide breach; wide separation; great difference; great divide; rift; void; abyss; gulf

CLICHÉD ALTERNATIVES: world of difference

year in, year out ✪✪

PLAIN ENGLISH ALTERNATIVES: all the time; every year; regularly; continuously; relentlessly

CLICHÉD ALTERNATIVES: with monotonous regularity; year after year; year upon year

yeoman service ✪✪

PLAIN ENGLISH ALTERNATIVES: great help; great utility; powerful aid; effectual service; invaluable assistance

CLICHÉD ALTERNATIVES: stout service

▪ *Origins* A yeoman was a freeholding farmer who was often called upon to do military service in English armies.

yesterday's man ✪✪✪

PLAIN ENGLISH ALTERNATIVES: a has-been; a loser; a dinosaur; a relic; someone whose time has come and gone

CLICHÉD ALTERNATIVES: a relic of the past; a hangover from another era

you ain't seen nothing yet ✪✪✪

▸PLAIN ENGLISH ALTERNATIVES: that's nothing; even more impressive things are coming; wait till you see what happens next

CLICHÉD ALTERNATIVES: if you think that was something, wait till you see what's coming next

you can say that again ✪✪

PLAIN ENGLISH ALTERNATIVES: that's absolutely right; that's true; I quite agree; I am in full agreement with you; I agree entirely

CLICHÉD ALTERNATIVES: right on!; you're not kidding; you ain't just whistling Dixie (US); well said; hear, hear!

you can't legislate for ... ✪✪

PLAIN ENGLISH ALTERNATIVES: you can't foresee; you can't predict; you can't expect; you can't anticipate; you can't be prepared for

you can't win them all ✪✪

PLAIN ENGLISH ALTERNATIVES: an occasional failure is to be expected; sometimes you have to admit defeat; no-one has a 100% record

CLICHÉD ALTERNATIVES: you win a few, you lose a few; you win some, you lose some; you can't be right all the time

you could have knocked me down with a feather ✪✪

PLAIN ENGLISH ALTERNATIVES: I was very surprised; I was astounded; I was dumbfounded; I was amazed; I was utterly taken aback; I was thunderstruck

CLICHÉD ALTERNATIVES: I was gobsmacked; I couldn't believe it

- *Origins* From the idea of being so shocked that one feels physically weak.

you don't have to be a rocket scientist to understand it   ✪✪✪✪✪

PLAIN ENGLISH ALTERNATIVES: it's not that hard to grasp; it's not that intellectually demanding; it's easy enough to understand; it's quite simple really; it's elementary

CLICHÉD ALTERNATIVES: anyone with half a brain could understand it; you don't have to be Einstein to understand it; there's nothing to it; it's not rocket science

- *Origins* See **it's not rocket science**.

you don't know jack   ✪✪

PLAIN ENGLISH ALTERNATIVES: you know nothing; you are ignorant; you have no idea

CLICHÉD ALTERNATIVES: you don't know the first thing; you know diddly-squat; you haven't got a clue

- *Origins* Originally American. 'Jack' is a shortened form of 'jack shit' meaning 'nothing at all'.

you must be joking   ✪✪

PLAIN ENGLISH ALTERNATIVES: you can't be serious; you're not serious; you're kidding; you can't expect me to believe that; that's ridiculous

CLICHÉD ALTERNATIVES: you're having a laugh; you're having me on; pull the other one

you pays your money and you takes your choice   ✪✪

PLAIN ENGLISH ALTERNATIVES: it's up to you; choose what you like; take your pick; whatever you prefer

- *Origins* From the kind of patter used by market traders or fairground barkers.

you're telling me!

you're telling me! ✪✪

PLAIN ENGLISH ALTERNATIVES: don't I just know it!; I know exactly what you mean; you are absolutely right; I know all about it

CLICHÉD ALTERNATIVES: don't I just know all about it!; tell me about it!

your guess is as good as mine ✪✪

PLAIN ENGLISH ALTERNATIVES: I don't know any better than you do; who knows?; who can say?; who can tell?; there's no telling; it's impossible to know

CLICHÉD ALTERNATIVES: it's anybody's guess; don't look at me; how should I know?

you've got another think coming ✪✪

PLAIN ENGLISH ALTERNATIVES: you will have to think again; you are wrong; you have the wrong idea; you will have to give the matter more thought

CLICHÉD ALTERNATIVES: you thought wrong; you will have to rethink the situation

you win a few, you lose a few ✪✪

PLAIN ENGLISH ALTERNATIVES: an occasional failure is to be expected; sometimes you have to admit defeat; no-one has a 100% record

CLICHÉD ALTERNATIVES: you can't win them all; you can't be right all the time

zero per cent finance ✪✪✪✪✪

PLAIN ENGLISH ALTERNATIVES: interest-free credit; interest-free loan

CLICHÉD ALTERNATIVES: nought per cent finance

   ✪ mild   ✪✪ highly unoriginal   ✪✪✪ irritating